THE TURNING TIDE

A
Biography
of the
Irish Sea

THE TURNING TIDE

JON
GOWER

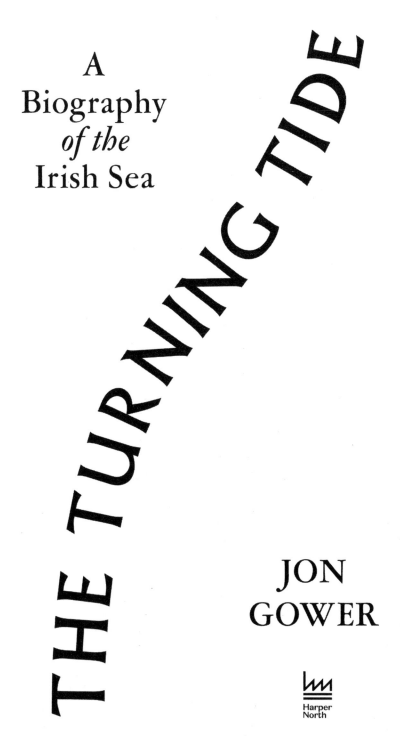

Harper
North

HarperNorth
Windmill Green
24 Mount Street
Manchester M2 3NX

A division of
HarperCollins*Publishers*
1 London Bridge Street
London SE1 9GF

www.harpercollins.co.uk

HarperCollins*Publishers*
Macken House, 39/40 Mayor Street Upper
Dublin 1, D01 C9W8

First published by HarperNorth in 2023

1 3 5 7 9 10 8 6 4 2

A catalogue record for this book
is available from the British Library

ISBN: 978-0-00-853263-5

Printed and bound in the UK using 100%
renewable electricity at CPI Group (UK) Ltd

Ports, Past and Present
Calafoirt, Inniu agus Inné
Porthladdoedd, Ddoe a Heddiw

To Claire, Paul and Olan

'He unloaded the lobster from the pot and put it in a tub, and then took out the spider crabs, their conkery shells crusted with acorn barnacles. He wondered whether the spider crabs being early was from some disturbance, perhaps flushed by the scallop dredgers out at sea, or some sign of unusual warming water. "Ah," thought Hold. "There just aren't any rules. Just the rule that says the sea will keep surprising you."'

Cynan Jones, *Everything I Found on the Beach*

CONTENTS

PART THREE – THE OPEN SEA

1.

A CHARTING

Knowing precisely where you are stops you being all at sea, so let's take our bearings together. As you hold a book open the two sides are not dissimilar to a ship's hold, carrying a cargo of information, maybe a little ballast but certainly a weight of stories. The spine of the book is perhaps the keel, gently cradled in your palms, as if in dry dock. And, staying with the conceit, reading a book is very often a journey, although this one is far from a straight line. For the sea is unpredictable, diverting and bounteous in its gifts and signals. We will thither and hither, sometimes loop back, sometimes make the same passage from port to port two or even three times, or veer around sharp rocks, or lose sight of the lighthouse. But we will get there. I know where we're going. If the weather allows and the tides prevail.

* * *

The Turning Tide concentrates on a section of the Irish Sea covered by the Imray C61 nautical chart, which unfolds to the width of my arms. It spans an area known as St George's Channel, found roughly between a line drawn from Dublin to Holyhead and another from Wexford to Fishguard, but also covering Waterford, the busy shipping lanes of Milford Haven and the former shipyards of Pembroke Dock. The sea always connects, so exploring its history takes us to the shipyards of Belfast and saintly outposts on the Scottish coast, or even

1

further out into the Atlantic. But in the main I stick to the C61, else I'd be writing a marine encyclopaedia.

When this landlubber started composing the book, I bought a copy of chart C61 and set it under the glass of my writing table. I was now not just writing *about* this stretch of sea but writing *on it*. Soon the quince tree outside, often busy with house sparrows, was replaced by an imagined horizon, an expanse of sea and the facing coasts of Wales and Ireland on either side stretching towards the neighbours' wall.

The sea, flowing as tides and currents, is never static, has no cut-off points and boundaries, so there is a connectedness to it all. The tide ebbs and flows as the earth turns on its axis, as the gravity tug of the moon interacts with the centrifugal force of the planet. Twice a day the sea claims parts of the land or yields to it. In the case of the Irish Sea, the moon's pull causes water to flow from the west around the island of Ireland and, in quotidian rhythm, from both the north and the south. This leads to some tidal oddities, such as the fact that a place like Courtown, County Wexford has not two daily tides but four weak ones. The lugworm in the sands must like it. In the south Irish sea the tidal flows are strong, as are the ebbs, while in the north-eastern portion they are slower, leading to large accumulations of mud and silt, such as those favoured by Dublin Bay prawns or langoustines, by feeding geese and wading birds galore.

This ceaseless movement of the tides is one of the more dependable changes of the sea, but this book logs some that are much less predictable, such as storms which can lead to shipwrecks or at least to seasickness. Tempests can also combine with the tides to heighten the impact of storm surges on the coasts, as happens increasingly as a consequence of the climate emergency.

When the weather's calmer – tending towards millpond stillness, even – the sea is a conduit, allowing craft to sail, linking one port to another, enabling historical and cultural connections which often go way, way back. The stretch of St George's Channel unrolled before me connects with the Irish Sea (beyond the quince, near the stone wall with its lush red agrimony) and beyond that the narrowing funnel of the North Channel's Straits of Moyle, lying between the

Antrim coast and the south-west Highlands of Scotland. Here the Irish Sea empties into the wild Atlantic before filling again, the sea's great daily pulse. On the chart's south, too, the waters of St George's Channel – named after the patron saint of England, provocatively separating Wales and Ireland – mix and churn with those of the Celtic Sea. And beyond that is the great, wide, open ocean, a reminder that we all live on some part of an enormous archipelago: let's call it the human domain.

The research for the book was supported by Ports, Past & Present, a project funded by the European Regional Development Fund to explore the heritage of five ports around St George's Channel, with the aim of developing cultural and other kinds of tourism. As a life-long naturalist it struck me that the five chosen ports – Dublin, Holyhead, Pembroke Dock, Fishguard and Rosslare – are all very close to superb wildlife sites, so I decided to visit them in turn, using public transport and, where possible, my bike. This took me to the screeching tern colonies of Our Lady's Island in South Wexford and to the bustling seabird cities of South Stack on Anglesey, and to appreciate the abundant natural glories of some of the Irish and Welsh islands. My nature itinerary also included the rarest goose in Europe, the Greenland white-fronted goose, which visits the Wexford Slobs in winter, at the same time as the brent goose starts to feed in urban parks and playing fields in Dublin, as its natural food sources, such as eelgrass in the waters of Dublin Bay, have declined.

Some people view the sea as an emptiness. They might look at the Imray chart's stretches of pale blue representing deep fathoms, and those in white for shallow water, as being somehow just so much brine. Yet the chart's bounty of detail shows sandbars and shallows, firing practice areas, buoyed entry approaches to harbours, and flashing lighthouses warning of jagged danger. And there is so much else that doesn't appear on the chart in front of me: the migration pathways of people and animals, bright schools of fish, drowned kingdoms, speeding porpoise, smugglers' caves, and seabird feeding areas, for example. There might be ghostly flotillas of moon jellyfish, the flash of sharks, or a bloom of tiny phytoplankton so substantial that they can be seen from satellites – providing a feast for zooplankton and a wide range of fish species besides. These, and the warm wash of the Gulf Stream's North Atlantic current, means that some 375 species of fish are found in Irish waters, while the seabird colonies of Wales and Ireland are supremely important for seabirds such as the Manx shearwater, the gannet and the storm petrel. So, not empty at all.

The apparent emptiness is, in truth, a place of fecundity, of wildlife plenty, of green energy source, submarine dangers and poet's inspiration. *The Turning Tide* sets out to chart a little of all that. What a huge, small word it is: just three letters. Sea. Now let's traverse one together, sometimes watching our wake swiftly dissipate as we cleave the waves. Bring a sou'wester.

2.

CROSS-CURRENTS

A *shirr* of water as sea-wavelets riffle among the pebbles and shuffle small stones. In open water, well out from the tideline, the wind rakes white catspaws to cap the waves. There are two people standing on the coast, who see something that makes them draw breath. This is Kerry, Ireland, and it is a red-letter day.

For in March 2021 a young Arctic walrus made a surprise appearance. Yes, a walrus, all bulk and tusks.

The heavy, elephantine animal was first sighted on the rocks of Valentia Island. Alan Houlihan, whose five-year-old daughter found it, was bowled over by its size: 'It was astronomical. It was the size of a big bull.' The huge-gourd shaped animal would have entered shallower water to find food such as shellfish, for which it has a suitably gargantuan appetite, eating several thousand clams a day.

The first record of walrus in Ireland was one spotted by a Mr Charles Ackroyd off the mouth of the Shannon. He was well acquainted with seals and so knew the difference between one and 'tother. In 1922 a walrus was seen in Dursey Sound in West Cork and believed to be a mermaid, while other sightings by fishermen of 'seals with beards' were treated as possible sightings. All in all, there have been some 22 confirmed Irish appearances of walrus, the majority off the coast of Donegal. But the history of the walrus in Ireland goes much, much further back. A right tusk which was found on the high-water mark on a beach at Hook Head, County Wexford was carbon dated to between 1038 and 1163 CE.

There have been many stories and sightings of mermaids, too. The Irish song 'An Mhaighdeasm Mhara' (Song of the Isles) tells of a mermaid called Mary Kinney, who is caught by a fisherman who steals the cap from off her head, causing Mary to forget her submarine past. They marry, as happens in such tales, but then her children find the aforementioned cap and give it to their mother who duly tries it on, remembers who she is and returns to Eirne: the open sea.

On the Welsh coast, too, there are many mermaid tales. There was the farmer in Aberbach, Pembrokeshire who kept one in a bath of salt-water, while another was often spotted near Carreg Ina at New Quay, Ceredigion. One more washed ashore at Conwy, and appealed to fishermen to restore her to the waters: they refused and were duly cursed. Conversely, the mermaid that appeared to a fisherman at Llandrillo yn Rhos brought luck. After being caught in some nets she was released, only to return some years later to warn the man who'd caught her about a storm that was on its way.

Not every strange creature in the sea is a mermaid, or walrus, mind. The *Dublin Evening Post* on 17 October 1850 contained a letter from a John Granville, who told readers about a trip he had undertaken that week from Holyhead. They had left the port at two o'clock in a yawl, a two-masted sailing ship, with the intention of idling the time away by fishing and shooting seagulls. They cast anchor about five miles out, dealt with 'the squeamishness which our short voyage had brought on, by liberal portions of cognac', then cast their lines into very deep water. He and his companions felt electric shocks as they did so, and their screams were accompanied by the sight of an enormous cod leaping out of the water. Still shocked, quite literally, they then saw 'the head of a most terrific looking animal, such as we had never seen before and hope never to see again. It was more like the head of a horse without ears than anything else, but about four times larger; its eyes were most filthy looking things, about nine inches diameter, and of a dark brown colour. It had a long mane on the top of its back, and a greasy matter floated about wherever it went, which had a most nauseous odour.' The creature was 120 feet long and despite being hit by large shot from two double-barrelled shotguns it hissed and 'ascended, with his head foremost, about four times the height of our boat, and immediately descended like lightning into the water below us, leaving nothing but the slimy matter I mentioned before ...' Fascinatingly, this serpentine monster was simply one of many: the mid-nineteenth century spawned an epidemic of such sightings, from Brazil to Boston. A mass delusion? Perhaps, but it was as if people *needed* to see these enormous creatures with their long necks and terrifying heads, rising up from the often abysmal depths at a time when scientific reason was busily explaining away the supernatural.

* * *

The walrus – this blubbery torpedo of a mammal – then submarined its way to south-west Wales, some 280 miles, or 450 km, to the south, where it appeared at South Beach at Broad Haven before obligingly spending time lounging on the slipway of the lifeboat station in Tenby, Pembrokeshire. It would have had its erratic journey decided in part by the currents and tides. The sea is amoebic, organic, elastic, full of ebb and flow and quotidian change. The Irish Sea opens out into the Atlantic at both ends and it is subject to an extra tidal flow inwards, which generally moves the water northwards across the sea's basins, deep troughs and underwater ridging. The sea is a conduit, carrying things with it, even from the Arctic.

A young adult, the walrus looked prematurely aged because of the heavy wrinkling of its deep brown skin. It was a long, long way from home but served to underline the connectedness of things, and how the sea between the two countries, indeed all countries, is fecund with sea-life. It became a tourist attraction, Instagrammed half to death by tourists on their leisure craft.

When the Arctic aquanaut took to the currents again, hitching a ride on the ocean's carousel of currents and tides, it moved on to Cornwall.

In this he was following an ancient route which Welsh saints took to convert people both in the south-west of England and in Brittany. The Welsh prefix *llan* is found in Cornwall as *lan*, and there are a great many on the map. Welsh saints such as St Pol de Leon and St Samson of Dol arrived there to proselytise, the Irish saint St Feock reputedly traversed the same stretch of sea riding on a granite boulder, and Cornwall's answer to Patrick and David was the sixth-century abbot, St Perrin, or Pira. They would have enjoyed the sight of the walrus: these were men at one with nature. St Kevin, whose refuge nestled in the Wicklow Mountains, is said to have been praying when a black-bird laid its eggs in his cupped hands, so he stayed on his knees until they hatched. St Ninian, who built the first-known stone church in Britain, was said to study in order to 'perceive the eternal world of God reflected in every plant and insect, every bird and animal, and every man and woman.'

The walrus in Cornwall wasn't just following the route of saints. As it submarined on to Brittany it was following a route also sometimes taken by seals. A female seal travelled from Ramsey island in south-west Wales to Porthscatho in Cornwall in the autumn of 1960 while a male, tagged on Ramsey on 21 September 1960, had reached Santona in northern Spain by mid-December of the same year, this constituting the longest seal sea-journey recorded. The fastest seal trip happened to connect with the Kerry coast again, as an animal tagged in Pembrokeshire on 22 October 1967 was spotted near Kerry Head on 7 November, the animal having traversed a distance of 309 miles in sixteen days. Our walrus's journey, meanwhile, continued to La Rochelle in France, then looping to Bilbao in Spain before spending three weeks off the south coast of Ireland. It was eventually then spotted much nearer its Arctic home, near Höfn in south-east Iceland. There he would hopefully put on sufficient blubber whilst feeding in the fjord to withstand the frigid black waters of the Arctic.

* * *

The walrus would have to navigate various dangers such as overcurious tourists on jet skis and invisible perils too, such as plastic. Some 100,000 sea mammals die each year trapped in such things as discarded nets, not to mention the disintegrating plastic that floats on the waves and sadly becomes part of the general food chain.

In 2017 a crew of women sailed across the Irish Sea from the English south coast to Belfast in a 72-foot expedition yacht called *Sea Dragon*, trawling as they went with a very fine mesh net to collect microplastics, from microbeads to nurdles to pellets of polystyrene, all sampled from the ocean's surface. They filtered their catch through sieves of various sizes before examining their find. It included bits of plastic with organisms growing on them and microfibres floating out of the gut of a fish. Even an eel which had been trapped in their engine water intake on leaving Cardiff, bound for Belfast, turned out to have a piece of hard plastic in its digestive tract. As crew member the writer and sailor Sarah Tanburn put it, 'Our fashion to drink water out of single-use plastic bottles is an incredibly destructive piece of very clever marketing. Bollocks to that. I don't want you marketing something that gets dumped on my street, gets into the ocean and damages the food chain. So how do we encourage people who want to be hydrated and be healthy to drink the very good tap water that we're blessed with?' In seas so rich with wildlife it is salutary to note that over half of all seabirds studied have plastic in their stomachs, and this particularly affects birds such as Manx shearwaters and storm petrels, who mistake floating plastic for prey. To underline the problem the *Sea Dragon*'s crew went to clean up a beach near Belfast when they made it to harbour there. They managed to fill 55 bags with plastic in 90 minutes, made even more telling by the devastating fact that this plastic is only used by humans for a few minutes, but lasts for centuries, never breaking down, only getting smaller.

The poet Jean Sprackland found the problem to be just as bad the other side of the Irish Sea. In an hour's beachcombing through the 'modern ribbon of debris' that is the strandline at Ainsdale Sands between Blackpool and Liverpool, she found over 300 plastic items. They included ten disposable cigarette lighters, 13 sanitary towel wrappers, 39 sweet wrappers, 26 cellophane wrappers from cigarette packets, plastic rope, fishing line, a Bart Simpson stencil, a shuttlecock and a plastic dinosaur. In an hour.

The pollution might not even be visible: man-made chemicals called polychlorinated biphenyls (PCBs) which built up in the bodies of seabirds led to the 'Irish Sea Bird wreck' of autumn 1969, when thousands of birds were washed up on shore, having been weakened by the effects of these toxic compounds and hit by a series of winter storms. The fact that such chemicals came from a licensed dump off the Clyde estuary in Scotland underlined how low-level pollution over a period of time could accumulate to create real trouble.

But plastic and PCBs are not the worst of the Irish Sea's pollutants. After the Second World War the British had to dispose of over 709,000 German bombs filled with tabun, a deadly nerve agent, along with sarin nerve gas and stocks of arsenic. Some were stored temporarily in Snowdonia while disposal facilities were prepared in RAF Llandwrog near Caernarfon. Work began on defusing them but it wasn't until 1954 that the decision was taken to dispose of them. The toxic bombs were taken to Cairnryan in Dumfries and Galloway before later sinking them north-west of Ireland by scuttling the ships that carried them in deep waters well beyond the edge of the continental shelf.

* * *

But let's return to our redoubtable Arctic mammal. The walrus was of great interest to the Vikings, whose names pepper the coasts of Wales: we have holm, meaning 'little isle', present in Grassholm, Priestholm, Skokholm and Gateholm; and we have Skerries, from *sker*, a lonely cliff, on both sides of the Irish Sea. The Irish Sea itself was a Celtic lake before the Vikings took control of its waters and bestowed new names such as Tusker, Waterford and Wexford, claiming by naming.

The Pembrokeshire town of Tenby was possibly a trading station for the Vikings, whose interest in walruses was more to do with economics than ecology. They made a lot of money from trading walrus tusk ivory, especially when the trade in elephant tusks was curtailed by the Moors when they took control over much of the Mediterranean.

Ivory was used to decorate medieval churches and to make luxury goods, as the crofter Calum McLeod discovered when he found an exquisite set of 93 chessmen on the Isle of Lewis in the Hebrides. The set, now divided and exhibited at both the National Museum of Scotland in Edinburgh and the British Museum in London features wild and staring-eyed rooks. These, intriguingly, were berserkers, baring their teeth, crazed warriors of old who would sometimes ingest hallucinogenic mushrooms before going into battle and thus do so when out of their maddened minds. Ivory was so favoured for such carvings that there's even a word for them – 'scrimshaw' – often referring to such items made by sailors and especially by whalers.

With walrus tusks, or sea-ivory, held in such regard by the Vikings it was little wonder that pieces of such ivory were discovered during excavations at Wood Quay in Dublin. The *Mare Clausum Seu Dominum Maris* – a book from 1636 by John Selden written to justify the maritime policies of Charles I – suggests that ancient Irish warriors were known to decorate the hilts of their swords with the tusks of sea-beasts, probably walruses. Such ivory was treasured in Wales as well. The laws of the Welsh king Hywel Dda demonstrate a Welsh delight in articles made either from the bones of cetaceans or the tusks of walruses. The 'judge of the court', when he swore his oath of office, was given a *tawlbwrdd* made of the ivory of a sea-beast as a gift from the King. The word translates as 'throwboard' and is described as a chess-like game played with 16 white men arraigned against a black king and 8 black men. The King's bard or favoured servant might receive one as a gift.

* * *

Some of the lighthouse keepers of the Irish Sea area played very long games of chess. Gerald Butler was a third-generation lighthouse keeper who grew up on Roancarrig light and lived in various lights such as Ballycotton, Mine Head near Dungarvan in County Wexford, and at Galley Head in West Cork. He remembers how the keepers would always be supplied with a Bible and the *Guinness Book of Records* to help settle factual arguments, and also how marathon chess games whiled away the hours for neighbouring and sometimes not-so-neighbouring keepers: 'We played chess over the radio, from one station to another, and you'd have a chess board, and the game of chess might last maybe a week. We'd set up the board and moves are all known, so you'd come on the radio and you'd call up and say "Look I want to move my queen to rook four" or whatever it was, and he'd do that and say maybe "Alright I'll come back to you tomorrow with another move." And you might give all night looking at it, and all the possibilities and such. Even when we were with ourselves we used to play chess quite a bit. It was fabulous: the chess games. I loved them. I really did.'*

Other keepers had a similar penchant for the game. Martin Murphy, who grew up near Hook Lighthouse, also worked for six-year stints on Inishtearacht, the outer Blasket Island, and Tuskar Rock, among other postings. 'You wouldn't pass the time lightly in places like that,' he says.† 'You would have to have hobbies. What people did in their spare time was as important as anything else, to keep their sanity. People became very good artists, rug-makers, and makers of *shillelaghs*, of keyrings, and so on. Most of us played chess and Scrabble. During the 2 to 6 watch at night, often one chess board would be set up on, say, the Fastnet lighthouse and another on Inishtearacht. People would play out their pieces, communicating by contact radio frequency between the two lighthouses, as if they were at the same station.' Murphy also recalled how some games went on and on, fruitfully eating up the long hours. 'Sometimes, you might not get the game finished and the board was left there with the pieces in the same place. After television came in, a lot of that changed.'

---

* Déirdre D'Auria, 'Reflections of a Former Irish Lighthouse Keeper', *Béaloides*, 75, 2007.

† *Irish Examiner*, 13 September 2013.

Picture the scene, then. In the monolithic granite lighthouse tower on Fastnet the player moves the white piece to start the game, his old fingers moving the king's pawn forward two places. He takes a contemplative draw on a long-stemmed pipe, shaped like the down-curved bill of a curlew. The fug of tobacco in the room offers a comforting aroma as the wind banshees outside. He waits for the reply. No rush. His studious lips purse in satisfaction as he has already started to claim the middle ground. Already! Ha! He has a choice of some of the oldest openings in the game – the Spanish Opening, the Italian game, the King's Gambit. He taps out the contents of his pipe ready to fill the bowl again. His opponent on Inishtearacht knows a loss is overdue, as they have long been rivals. One day he would like to meet him, shake his hand, thank the old man for evenings of such absorption, making time run quickly which was, for him, for them, all of the game.

* * *

The recent intermittent chess game between the UK and the EU as a consequence of Brexit has seen an imaginary border drawn down the Irish Sea, even if some of the key players aver it doesn't exist in truth. It's tempting to imagine one side negotiating while wearing welders' goggles and clumsily moving the pieces with oven mitts. But the satire's more than well-provided in Twitter feeds such as that of The Irish Border, @BorderIrish, an account that ran for two years and penned its own obituary in the *Irish Times*:

> We've ended up with the Northern Ireland protocol, which means the UK leaving the EU politically but leaving Northern Ireland behind economically.
>
> Or, as people love to say, with a border in the Irish Sea. There's only one Border in Ireland, I'll have you know, and it's not that one.
>
> The Irish Sea border will be a kind of franchise operation. I'll be contracting out to the Irish Sea border the actual work of

bordering while I go on doing absolutely zilch and getting all the glory of being invisible in a post-Belfast Agreement kind of way.

It's tempting to see the Brexit and post-Brexit negotiations as being more like snakes and ladders than chess. The veteran Brexit observer Fintan O'Toole has suggested how easy it was to turn patrician languor, the affected boredom about Europe expressed by many intellectuals, into the sense 'that the whole thing is a jolly game.' But with the Northern Ireland protocol depending on it, and thus a fragile, tentative peace, it had to be more than a game, it had to be taken seriously. 'There will be no border down the Irish Sea ... over my dead body,' the British Prime Minister Boris Johnson told the *Irish News* in August 2020.

Cartoons in recent years have drawn a line down the Irish Sea, representing that self-same border. But if it's true that nature abhors a vacuum, she certainly dislikes straight lines. The only ones connected with the Irish Sea are man-made, such as those that demarcate the various areas of the Shipping Forecast – Lundy, Fastnet and, of course, Irish Sea, all dating back to 1924 when the mantric shipping news and forecast was first broadcast. Before that, sailors would trust to their instinct as they judged wind direction, the state of the sea, watched the shapes and formation of clouds, took bearings from the sun and stars, used smells, and even watched the behaviour of fish, sea mammals, and birds.

Some other straight lines go under the sea in the form of underwater cables which, even today, carry more data than satellites and landlines, so are crucial components of the global economy. They were invented in the Victorian era, using copper wire as the core. This was at a time when the British Empire could avail itself of plentiful supplies of gutta percha, the rubber-like substance harvested from trees in Asia and Australasia, while the cables were often wrapped in iron wire to strengthen them as they were sunk. In 1855 the Electric and International Telegraphy Company used the *Monarch* to lay a cable connecting Howth Head near Dublin with Holyhead, allowing news and information to travel swiftly. Cables were also set down along a 63-mile stretch of sea between Wexford and the Pembrokeshire haven of Abermawr. When this terminal was dismantled in the 1920s local fishermen, not short of ingenuity, recycled the abandoned wire to fashion lobster pots.

In 1937 the *Faraday* was laying more cables between Wales and Ireland. Cables were also laid across entire oceans, of course, and some of that happened with the help of an amazing character called Captain Robert Halpin. Born at the Bridge Tavern, Wicklow, he went to sea at the age of 11, joining a brig called the *Briton*, which crossed back and fore to Wales but also ventured to Quebec. The young man crossed the Atlantic four times, gaining a master's ticket. Eventually he commanded what was the biggest ship in the world at the time, the Isambard Kingdom Brunel-designed SS *Great Eastern*, which set out to successfully link Europe with America by cable, earning him the nickname 'Mr Cable'. Halpin, true to this nickname, connected continents.

*   *   *

The sea was an often-used measure of what kept countries separate. Indeed a sea can defined as a portion of the ocean that is partly surrounded by land. Making the case for a form of self-government for Ireland, for instance, the British statesman and Prime Minister William Gladstone drew on Henry Grattan, who had opposed the Union in 1800 on the grounds that the Irish Sea made for inevitable separation, even as threats from overseas demanded a secure connection. Ireland, he wrote, 'hears the Ocean protesting against Separation, but she hears the sea likewise protesting against Union; she follows, therefore, her physical destination, and obeys the dispensations of Providence when she protests, like the sea, against the two situations.'*

---

* Claire Connolly, 'Too rough for verse? Sea crossings in Irish Culture', in Leerssen, J. (ed.) *Parnell and his Times*, Cambridge: Cambridge University Press, 2020.

But countries often define themselves by, and certainly defend, their territorial rights. Halford John Mackinder, writing in 1902 in his *Britain and the British Seas*, described the Irish Sea both as a 'British Mediterranean' and also as 'a land-girt quadrilateral, wholly British, whose four sides are England, Scotland, Ireland and Wales.' The north Channel, meanwhile, was 'not merely British on both sides, but also remote from all foreign shores.' It is set, Mackinder averred, 'midway along the "back of Britain", a private entry as it were to Liverpool and Glasgow.'

A little over a decade later that 'quadrilateral' was under attack. To combat the privations wrought by German U-boat attacks in the First World War, Britain set huge fields of 6,000 mines in St George's Channel to protect access routes along the backbones of supply connected to Liverpool and the Clyde. In response the Germans laid their own minefields off the south-west coast of Wales to deter shipping from entering or leaving Pembroke Dock and Milford Haven. Which begs the question: how did ships find their way through the dangers posed by their own countries' mine-defences? The 1940–1943 *British Offshore Minefield Chart* usefully marks a 'Secret Gap' in the fields off the coast of Wexford, through which ships could manoeuvre. A Secret Gap. It's a bit Monty Python, but it worked in large measure.

* * *

The Irish Sea is essentially the result of a great ice gouge, created by an enormous glacier that moved incredibly slowly but equally powerfully southwards from its original location in Scotland and Ireland, scraping across the Isle of Man, Anglesey and Pembrokeshire, 700km from its source to its southernmost edge. When it reached the narrowing constrictions of St George's Channel there were two rumbling ice streams in play: the Irish Ice Cap to the east and the Welsh Ice Cap to the west. Once through that narrowing throat the ice widened out where the waves of the Celtic Sea move today. It eventually created a sea, but it shaped the land on either side as well.

When the tide's out, or rather far out, on either side of the Irish Sea you can sometimes see petrified forests of pine, oak, hazel, willow and birch, dating back to 4500 BCE and the end of the last Ice Age, when sea levels around the coast were much lower than they are today. As the ice retreated, the waves inundated large areas of the Irish and Welsh coasts, drowning the trees where Mesolithic and Bronze Age hunters would have operated. Their presence is evidenced by simple tools fashioned from antlers which have been found in peat surrounding these tree stumps. After winter storms or at very low tide these rise again, black stumps in the sea telling an old and powerful tale about geology and previous climate emergencies. We are not the first to face nature's dramatic changes, although we are the first to have caused them ourselves. Welcome to the Anthropocene.

The earliest inhabitants of the shores of the Irish Sea – which has also been provocatively described as the Welsh Sea and even the Manx Sea – were primitive beachcombers. They scavenged like gulls for food such as oysters and went fishing with harpoons made from antler and bone. They also picked at the land's plenty: at that time a wildwood covered it like a thick blanket, before flat axe met forest to usher in the Neolithic age of settlement and eventually agriculture. Hunters went after seal, deer and porpoise, catching salmon, gathering seabirds' eggs and harvesting mussels, all with simple tools. Axe factories produced items of very early trade, underlining links and interconnectivity between disparate, remote communities, all linked together by the sea-lanes.

Such tools – made of stone rather than flint – were a feature of the Irish Sea area, with primitive manufactories at Penmaenmawr in north Wales and at Mynydd Rhiw at the western edge of the Llŷn peninsula. There were other early trade items, too: porphyry was extracted in the Preseli mountains in Pembrokeshire and on Lambey Island near Dublin, while obsidian was obtained on the Scottish Isle of Arran and at Pike O' Stickle above the Langdale Valley in Cumbria. Indeed, tools from here were traded as far away as the Rhineland, the Channel Isles and the Baltic coast of Poland. On the eastern edge of Europe these might have been exchanged for amber, while jet from North

Yorkshire was similarly traded, as were ceramic goods later on. And, of course, copper from north Wales, mixed with tin from Cornwall and thence carried by sea, made bronze possible, ushering in the Bronze Age. Trade routes from Ireland carried gold and copper, dogs, slaves and hides, while incoming commodities in the Celtic era would have included wine, wheat, oil and luxury goods. A lost Irish legal text, *Muirbretha*, gives us a sense of others when it lists the cargoes of wrecked ships: 'hides and iron and salt … foreign nuts and goblets and an escup of wine and honey if there is good wine and honey', while other goods listed included silver and gold, horses and fur.

All this mercantile traffic along the shorelands of the Irish Sea, and indeed the Atlantic fringes of Europe, long unified their various peoples. As the archaeologist V.G. Childe put it, 'the grey waters of the Irish sea were as bright with Neolithic argonauts as the Western Pacific is today.' There was prehistoric trade in a range of goods, such as Irish gold lunulae and leather crossing the sea, before moving overland across north-west Wales or across Cornwall.

According to Pliny, the people of Britain sailed abroad in vessels of wickerwork covered with hide, thus possibly describing Irish curraghs or Welsh coracles, both being simple craft that could nevertheless withstand severely testing seas. The larger of such craft, built on the same principle – with a wicker framework and covered with many layers of hide – could carry a crew of twenty men and were robust enough to cross the seas to Iceland, though what they carried precisely, or why they ventured in the first place, is lost in the sea-mists of time.

* * *

The Neolithic Boyne culture saw the main landfall of the Passage Grave people around the Irish Sea Basin. They built a class of tombs, huge megalithic memorials each furnished with a narrow passage so that the homes of the dead could be visited repeatedly. There is evidence of contact between disparate places such as the Isle of Man, Anglesey and the Llŷn peninsula, as well as western Pembrokeshire and, of course, with Ireland. This connected the story of the superb burial mound at Newgrange, in what is nowadays County Meath, with people who wandered from Almeria in Spain, travelling thence to south-west Portugal, via the Gironde estuary, to Finisterre in Brittany, to finally reach the valley of the Boyne. Their passage graves are also found in Co. Waterford and on Llŷn and Anglesey in Wales. They evidence the way in which culture, goods and indeed language travelled from the Mediterranean along the western seaboard of Europe, along the edge of the Irish Sea. V.G. Childe in *The Prehistory of European Society* suggests close parallels between the spread of the Megalithic culture along the Western sea-routes and that of the Celtic saints three thousand years later: 'Are not the Megalithic tombs of Britain the counterparts of the Celtic chapels founded by the Welsh and Irish saints in much the same parts of the British Isles? If so, their founders might be called "megalithic" saints and owe their authority and status to spiritual prestige rather than to temporal power. In this way missionaries from the South-west won the allegiance of a British Neolithic peasantry by their reputation for sanctity or magic power ...'

* * *

People from each of the facing coasts of Wales and Ireland left their mark on the other. Irish-speaking people from Leinster settled on the Llŷn peninsula and left their names behind. The name Llŷn itself is cognate with Leinster, while the name of the picturesque port of Porthdinllaen explains that here, once, was the 'harbour of the fort of the Leinstermen.' Further evidence of the association is apparent in the name of Iron Age remains such as those near Holyhead, dating from around 600 BCE, known as 'Cytiau Gwyddelod' – the Irish Huts.

* * *

The early middle ages saw parts of Wales subject to small-scale invasion by various pagan, Goidelic Irish tribes such as the Deisi – from the Cork and Waterford area – who were key in the foundation of the south-west Walian kingdom of Dyfed. Settlers, perhaps, rather than invaders, they may quite literally have burned their boats when they landed. Some have it that they had been driven out of Ireland by Cormac Mac Airt, lord of the Fenians, who was disfigured while battling them: a real face-off battle.

They brought and left bits of language. There are many places called Cnwc in south-west Wales, connecting with the word *cnoc*, meaning hillock. Certainly a royal dynasty emerged in the extreme south-west that had clear origins in Ireland. There was influence further inland, too, where the small kingdom of Brycheiniog could trace its lineage to the marriage of a Welsh princess and an Irish prince from Pembroke, or possibly from Ireland.

* * *

One of the most distinctive of the imports from Ireland was Ogham, a stroke alphabet. There are seven sites in west Wales, and in landlocked Brycheiniog more than anywhere else, where Ogham memorial stones are still standing, with simple 'letters' notched on the edges. In Ireland tombstones were inscribed in Ogham alone but in southwest Wales they are bilingual, inscribed also in Latin as the Irish settlers mixed with Gallic Christians. I remember seeing the language for the first time etched into a stone outside Cilymaenllwyd, the big house that overlooked the south Wales village of Pwll where I grew up. It was hard to countenance the fact that these simple chisellings had meaning.

The series of such notches could be cut easily and clearly into both wood and stone. The resulting alphabet included eighteen letters, each one associated with an animal, a bird or a tree, or a colour, whilst also having some sort of divinatory role. It was a sort of lexical three-for-one deal. So the letter 'R' stood for *ruis* and was variously denoted the elder tree, *rocnat*, the rook, and the colour of red blood. 'D' stood for *dair*, oak, and was associated with *dreoilin*, or wren, and the colour black. Some letters linked to days of the week, so 'B' stood for Birchday or Sunday, while Tuesday was Hollyday, not to be confused with a holiday.

The Irish Fenni and Ui Neill tribes crossed to Wales as well. In the north of Wales the chieftain Cunedda Wledig possibly campaigned against them before he settled there at the beginning of the fifth century, a move made in response to a request by the Romans who wanted to deal with the threat of such Irish invaders. Cunedda, chief of the Votadini tribe, took his sons, along with a fighting force of 1,000 men, down from the Firth of Forth near North Berwick and Edinburgh in 425 CE and eventually established his own royal dynasty in Gwynedd, after causing 'enormous slaughter' so that the Irish 'never came back to live there again.'

According to some chroniclers the Irish influence extended over the Britons, and in particular the west Britons, until the early Christian era ushered in a period of retreat. Cormac of Cashel, who died in 908, sketched out the map of such influence in his *Glossary*: 'The power of the Irish over the Britons was great, and they had divided Britain between them into estates … and the Irish lived as much east of the sea as they did (to the west), and their dwellings and royal fortresses were made there … And they were in that control for a long time, even after the coming of St Patrick.'*

The Irish certainly settled Kerno, or Cornwall, and might even have ruled there in late Roman times. Irish migrants crossed the North Channel in the first half of the first millennium to claim lands where once lived the Picts, colonising three places: Islay, Kintyre and Lorn, collectively called 'Ar-gael' or Argyll, which translated as the 'Eastern Irish'.

The eleven Welsh folk tales collected in the *Mabinogion* show the constant traffic between Wales and Ireland, including princesses, starling-messengers, giant warriors and invading armies. Language, too, provides evidence of interchange. The Celtic languages – spoken

---

* Norman Davies, *The Isles*, London, 2000.

by a people the Greeks knew as the *keltoi* – were a form of cultural currency, with dialects of a common prototypical language being spoken right down the Atlantic seaboard of Western Europe, intelligible from the Algarve to the coasts of Scotland, thus for five hundred years facilitating trade in pottery, weapons and axe-heads, not to mention exchanging ideas about anything from religion to politics, the littoral gossip of the day.

* * *

Languages sometimes overlap, as do waves. A wave, in Welsh, is *ton*, plural *tonnau*. The principal Irish word for wave is *tonn*, which can be both a single wave or a whole ocean. In Irish myth there are three great waves which crash and thunder around the island's coasts, *Tonn Tuaithe*, *Tonn Rudhraighe* and *Tonn Clíodhna*, Clíodhna's wave: together they 'thundered a welcome' to Lugh after he left the magical realm of Tír na nÓg, the Land of Youth. Clíodhna was a goddess who cared for three magic birds with healing voices that could cure all ills, who took the shape of a wren to escape the sea god Manannán but drowned as she did so.

Meanwhile the word *long* in Irish, meaning boat, echoes *llong* in Welsh, both stemming from the Latin *longa*, while a certain kind of small boat is *currach* in Irish and in Welsh is known as *cwrwgl*. Meanwhile the name for a fish that was hugely important in both countries, the herring, is *scadán* in Irish (in which language it also means 'thin man') and *ysgadan* in Welsh, a species that was pretty much a silver currency all of its own in the heyday of fishing.

Thus the connections run deep and long. Pytheas the navigator referred to a people he called *Pretanike* which derived from a Celtic word meaning Painted People, or the People of the Designs, referring to the widespread use of skin on ink, the tattoos which long prefigured the Celtic knots and loops that commonly decorate bodies nowadays. These were Celtic connections which interlaced over long periods of time and often intimately so, like swirling fans and fronds of kelp, drifting together but also discernibly separate in themselves.

PART ONE

ISLANDS

3.

ISLAND OUT OF TIME

'And at the close of the seventh year they went forth to Gwales in Penvro. And there they found a fair and regal spot overlooking the ocean; and a spacious hall was therein … And that night they regaled themselves and were joyful … And there they remained fourscore years, unconscious of having ever spent a time more joyous and mirthful. And they were not more weary than when first they came, neither did they, any of them, know the time they had been there.'

*'Branwen, Daughter of Llŷr,' being the
2nd Branch of* The Mabinogion *

If you take the ferry from Rosslare to Pembroke Dock, or vice versa, and the visibility's good, you'll be sure to see 'Gwales in Penvro', being the island of Grassholm, which lies 14 km off the Welsh coast. Indeed, on a clear day it's pretty hard to miss because of its striking colour scheme of black and white, like an outsize photographic negative.

The black is the basalt rock of which it's composed, evidence of ancient volcanic eruptions hereabouts, when the sea boiled and

---

* Leopold Classic Library edition, ed. Owen M. Edwards, p. 32.

sputtered and molten rock spewed forth before solidifying in a hiss of immersion-heated spume. Geological high drama. The white colour, at least in summer, is made up of sentinel ranks of nesting gannets, spaced out at equal intervals, a veritable pixillation of them on the rocky surface. Flying over them is a snow blizzard, *fflwch eira* in Welsh, a whirling flurry of wings, when the starch-white birds veer and turn in their thousands. In winter, when the birds have dispersed to warmer climes, what you see is matt-white guano, or droppings, covering the island in near-harvestable amounts. On south American coasts and islands they gather seabird droppings to make a rich and stupendous fertiliser despite the equally stupendous stench. When the copper trade in Wales was in its heyday, cargoes of the metal would travel to Chile and the boats would return full of gag-reflex-inducing consignments of guano. Think tons of rotten fish cooked in the sun and then carried across an ocean.

The gannet, or *hugan* in Welsh, is a common sight in the seawaters between Ireland and Wales, with its startling white plumage, cigar-shaped body and six-foot wingspan tipped with black primary feathers, as if dipped in Quink ink.

We may associate seabirds with islands – puffins standing sentinel on ledges, guillemots in serried ranks on slim ledges – but this is only a temporary habitat. On land they are edgy, twitchy, vulnerable to predation. Just take a look at auks such as razorbills and guillemots on their breeding ledges in early spring, just after they've come in off the sea, how jittery they are. They fly to a ledge, then skitter down to the waves before returning again, neurotic, exposed. But we humans tend to see them as birds of islands simply because we are hardly ever able to see them out over open ocean. For such pelagic species the sea is their true habitat and land is a dangerous place of brown rats and other ground predators, gluttonous gulls and, of course, human disturbance. These are, after all, sea birds and therefore gannets and the like spend most of their lives way out there, quartering the waves on uplifts of wind, their outstretched wings barely moving, riding the air like outsize paper planes. They only rest on the waves when they have to, staying far away from shore, other than when that ancient urge to breed takes them to isolated headlands and islands.

The Latin name of the gannet, *Morus bassana*, refers to one of its most famous colonies, Bass Rock in the Firth of Forth. It was celebrated by William Dunbar, as long ago as the fifteenth century:

The air was dirkit with the foulis
That came with yawmeris and yowlis
Whith shrykking, screeking, skyming, scowlis,
And miklie noyis and showtes.

The gannets didn't just inspire screeking poetry: they inspired covetousness, too. The Prioress of North Berwick, on the mainland opposite, petitioned the Pope for tithes to be claimed from the Bass Rock's owner, payable in the form of barrels of gannet grease. Slick work. Early sixteenth-century visitors noted and heard the 'shrykking' birds on this great slab of geology: 'Near to Gleghornie, in the ocean, at a distance of two leagues, is the Bass Rock, wherein is an impregnable stronghold. Round about it is seen a marvellous multitude of great duck that live on fish.'

The 'great ducks' are easy to spot when patrolling the waves for a flicker of herring-silver, but when they plunge-dive for fish they are simply unmistakable. From a height of up to 140 feet they collapse their wings, their bodies becoming living spearheads. They plummet towards their prey at a speed of up to 60 miles per hour, or as the poet Christine Evans has it: 'Gannets fall/as if fired back/by sky they have stretched/with their slow, strong wing beats.' Before they hit the surface of the sea, small air sacs in the head fill up, like the airbags that cushion a human car passenger from impact. The fine nature writer Tim Dee has captured the kinetic vibrato, the sheer thrill of this avian spectacle – which easily rivals that of African Big Game – and the plunging exhilaration of the dive: 'Again and again they do the same thing to catch their food, but each dive shines. Nature's repetitions are never boring. Every time it is like witnessing a fresh marvel in a new world; their visible decision-making, with its corrective twisting and corkscrewing, the rapid origami of themselves, and then their brilliant white match strikes, fizzing into the water (at 60 mph) to leave puffs of lit sea spray. It is hard not to blink and hold your breath as they go in.'*

'The rapid origami of themselves' – a phrase worth repeating! The Grassholm gannet colony numbers some 100,000 living origami fold-outs, in total made up of 36,000 pairs, with the remainder being non-breeding birds. A 1934 documentary film about this colony, *The Private Life of the Gannets*, made by the renowned biologist Sir Julian Huxley, became the first wildlife film to ever win an Oscar. Its producer, Alexander Korda, had attracted huge audiences and garnered much acclaim for his *The Private Life of Henry VIII*, released the previous year, hence the title.

With Korda's blessing, Huxley borrowed one of London Films' best cameramen, George Borrodaile, along with all the apparatus for film-ing, before obtaining tents and stores for a fortnight, including seven casks of water and one of cider. They set off on the steam tug *Taliesin* to film the intimate story of a bird that, unlike Henry VIII, tends to mate for life.

Gannet mating displays are complex and ritualistic. A bird return-ing to its companion on the nest will often present some strands of seaweed by way of bouquet, extra nesting material presented in a small act which is often the precursor to a more elaborate show. The birds bow their heads, they preen themselves under the wing, much as great crested grebes do on mainland lakes. The gannets might inter-twine their necks, cackling loudly and clappering their beaks in the ecstasy of the moment. Occasionally a bird left alone on the nest will be so overcome by emotion that it will perform a display all by itself. It's a sad case of solipsism and showing off. The resulting film did very well, as Julian Huxley recalled in his memoirs: 'It had a long run in cinemas all over England and America, as well as proving useful to departments of Zoology by illustrating the breeding biology, the strange mutual displays of the birds and their aerodynamic skill. The

---

* Tim Dee, *A Year on the Wing: Journeys with Birds in Flight*, Simon and Schuster, 2009.

end of the film was supplied by my old friend John Grierson, "father" of documentary films, who chartered a herring boat to take close-ups of gannets diving for fish – a beautiful sequence in slow motion.'*

John Grierson had already given the world genre-defining documentary films such as *Coal Face* and *Night Mail* – and had even coined the very word 'documentary' in a review. He now added a beautiful visual flourish to this latest film's end, showing the usually aeronautic birds turn aquanauts, a 'regular bombardment of birds' as the script has it, all hitting the water with a sherbet fizz before spear-heading for their prey. There are shots which show these fine avian spear fishers twisting and snaking underwater, exhibiting a rabid gluttony. Their binocular vision underwater helps guide the gannets to their silvery prey like sleek white torpedoes, trailing big champagne bubbles of air.

The film crew also had the benefit of local knowledge, as Huxley was joined by the naturalist R.M. Lockley, who brought his wife along as a sort of ersatz honeymoon. They found the gannet colony enchanting. As Lockley wrote in *I Know an Island*, the birds 'spread below you like some rare ballet in blue and silver and gold … and each bird was as beautiful to look at as the whole colony itself.'†

The Private Life of Gannets has been described by WildFilmHistory as a 'truly landmark film … with groundbreaking footage … shot with the support of the Royal Navy … [revealing] the incredible private life of these birds as they squabble over territory, perform spectacular dives and regurgitate fish for their young.'

* * *

According to *The Mabinogion*, the island of Gwales is a place out of time. One story concerns the Welsh princess Branwen, who marries the Irish king Matholwch, who imprisons her in a cell. From there she sends a message, via a starling, to her brother, the giant Bendigeidfran (Brân the Blessed) – who also doubles up as the Celtic god of

---

* Julian Huxley, *Memories*, London, 1970.

† Ronald Lockley, *I Know an Island*, London, 1947.

regeneration – to ask for help. There's always avian two way-traffic across the Irish Sea. The starling went one way, flying east – just as there's a bit of folklore that says the magpie first came to Ireland from Wales, flying west, landing in the Barony of Forth near Wexford harbour. Here it established a two-tone nesting colony to celebrate its arrival. There's often an interchange between Irish and Welsh populations of birds, from geese to terns to gannets.

But I digress. Bendigeidfran promply strides through the sea to rescue Branwen and a bloody battle ensues, during which the giant is mortally pierced by a poisoned spear. As a consequence he orders his men to cut off his own head before bearing it back to Britain to be buried. Seven survivors of the battle are entrusted with the regal cranium and, in keeping with the stretched time-beats of myth, spend seven years feasting in Harlech on the north Wales coast before moving on to Gwales, where a stately hall awaits them. Gwales, Grassholm, turns out to be a little bit of paradise for them, because here they can forget all their woes and there is plenty of everything. No one gets any older, despite their staying on the isle for eighty years, and to top it all Bendigeidfran's head proves to be surprisingly good company, even if it is detached from his body: he is one of the very original talking heads.

But all good things must end, and the soldiers ignore a warning not to open a door that faces out towards Cornwall. When they do their minds flood with appalling memories, the past pours in and with it the grim realisation that their lord and master is long dead. Branwen, meanwhile, has already returned to Wales, to Anglesey, where she sees the damage she has wrought. Or, as it says in the poet Tony Conran's play, *Branwen*, she 'looked at the land made desolate/And remembered Ireland and the people dead/"I am a curse to the world," she cried/"Two good islands/Have been destroyed because of me."'* The realisation is too much for her, and her heart breaks.

This sort of tale isn't confined to the Welsh, of course, and there are many international variants. The Irish have their *immrama*, or

---

* Tony Conran, *Branwen and Other Dance Drama*, Llanrwst, 2003.

sea-journeys, which tell of heroes setting sail for such islands, sea-girt rocks bathed in happiness where there is a plenitude of food and drink, where magical music is heard and time stands completely still. But time, that old stalker, has a habit of catching up with even such mythical travellers, much as Osian in the fabled Tír na nÓg ages so quickly his body flakes into ash. In that sense Grassholm resembles Tír na nÓg, a portal to another kind of time. And sometimes gannets themselves appear directly in such myths and ancient stories, such as the one in Homer's *Odyssey*, which turns out to be the sea goddess Leucothea in disguise. She advises the shipwecked Odysseus to discard his cloak and abandon his raft before offering her veil to wind around our hero so he can save his life. It's a story one can imagine the old gods sharing with delight and, as one writer put it, myth is after all only very old gossip.

*   *   *

Grassholm was long associated with supernatural goings-on, which persisted at the tail end of the nineteenth century, as a report about one Captain John Evans attests. In 1896 the *Pembrokeshire Guardian* redacted the ghostly tale: 'Once, when trending up the Channel, and passing Grassholm island, in what he had always known as deep water, he was surprised to see windward of him a large tract of land covered with a beautiful green meadow. It was not, however, above water, but just a few feet below ... so that the grass wavered and swam about as the ripple flowed over it, in a most delightful way to the eye, so that as he watched it made one feel quite drowsy. You know, he continued, I have heard old people say there is a floating island off there, that sometimes rises to the surface, or nearly, and then sinks down again fathoms deep, so that no-one sees it for years, and when nobody expects it comes up again for a while. How it may be, I do not know, but that is what they say.'

Other sources from the same period suggest that fairies lived among the underwater meadows of seaweed surrounding such islands. They were called Plant Rhys Ddwfn, Deep Rhys's Children, likely a corruption of Is Ddwfn, the children of the underworld. The common name in Welsh for this Celtic underworld was *Annwfn*, and Grassholm was believed to be a sort of portal to it, being out of, or apart from, conventional time and the rules of physics. A thin place, where the boundary between this world and another is insubstantial as gossamer.

Nowadays the fairies are gone – as best we mortals can ever know – and the island is simply home to the fourth-largest gannet colony in the world, after Bass Rock, far-flung St Kilda, Scotland and Bonaventure Island in Quebec.

* * *

There was a time when Grassholm belonged to another species of seabird altogether. It used to be the kingdom of the puffin, that clown-ish, parrotish member of the auk family with the sad Pagliacci-like tears in its eyes. Puffins once nested here in abundant numbers although it is likely they undermined themselves, quite literally, by digging too many tunnels into the thin layer of island soil. The turf canopy overhead completely collapsed.

The gannets probably arrived after their colony on Lundy Island in the Bristol Channel was sacked by people. The Pembrokeshire colony was probably established in 1820, and by 1890 it had grown to 200 pairs. Sadly a naval party landed here that same year, callously shoot-ing many birds and destroying all the eggs. The crew from the *Sir Richard Fletcher* might have got away with it had it not been for a key eye-witness. The artist and founding father of the National Museum of Wales, Thomas Henry Thomas, was paying a prolonged visit to the island at the time, in the company of three companions. Thomas was an interesting man, being the discoverer of the first dinosaur foot-prints in Europe and the illustrator of a guide to British goblins. More pertinently he was an artist who covered news stories for the the *Graphic* and the *Daily Graphic* newspapers. He was on hand to record the wilful destruction by the sailors, using his pencil to detail this heinous wildlife crime. Questions were asked in the Commons. A successful prosecution of the culprits ensued in court in Haverfordwest, backed by the Royal Society for the Prevention of Cruelty to Animals, a triumph for sketch-book journalism.

*   *   *

My own experience of visiting the island showed how human life can intrude and despoil even remote rocks. I was working in the 1990s for the Royal Society for the Protection of Birds, which had established Grassholm as its first reserve in Wales in 1948. In the company of species officer Iolo Williams, now a well-known and much-beloved TV presenter, I visited the island at the end of the gannet breeding season to perform a task which underlines just how profligate a species is homo sapiens sapiens.

As we approached the island the air was awhirl with birds, a white-out blizzard of them, the birds being animatedly splashed onto the cerulean canvas of sky – sharp dabs of startling white, the colour emphasised by the contrast with the birds' wing tips the colour of tarmac. Even at this time of year, the tail end of the nesting season, the air was seething with birds, with individual birds seemingly float-ing along within the aerial mêlée, each great tail acting as a paddle, correcting its path along the air-streams. But just as the sense of sight was seemingly assaulted by the thousands of birds, so too was the olfactory sense, as the stench of decaying fish grew stronger, edging from a clean white smell of cod to darker tones of dogfish, putrescent pollack, dessicated herring. It was a solid phalanx of smell to match the wall of sound as the remaining gannets screeched their collective unhappiness at the appearance of this boatload of intruders.

There was beauty, too. Up close the birds showed blurts of colour – a golden sheen to the head, bright blue bills and bright blue rings around the eyes, tones and hues quite lost to the long-distance observer. They are not just black and white.

In their breeding areas the gannets gather all manner of material with which to construct their nests, much as magpies do on land, using whatever they can find, often seaweed and kelp. Unfortunately, nowadays, they scoop up many other things which they integrate into the untidy gannet nest-mounds: the birds are site-faithful so return year after year to the same nest site, building it up by accretion year on year unless a storm blows it away. A nest might be constructed from seaweed, or a plant that grows on some part of the island, but then extraneous, man-made items might be included – a panoply of things such as synthetic rope, plastic, the tops of six-packs of beer, or, dangerously, lengths of mono-filament fishing line. This means you see a welter of unnatural colours, the orange, reds and blues of man-made materials – polypropylene, nylons, braided polyesters, Dralon and Dyneema polyethylene. Such materials are designed not to rot and decay and thus to last a very long time. They thus make a problem that simply does not go away, as the slow suffocation of the seas so sadly attests. This isn't entirely new. The great Irish naturalist Robert Lloyd Praeger, writing in 1937's *The Way That I Went* noted that gannets built their nests out of pretty much anything, including 'strings of onions, blue-castor oil bottles and a child's tin clockwork steamer.'

Sadly the adults and especially the young birds can get their legs entangled or trapped in their own nests, and Iolo and I were there to release them from all that polypropylene and Courlene netting. If the bird's struggles had led to its leg being too tightly wound into the plastic we might have to amputate it, although happily studies have shown that young birds mutilated in this way still make it to their winter fishing grounds off the coast of west Africa. They then return to Pembrokeshire the following spring to begin to look for a mate. We released some by painstakingly unwrapping cords and twists of plastic, noting the irony of such a remote rock resembling a municipal dump. What a profligate species we are.

Tragically not all the entangled birds survive, and an estimated sixty-five die each year on Grassholm, though this does not impact on the overall population. This had remained buoyant until the outbreak of avian flu in the summer of 2022, which led to the death of thousands of birds. The young birds are very different to the adults, a completely different colouration of dark grey and slate grey, with the sooty brown upper parts and wings spattered with white like the overalls of a painter and decorator. Some had already left the island on their maiden flights although these sad specimens just sat there, twisted into immobility, trapped in the bright, indestructible detritus of the modern age.

That said, it was still a grim and grisly business, so to introduce some light relief to the proceedings I started to talk about *The Mabinogion* and the essential timelessness of the place. Iolo playfully scorned my romanticising. Above us small birds turned in the sky. On closer observation it turned out to be a small flock of redwings – birds of winter coming in from Scandinavia and Russia, and some swallows, birds of summer, setting off for the reedbeds of South Africa. All commingling as if this place really was the crossroads of the seasons. 'More things in Heaven and Earth than are dreamt of in your philosophies', as Hamlet tells Horatio.

And science can be just as magical. It's been proven that a single starling, part of a flock or murmuration – within which thousands of birds might wheel, bank and veer – will take its coordinates from seven nearby individuals: genuine aerial formation flying. As we know, in the tale of Branwen the imprisoned princess sends her impassioned plea for help via an avian messenger, a starling which flies across St George's Channel, as the birds overhead must have done. So those massing above us might too be messengers, portents of season's change, flying wing tip to wing tip before bulleting on and ever onwards over the ceaseless waves, crossing the islands, heading for land.

* * *

The great nature writer and polemicist Rachel Carson suggested in *The Sea Around Us* that man's enduring interest in places such as Grassholm has much to do with the elements: 'Islands have always fascinated the human mind. Perhaps it is the instinctive response of man, the land animal, welcoming a brief intrusion of earth in the vast, overwhelming expanse of the sea.'* That sea, those *seas* are the true

---

* Rachel Carson, *The Sea Around Us*, New York, 1951.

habitat for the gannets, the North Atlantic ocean a vast feeding area for this great peregrinating species. On land, their breeding season is merely a brief intrusion into their skywheeling, squid-spearing, Atlantic lives. Six brief and frenetic months, when they reconnoitre the waves in freewheeling white squadrons, like artist's brush-splashes of titanium white against the blue-washed canvas of a striking cyan sky.

4.

PIRATE ISLE

Cycling from Rosslare to Kilmore Quay on the South Wexford coast takes you on the EuroVelo 1 route, doubling-up in parts as the so-called Norman Way, with its time-fractured churches such as St Iberius', now basically just an arch. You can spin past single tower castles such as Ballyhealy which solidly contribute to the pub quiz factoid that Ireland has one of the most castellated landscapes in the whole of Europe. The route takes you through gently undulating countryside punctuated with thatched cottages and tidy farmed fields, with here a Norman windmill, there an ornate bungalow almost steampunk in its garish anachronisms, built maybe by a Euromillions winner.

I stop for a rest and squish a purple mouthful of blackberries on the edge of a cornfield in which some hooded crows are picking at something bloody. The Irish name for this species is *badhbh*, a tricky homophone, being a word that sounds exactly the same as another, in this case denoting a female fairy. The two meanings blur to create a sort of phantom bird, that is if you're one of those people prone to such spectral ornithology. I press on, enjoying the laving, honeydew sunshine and the safety of dedicated cycle lanes.

* * *

Kilmore Quay is enjoying a morning of sharp sun and post-lockdown business. Children buzz and weave excitedly along the wide harbour walls and the 'Lick'd' ice-cream stall is starting a procession of children bearing cones – quite a feat considering it's barely ten o'clock. I find the small sign for the 'Saltee Ferry' above a metal gate and gangplank, around which milling holidaymakers snapshot the gathered trawlers – some of them rather rusty crates which work the rich Nymph Bank, the East Bank, and other fishing waters. Some animated naturalists, weighed down with daunting binoculars, are talking about the sort of rare birds that can cause their blood pressure to rise with excitement. Saltee gets its fair share. Red-flanked bluetail. Hoopoe. Baillon's crake. They can get a birder into a fair old tizz. Not for nothing are they known as twitchers.

The ferry is a small twelve-seater boat, suitable for what is usually just a twenty-minute trip, today through an azure lake full of turquoise tinged waves. The nut-coloured crew are young sea-gods burnished by the sun, barefoot and carefree. The sea is as blue as the hyacinths that grow on the island and we speed on as if through the Mediterranean.

On the short crossing we pass one of the notable features of the island approaches, being St. Patrick's Bridge, a rainbow-shaped shingly bar of rocks in the water, like a land bridge that's been subsumed by the waves. A geologist once suggested that this is a ridge marking the limits of the Irish Ice Sheet which, as it melted, left boulders, stones and shingle in its wake of cold water. Some of these glacial erratics are very big, and one in particular – St Patrick's Rock – is big enough to command its own little legend or two.

One goes like this, sounding like something out of an ecclesiastical Marvel movie: St Patrick, keen to visit the Saltees, borrowed a local fisherman's boat for the purpose. It leaked, however, and Patrick had to swim for it. Wet and angry, he cursed the boat, which immediately turned to stone, and so he promptly built a rocky ridge out to Little Saltee. Another story that explains the name involves Patrick chasing the Devil, a pursuit that started in the Galtee mountains (the Galtees) and ended, rhymingly at the Saltees, a hundred miles away. Beelzebub had to take a big bite out of a mountain to get through, so to further impede his progress Patrick threw a boulder at him, which landed in the sea. Thus was born St Patrick's Rock. It apparently still has his finger marks on it. But wait, in the Hollywood film there's often that extra, unexpected ending: the Devil was making his getaway, swimming determinedly to safety, when Patrick pelted him with smaller rocks until Beelzebub was forced to drop the big rock he was carrying in his mouth, which eventually became Little Saltee. Roll end credits. Other rocks commemorate a wreck in the area, such as Privateer Rock, the privateer in question being the *Faery Queen*, wrecked in the late nineteenth century with its cargo of muskets bound for South Africa, and Water Witch Rock, named after a steam boat that sundered here in 1833.

*   *   *

On the brief journey we skirt Little Saltee, now given over to a bawling nursery of Larus gulls which squawk and cry, acting as if they're starving. As we transfer in the ungainly manner of landlubbers from the ferry to a pair of inflatables to take us to shore, the young lads warn us it's going to be a 'wet landing'. They mean that you have to go barefoot, wading ashore through fronds, drifts and aromatic tangles of seaweed. There are pirates' belts of kelp, loosened in clear, clear water where their long trunk-like stems, or 'stipes', seem to form an understory for this floating forest. Then you tread dry land and crunch seaweed underfoot. There's an Irish word, *turscar*, for 'the washed up refuse of rotten seaweed and shellfish found on the shore.' This green mulch of sun-baked kelp zings with sandflies. The pebble beach scrunches as your bare feet finally make dry landfall after sploshing through what used to be seen as beds of food. *Feamainn* and *sleabhac*, seaweed and sea vegetables, were important for Irish society, providing calcium and minerals especially important in the lean months of winter. The seaweed, or *woar*, was much more than food. It also made excellent fertiliser, gathered after winter gales and carted to cover the fields. A report about the island in 1837 noted that 'from its abundance of seaweed found on its shores, it was rendered particularly fertile.' Walking through the green wracks felt delicious, an open-air New Age therapy foot spa. Highly recommended.

There's a lovely word for beachcombing – 'progging' – which I first encountered on Smith Island in Chesapeake Bay. I guess fossicking is a close equivalent, but the tideline on Saltee is ideal for this sort of ambling going-over. There's the egg-case of a skate or dogfish, known as *sparán na caillí*, the purse of the dead witch, and a dead jellyfish looking like an exhausted balloon. A myriad of sandflies dance busy aerial jigs as you turn anything over.

On land proper, the island is fair drenched by sunshine, the heat bringing out the green tang of bracken as you brush past. Smart oystercatchers, in their tuxedo black and white plumage, with their cherry-red bills, eyes, and reddish-pink, flesh-coloured legs are progging around the seaweedy shore near Middle Quay. In Irish the oystercatcher is *Griolla Brighde*, which translates as 'Servant of St Brigid', the same saint's name that occurs in St Bride, as in St Bride's Bay in Pembrokeshire. Legend has it that Brigid crossed the Irish Sea in a boat made from a single sod of earth. It sounds really uncomfortable and makes me glad I went with Irish Ferries.

I have a lot to thank oystercatchers for. When there was a cull of the birds on the Burry estuary in the early 1970s I was asked to do a TV interview to defend them, as they had been wrongly accused of depleting the cockle stocks out on the sands. As a schoolboy this was all very exciting, but it also led to more and more broadcasting opportunities, often allowing me to see things I might not otherwise have been able to, adding to a sense of gratitude that still informs my days. It's the same feeling of blessedness that had the writer Barry Lopez bending his head reverentially in the direction of a Lapland bunting in *Arctic Dreams*, a thankfulness for natural things, for having a sentient place in the pattern of things. Even now you can learn things each day, such as the fact that oystercatchers have small sensors located at the tips of their bills which help them locate the worms and tiny crustaceans on which they feed, their probing akin to metal detecting when the tide is out and the sand ridges glisten.

*   *   *

The walk around the island takes you through shoulder-high bracken, which hides tripwires of bramble. Seals, Ireland's largest marine predators, snout around in clear water offshore and then drift with their noses out of the water, looking like huge sunken bottles or plump grey gourds as they bob about, take a floating nap. The Latin name is *Halchoerus gryphus*, the 'hooked nose sea pig', although that description doesn't match up with the doe-eyed sea mammal dozing serenely beyond the wracks of kelp.

The seal has an intriguing life story. In September a cow drops a calf which feeds on very fatty milk, sufficiently rich to gain around three pounds in weight per day. The milk supply dries up after about two or three weeks, so the pup is left with a formidable bull, or 'beach-master', to guard it, as it lolls on the shingle in the company of other pups. They eventually change coats, from white to a dappled, spotted grey and eventually set off on their wanderings, some venturing to Wales, others to the Bay of Biscay or to emerge in the English Channel.

Lunch today is all about fish. I have a tuna sandwich as I watch a busy cormorant troubling the local fish stocks – as its overstreched gullet amply demonstrates. The Irish name is *cailleach dhubh*, the black hag, and this one is a pretty replete black hag, seemingly very satisfied with its piscivore's lunch as it struggles to get airborne. It contrasts so very much with the dainty kittiwakes that fly into view, moth-buoyant in flight and almost dove-like in their expression, so unlike the piratical, gimlet fix of the larger, Larus gulls which keep an opportunist yellow eye on everything.

A pair of chough needle in some low maritime turf, their matching red, decurved bills and legs as distinctive as their wild caw as they fly away on splayed black wings. They love probing in low maritime heath and there's an amplitude of such habitat on the rising land.

There's a belief in western Britain that King Arthur did not die but was resurrected as a chough, explaining in part why this bird is the emblem of Cornwall – with its wealth of Arthurian links – and is known as *Bran Gernyw*, The Crow of Cornwall. The red colour of its bill and legs connects with a strange folk tale, collected by Daniel Defoe in *A Tour Through the Whole Island of Great Britain*, which portrays the chough as a sneaky arsonist, carrying burning wood to set light to thatched roofs. Interestingly, the population of chough that is now consolidating in Cornwall derives from Irish stock, as genetic studies have revealed. Worryingly, south Wexford has a lot of thatched roofs!

*   *   *

The Saltees are the only islands on a long, long stretch of coast from Ireland's Eye off County Dublin to Sherkin off the south-west tip of County Cork. They are made up of tough rocks that have withstood time and tide, or, to be exact, tough pre-Cambrian granitoid gneiss, not that it's ever going to come up as a question in Trivial Pursuit. They were also one of the first Irish islands to be deserted, before the Blaskets, or Innishmurray off the Sligo coast. The rocks here are deeply fissured and pock-marked, long gnawed-over by the ravenous waves and given to cave formation. The islanders and fishermen have baptised a great many of the island's features: Tommeen, Ardheen, Cat Cliff, China-shop, Happy Hole, Wherry Hole, the Otter's Cave, Devil's Den, the Giant's Chair, and Makeston – the 'makes' stone, deriving from the fact that the local name for the kittiwake is make. Then there is Dead Man's Shoal, which records the place where a schoolboy fell from the top of Celbooly cliff into the maw of the sea.

Then the land out towards the western edge of the island rises and my arthritic knees start to clack like outsize knitting needles as I climb. The smell of the gannetry begins to insinuate itself into your nostrils. It's that moment when grandmother rediscovers the tin of sardines she's hidden under a cushion, away from the cat. But as you climb the smell intensifies until you gain more height on South

Summit and reach the actual gannetry at Seven Heads. There's the rank smell of the place – fish cannery with overtones of old cod – and there's the noise of it, as the wheeling birds utter raucous, throaty, vibrato calls, which evoke the sound of a Soviet-era helicopter, its rickety rotors needing some attention.

But what a sight, too: thousands of these dazzling white seabirds with their six-foot wingspans, wheeling in the air while some stand sentinel at what's left of the nests they built from sea-campion at the start of the nesting season, their great bills cropping this material like secateurs. This year's chicks are in various stages of development, the newest covered in grey powder puffs of feathers while the older young-sters are developing youthful plumage markings in brown and white, like starlings on steroids.

* * *

The magic of the place is that you can sit just a few yards away from them, close enough to appreciate the buff yellow tinges of the neck and head and the arresting blue of their eyes. Some birds bicker with their neighbours, or pairs indulge in beak-rubbing and entwining of necks to mark the return of a bird to the nest, perhaps reinforcing the bond between them.

In recent years the gannets have expanded to other locations such as The Megstone on Great Saltee, so there are now three sub-colonies on rocks along the island's southern edge. Here the snowy-white birds sit in serried ranks on bare rock, chattering and squabbling as their lives are lived in such close proximity to each other. This gannetry is the smallest of the three colonies in Ireland and was only established a little under a hundred years ago when two pairs nested in 1929. Its burgeoning is a success story in and of itself.

The gannetry has been growing year on year, from one or two pairs through the 1920s, 1930s and 1940s, then swelling in number to sixty nesting pairs in the 1960s. There were 700 pairs in the 1980s, when a subcolony was formed on the Megstone. By today the numbers on the Saltees have reached over 2,000 pairs. The Great Saltee gannetry has been pronouncedly expanding of late, as Tony Murray, the conservation ranger from Ireland's Parks and Wildlife Service explained to me: 'It was generally right at the western edge of the island but it's stretching back east now. Some species of seabirds seem to be doing OK, including gannets. In the past it's been found that they've been bringing in processed fish that's been jettisoned, or bycatch, so that clearly suits gannets. They don't have to eat live fish. Fisheries, the way we humans fish and what we fish is clearly to the benefit of some species like the gannet, but clearly have a negative impact on other ones. The numbers of shag out here are dropping so that has to be down to lack of grub, you know.'

The Saltee gannetry is dwarfed in size by the biggest colony in Ireland, on the uninhabited Skelligs off the coast of County Kerry. This is a spectacular pair of islands, with 70,000 birds present in the breeding season. During the Famine, Blasket islanders rowed here to harvest the gannets; nowadays the birds are totally protected by law. Irish and Welsh colonies can interchange members, and as one dips or declines, numbers in another might thus swell accordingly. Immigration from overflowing colonies such as that on Little Skellig probably boosted some irregular but substantial increases in numbers on Grassholm. Generally, gannets are doing well, in contrast with so many other seabirds such as puffins, whose populations have crashed owing to a shortage of sand eels.

Tony Murray particularly enjoys watching the gannets build nests in the spring: 'Any time I'm out there at the start of the breeding season their beaks crop sea-campion or thrift, which is a very waxy kind of plant, and you'll see them flying off with mouthfuls and mouthfuls of this to build a nest. They do use seaweed as well, and driftlines and random bits of nets and ropes that they find. And that can be a problem for the chicks which can get a foot tangled in them and certainly some of the nests on Saltee can be substantial enough to act like traps.'

One of the other typical plants of Saltee – if you ignore the bracken which threatens to engulf everything – is sea-pink or thrift, which grows in candyfloss cushions of pale pink inflorescence. The Welsh name is *Clustog Fair*, Mary's pillow, while the Gaelic is *tonna chladaich*, which translates beautifully as 'beach wave'. Where it grows in profusion it really is a sea of flowers, pinkened as if by sunset. But before I'm accused of being too dimissive of bracken I should perhaps give one small and almost holy fact in its defence: in Ireland it's sometimes known as the fern of God. Proof of this can be obtained by cutting the stem into three sections, each spelling out the letters "G," "O" and "D" respectively. She, or he, moves in mysterious ways.

Tony Murray is very keen to rid Great Saltee of rats, knowing this could signal much better seabird numbers, and after years of concerted work it looks as if he's winning the battle: 'We had the RSPB over, just to see if this was a good candidate – is it far enough offshore, is it below a certain size, the topography, the vegetation? We had to do some vegetation work so we could create transects – the bracken is six foot high in places and intertwined with bramble, so it's just impenetrable. Then we laid out bait stations, which were spaced a minimum distance apart. The weather played in our favour because it was a rough winter: the rougher the better from the eradication point of view. We had a hundred monitoring points on the island, and each has a wax block tethered inside it – rats have two front teeth which gnaw parallel lines down them. Over the winter we also had trail cameras and ink pads over which the animal would run and leave footprints and snap traps as well, so we had a myriad of ways to find the animals. There have been no signs in the last year so hopefully it's been a success.'

I ask him how soon one might expect to see a rise in seabird numbers on Saltee? 'It seems to vary from place to place. Some places get a bounce much quicker. The Manx shearwater chicks from last year probably got eaten. This year that wouldn't have happened because there were no rats here so we may not see a bounce until those birds leave, come back and start breeding at about the age of seven so we might not get a bounce in numbers untill 2028.'

One of the main beneficiaries of rat eradication on Saltee would be shearwaters. The population is currently 150 pairs, but Tony hopes that would be boosted significantly. There are plenty of rabbits out there, so there are plenty of holes – ample burrows for shearwaters to occupy, so he hopes they and other burrow-nesting species such as the puffin will benefit. Even if it takes seven or eight years, Tony reckons it'll be worth it.

* * *

The island may be given over to the birds nowadays but in the past it offered safe haven for pirates, who took advantage of the island's proximity to the main trading routes from Britain and Ireland and out into the Atlantic. They added their own brand of human danger to the reefs, rocks, shoals and islands of this wild stretch of coast, where fierce tidal currents can almost casually sweep vessels to their doom.

One of the most notorious pirates was Alexander Vailes, who preyed on merchant vessels using Waterford and Ross as bases. On one occasion he swooped on a French ship right under the fort in Duncannon on the Suir-Barrow estuary and pillaged '46 tonnes of wynes which was presently brought by the said pyrates to Waterford and there sould to the inhabitants thereof.' Things came to such a pretty underpass that ships could hardly leave Dublin, Wicklow, Waterford or Waterford without fear of capture. Captain Richard Plumleigh, writing to the Admiralty on 2 September 1632, informed them that 'I have had the chase of 2 or 3 Biskayners around the Saltees and have pursued them into the shallow waters and home to the very Rocks; that by such rough dealing with them they may be advised to forbeare troubling the trade of this Kingdom and pillaging the poore Fishermen upon the coast.'

One of the most memorable pirate stories on this stretch of coast concerns the *Sandwich*, a ship bearing a huge fortune, no fewer than 250 sacks of Spanish dollars, which it had picked up in the Canaries on its return leg to London. The bo'sun and sea cook persuaded two other crew members to kill the others on board, despatching seven out of the eight in cold blood.

The murderers, a Dickensian-sounding roster of villains – Gidley, St Quintin, Zekerman and McKinlie – duly launched the ship's longboat, filling it to the runnels with dollars, gold dust and ingots, all in all two tons of lucre. Their plan was to scuttle the boat and watch the *Sandwich* sink, but it failed to slip under the surface of the waves. A Canadian captain, sailing past the vessel at the mouth of Waterford harbour, therefore chanced upon a crime scene complete with an amplitude of clues. As the murderers rowed to shore they had to jettison gold over the side to lose weight, all in all the most expensive ballast ever. It's little wonder that their landing place is still called Dollar Bay.

The dastardly criminals, meanwhile, landed at Fisherstown, just south of New Ross, having buried most of their loot downstream, on the edge of the estuary. They took enough money with them to get rat-arsed in the Ballybrazil Inn, where they were foolish enough to flash the cash, spilling silver dollars on the bar like beer slops. A large amount was stolen from them but being seven sheets to the wind they didn't realise that at the time, too busy were they roistering and buying pistols at inflated prices.

In the morning they set off for Dublin, stopping at an inn where they idiotically gave the maid a necklace and gold earrings that had belonged to one of their victims, being the captain's wife. They also made themselves extremely obvious by trading pieces of eight with a moneychanger. By the time they had reached lodgings at the Black Bull Inn on the western edge of Dublin the law was well and truly after them, and following a speedy trial the men were executed on 3rd March 1766. Gruesomely, their bodies were exhibited in metal cages on the banks of the Liffey, a stark warning to others, a grisly display of rotting flesh and bones, a quartet of hapless murderers swiftly brought to book, a book that is in itself a tale of grisly maritime horror.

5.

ENLLI

Viewed from the mainland, from Uwchmynydd, the island squats on the horizon, a brontosaurus hump breaching the waves. It's a place of mewling gulls, keening seals and ancient sanctity. On a map, Ynys Enlli or Bardsey is an apple just out of reach of the gnarly, extended arm of the Llŷn peninsula.

The Vikings named so many of the Welsh islands – Grassholm, Skokholm, Anglesey, Skomer, Steep Holm – and to these marauding plunderers, Enlli, a.k.a. Bardsey, was Bardr's isle, whoever he was. There is a prettier, poetic etymology which suggests it was the Bards' Isle. Certainly there's one bard, Christine Evans, who lives there for much of the year, taking it as the subject of much of her art. The late, great poet R. S. Thomas also knew the island well and could almost see Enlli from his last parish posting, at St Hywyn's in Aberdaron. Whichever is the correct explanation for the island's naming, it is so much more than a rock enduring in the sea.

Enlli is set along well-established trade routes: it was known to the Phoenicians for instance; Ptolemy knew it as Edri, and included it on the first-ever map, or at least the first extant map, of the Irish Sea; Pliny called it Andros.

This sea-girt isle, viewed from the mainland, is today raked by sunlight. There's a jagged set of rocks set in the middle of Bardsey Sound called, tongue-twistingly, *Gorffrydiau Caswennan*, whose spiked dangers reputedly wrecked the Gwennan, King Arthur's ship.

Indeed, some believe Enlli to be Afallon, or Avalon: Avalon means Island of Apples (the Welsh word for apple is *afal*) and this was the earthly paradise to which the wounded Arthur was taken. A rather shrivelled and unique apple variety, *afal Enlli*, does grow in sheltered spots – I have one growing outside my study window, though it has yet to fruit. One imagines it being tastier than other indigenous Welsh apple types such as *twll tun gwydd*, the goose's arse, luckily so-named because of the way it looks rather than the way it tastes. Apples abound in myth of course: there's an Irish tale in which a Celtic god has a tub of sacred apples from the Otherworld. They're bite-sized tales.

Because the Ordnance Survey maps covering Wales are thoroughly bilingual nowadays, the marking of Ynys Enlli as that humped, sea-bound rock sets it in swirling context, translating as 'the island in the tides, or flood tides.' The spuming, thrashing winter swells inspired the medieval poet Bleddyn Fardd to sing about 'white waves that make loud the holy land of Enlli.' It's not a place you'd get to by pedalo, that's for sure.

There's a story told about winter gales so tempestuously strong that when the islanders came over to nearby Aberdaron in the spring they were all bald, their hair having been blown to Wicklow. It's probably the Llŷn peninsula equivalent to an urban myth, born out of the mainland envy of the islanders' renown for catching lobsters. Truth is, the fishermen of Enlli simply whistle at the sea and the big-clawed crustaceans climb into the pots, obedient as sheepdogs. Comes from years of practice.

Enlli has other names and monikers, too, not least 'the island of twenty thousand saints'. In medieval times the faithful would calculate that three trips here was equivalent to one to Rome, which explains the sheer numbers of saints, or pilgrims, who braved the treacherous crossing. Nowadays it's thirty quid, there and back.

To get to the island you have to cross Bardsey Sound: it's a Chartreuse surge, a racing stretch of fast and dangerous water. In places it is as smooth as green panes of plate-glass – both cathedral and aquarium – and as sleek as seal pelt, while in other places deceptive, unseen currents run just under the sea's surface, like fast streams cutting across fields.

As Enlli lies off the end of a peninsula it's a place where currents meet and clash: the sea can therefore boil and thrash, veritably explode with spume, hit the shore like geysers going off. Little wonder, then, that the island has a long and terrible history of shipwrecks, ships turned to matchsticks when pounded relentlessly against its jagged, deadly edges.

*   *   *

There is little that thrills me in life as much as heading for an island, and Ynys Enlli holds a special excitement, sending little pulses of electricity coursing through the veins.

Tongues of waves lick the sides of the boat leaving Porth Meudwy, the hermit's cove. As we move out to open water smutty plumes of diesel follow in our wake, along with lesser black-backed gulls that fly alongside like police outriders. In mid-channel an arctic skua, passing through on passage, lives up to its piratical reputation as it dive-bombs some guillemots, trying to force the auks to disgorge their catch. A nervous one surrenders its lunch in a spray of sand eels.

And then the island proper, Ynys Enlli, Bardsey, hoves into full view. While the eastern hump of Y Mynydd, The Mountain, at 548 feet, is a mere bagatelle of a climb, it is made of tough stuff, Precambrian rock, 600 million years old – some of the oldest rock on earth. It certainly makes the human timescale seem like a pitiful trifle, a mere instant. Y Mynydd commands the view as one approaches by sea: once on land the westerly edge of the island looks surprisingly inhabited, with a succession of houses. These nestle in pairs – Tŷ Nesaf and Tŷ Bach, Nant and Hendy – and are arranged at generous intervals along the A1, the ironically named cart track that runs south to north from Y Cafn, the artificial harbour dynamited into existence by Trinity House. At its widest the island has a girth of a mere half a mile and it's a mile long. But it has incredible depth of history. St Cadfan built a monastery here in the sixth century. Pirates and smugglers have used it as a base. It's drawn holy seekers, twentieth-century survivalists, crab fishermen, and twenty thousand saints. As the archaeologist Mary Chitty put it: 'Trying to spell out the history of the island is like watching the island itself from the headland. Sometimes the outline is clear and hard, its detail visible; more often in shifting gleaming light and shadows it seems to dissolve and float away. Sometimes it disappears altogether in the fog. Then only the mountain saying amen to the lighthouse tells us Bardsey is still there.'*

The lighthouse was built on the southern islet of Enlli in 1821 at a cost of £5,470, with a staggering £3,000 outlay for the lenses alone. By day it's a 100-foot high limestone tower composed, Lego-style, of horizontal red and white blocks. It's the same colour scheme as an old-fashioned barber's pole, and pretty distinctive in the realm of lighthouse design in being so square. The lantern houses five heavy lenses, sitting on a bed of mercury, surrounding a bulb which is only 400 watts. The mercury is the ingenious answer to the problem of a lens being too heavy to rotate: floating it on a bed of quicksilver means you can turn it with a finger.

The lighthouse keepers are long gone from the place – it was automated in 1986, with the last principal keeper, Harry Whitehouse, retiring that same year – and the light is now operated from the Trinity House command centre in Harwich.

The poet Christine Evans lives on the island and knows its flashing stroboscope like some people know a kitchen clock:

> Outside's a swirl of black and silver.
> The lighthouse swings its white bird round
> as if one day it will let go
> the string, and let the loosed light fly
> back to its roost with the calling stars.†

---

* Christine Evans and Wolf Moloch, *Bardsey*, Llandysul, 2008.

† Christine Evans, 'Enlli', in *Selected Poems*, Bridgend, 2004.

Paradoxically, Enlli's was a deadly light, a real killer. Flashing distinctively five times every fifteen seconds, it was notorious for luring migrating birds to their deaths. The phenomenon, peculiar to just a handful of locations in the UK, is known as an attraction. On the most notable occasion in 2003 up to 40,000 individual birds from a wide range of species were attracted in a single night, many striking the tower, stunned to the ground. Luckily the deadly, rotating light was replaced by bird-friendly red LED lights in 2004.

Many species migrate at night, using elements of the night sky to navigate – literally the stars to guide them by. The light of the moon, too, can illuminate the land underneath these peregrinators. Gargantuan numbers of waders, warblers and thrushes fly purposefully through the dark along with a range of other species such as terns, larks, rails and starlings, all subject, in the past, to being misdirected by the Enlli light, while even seabirds such as storm petrels and shearwaters can also be drawn in to deadly effect. There have been rarities, too, with thrush nightingale and red-eyed vireo on the grim tally.

Historically a log was kept of such deaths. The lighthouse keepers' notes were a useful source of information for visiting naturalists, such as that kept by the appropriately named Eagle Clarke, who analysed the logs for the 1870s and 1880s.

* * *

It takes a particular combination of circumstances to occasion an attraction: a prominent moon is usually required, and then a rapid change in the weather. If conditions turn inclement the migrants seek out other sources of light, such as the flashing of the lighthouse. I recall one such night from 1976, when I had my first job as assistant warden.

I approach the possibility of such a deathly spectacle with a mix of dread and fascination. The air is still, poised, inky-black, but then the velvet is rent, as the night sky starts to rupture and as the lighthouse beams send out their candles. The attraction starts.

The first birds to arrive are the jigsaw birds, random avian body parts caught in the slow stroboscope of the light. There are brief flashes of wing, quick glimpses of tail, dismembered birds' heads with lit hints of beak and bill. Then, finally, when they're fully hypnotised and are turning in helixes and spirals, trapped within the light's ambit, you can recognise them as birds, the pieces now all fitting together, spectral white species fluttering through space.

They are all mesmerised like moths, as if drawn to a candle, except this one is equivalent to 90,000 candelas. In they come, wings beating like metronomes, the quietest storm. In olden days lighthouses actually used candles as a light source, as they had a constant, consistent glow, though possessing very little individual power. One answer was to group them together, as was the case at the Eddystone lighthouse: in 1759 this sported a two-ring candelabrum holding two dozen candles. There were practical problems to using candles, not least the fact that the wicks had to be regularly snuffed, and keepers – their nerves presumably jangling and on edge – were given reminders of wick-snuffing duties by a clock that struck every thirty minutes. These were eventually replaced but had their own drawbacks. Lamps burning oil, then sperm oil, then ultimately vegetable oil, produced soot and so the glass had to be cleaned all the time. A keeper's lot was not a happy one.

To mitigate the deadly effects of the Enlli light, various devices have been employed over the years, such as floodlighting the tower to lessen the dazzle of the lamp, and setting roosting perches on top of the lantern, although these proved to be of limited effect. Initially, indeed, this idea was as much a curse as a benefit to the birds, as many were killed by colliding with the lamp and surrounding buildings. But in 1978 a 'false' lighthouse was built close to the original structure to draw birds away from the dangers and into the safer territory of the maritime heathland, where up to 3,000 individuals of a range of species roost overnight before continuing on their long journeys. A system of illuminating bushes on the ground also proved to be efficacious.

I remember how the morning after an attraction could reveal a grim harvest of avian corpses, like an open-air homework exercise for taxidermists. The macabre haul might include no fewer than 120 dead grasshopper warblers, or 'groppers' as they're known in the birding trade. Enlli ranks as one of the best places to see this secretive skulking species, which is in decline as their wet habitats disappear. Their little gropper bodies weigh next to nothing in the palm of the hand, where their plumage – camouflage brown streaks and striations of olive, is ineffably beautiful, if sadly so. Such a small thing to fly so far.

The grasshopper warblers aren't the only fatalities. Overnight it has rained dead sedge warblers by the score, and over a hundred willow warblers, littered over the short grass. There's a plump wood pigeon, its dove-grey feathers hardening with rigor mortis into rigid slate, a half dozen sandwich terns, several black-tailed godwits – their long bills like kebab sticks – and a tragic group of fallen whimbrel, stunned out of life. Finally, there's one little egret, its startling white plumage reminding one of the kind of sombre lilies you find in a chapel of rest.

After an attraction, dawn's macabre crop of corpses might include hundreds of birds from a single species, a massacre of redwings or a wastage of willow warblers. At one stage things were so bad that the Royal Society for the Protection of Birds made a film about the island with the subtitle 'A Death Trap', as if Charles Bronson had been appointed keeper. It shows ghostly flights of birds winging in towards the light and, consequently, a funeral or funereal procession of volunteers carrying wooden boxes to pick up dead or fallen birds. To list the species lying there is to write a litany.

* * *

Despite the strengthening gusts, the little cove at Solfach – protected by a curve of sandy banks – is tranquil, with rock pipits animatedly picking among the seaweedy jetsam for sand hopper hors d'oeuvres. Where they prog and pick there are plastic drinks' bottles newly washed ashore, a reminder of human profligacy even in this seemingly pristine and untouched place.

But stuff washed ashore, flotsam, or *broc môr* as it is known hereabouts, can have its uses, and wood in particular has been an invaluable commodity. An old story recounts how the sea offered up its bounty to a starving Enlli hermit in the shape of a freshly dead stag to grace an ascetic's simple barbeque, his fire and complementary stick. In the early nineteenth century islanders tasted oranges and lemons for the very first time after a vessel from the Azores ran aground and shed its ascorbic cargo. Once someone on Enlli found a complete lifeboat, which they kept to use as – well, a lifeboat – and in some of today's island homes there are articles of furniture, even the occasional chaise longue, built simply from driftwood and patience. Competition for wood for the fire or for fencing was often fierce and R.M. Lockley – an islander visiting other islanders by way of a busman's holiday – would often find Enlli's inhabitants prowling in the half light as he returned from a vigil at the lighthouse: 'There is a wonderfully healthy competition in the hunt for driftwood, in which the rule is that the first man to throw a plank on the greensward gets it. Anything larger than a pencil is eagerly snapped up.'

*   *   *

One of the most poignant memorials on Enlli is a small promontory called Trwyn y Fynwent, or Graveyard Point, commemorating the place where a Trinity House supply boat was dashed and smashed against the rocks in November 1822, not long after the building of the lighthouse. Half a dozen souls were lost in a whipping, treacherous squall, including the daughter of the skipper, who was returning from a trip to buy her wedding dress. A local poet, Ieuan Llŷn, penned her a lengthy lament, remarking, sadly, how her dark, long hair floated like seaweed, tantalisingly out of reach of the islanders' outstretched, helping hands.

Not everyone likes life on Enlli. One wannabe modern hermit lost his mind and had to be winched off by helicopter. The Bardsey Trust, which now administers the island, always makes sure that employees have companions to keep them on an even keel. And the occasional poet, such as Harri Webb, ladled out scorn for the place, just to cheer himself up:

No, I've never been there, with luck never shall,
Would be bored stiff in five minutes. All islands
Of this size are horrible alike, fit only
For sheep, saints and lighthousekeepers …
Almost, but not quite, nowhere.*

But while Webb couldn't abide even the thought of the place, it remains for many – be they people or birds – an important destination. For the artist and writer Brenda Chamberlain, who lived here between 1947 and 1961 and wrote a simply marvellous evocation of the island in the form of *Tide-race*, Enlli was both 'sanctuary and prison.' There is that about islands, there is that dichotomy. They can offer an illusion of freedom, despite being surrounded on all sides by the waves. But they can make very excellent prisons, too. Think of Robben Island, Rikers Island, Alcatraz. Storms can maroon, and getting off the island can be a tricky business when the winds change from keening to battering.

What seems nowadays to be fiefdom of the wind, an island in its blustery thrall, used to be its own kingdom with its own ruler. Enlli was once owned by Lord Newborough, and he and his wife Maria Stella would graciously visit and distribute gifts of ribbon for islanders to wear in their hats. The same largesse led to them bestowing the place with a crown – albeit not one of solid gold but of baser metal. Lord Newborough was a king maker, on the island he owned.

The full origins of the tradition are lost in the fog of time, but a letter from one of Lord Newborough's workers suggests that one king died in 1826. The first named incumbent of the title King of Bardsey was one John Williams, who drifted from this life in 1841, the day after his son John Williams II was born, too young to inherit the title. Crowning ceremonies – the crown itself was made of tin – were reputedly held at the Narrows, the little isthmus between the two principal parts of the island. They apparently involved a little silver snuff box,

---

* Harri Webb, 'Enlli', in *Collected Poems*, Llandysul, 1995.

with the man-who-would-be-king standing on a chair for the ceremony.

The most famous member of the royal succession was Love Pritchard, whose reign over the island included the great, sad exodus of 1926, when he himself took pictures of a little flotilla of boats taking people away from their Bardsey, at a time when other islands, such as the Arans, were similarly being depopulated. By that time the lack of young men on Enlli was a matter of concern, for as the King told the *Daily Sketch* for an article called 'Life Too Dull: Why Bardsey is being deserted', 'We have not enough men to row boats off for us and look after the cattle.' The mainland attractions of cinema and wireless seduced the young men, who couldn't wait to leave. But Love Pritchard looked every inch the king, with his flowing Neptune beard and bardic locks of hair. Artist Brenda Chamberlain, in her haunting memoir of island life, *Tide-race*, penned a briny vignette as she recalled her first regal encounter: 'He had a light metal crown chased with a design of seahorses and shells, worn slightly side-ways on his head, and in his crab-like fingers he held a plug of twist from which he was cutting thin wafers of tobacco. By his side lay an empty rum bottle. He was gross with majesty, and must have been a good trencherman and a heroic drinker. He reeked of fish and salt and tarry ropes.'*

Another writer, the South African poet Roy Campbell, became the King's 'chief adviser concerning his home policy: and cheating the tax collector', and recalled him as a strong man who even in his eighties 'could pick up a sack of flour with one hand and lay it over his shoulder as if he was a feather.' The king is now long gone, the island now the realm of seals and shearwaters.

The shadows are lengthening: time for a last round of the birding hotspots to see what's come in. The island's withy-beds, willow plantings, are always worth a gander: you may see a bright flick of colour, a redstart's tail, or see willow warblers, weaving their way through the foliage, alert for insects. For avian visitors, finding food in these green oases can be a matter of life or death and it always seems nothing

---

* Brenda Chamberlain, *Tide-race*, Bridgend, 1996.

short of miraculous that often very small birds can traverse huge tracts of sea and land, following the lengthening days which act as a grail for migrants, and make landfall on this rock.

At one end of Enlli there is a gathering of religious buildings, including a chapel with an asthmatic organ. There's a stone cross and the remains of a monastery. It's still a sanctuary, as the little birds which flit around the buildings attest.

A branch quivers inside a stand of island conifers. A blur of feathers shakes itself. It's a goldcrest, our smallest bird, less substantial than my thumb. It has three minuscule crystals of magnetite embedded in its head to help it navigate. I watch it awhile as it feeds frenetically, needling about in the small pine plantation at the northern end of the island, a stoic traveller, finding sustenance on this Holy Isle, fattening up before flitting off into space, once more launched on its daunting peregrination, its most determined journey.

The gold-streaked crown of the little traveller flashes in the caught light of the westering sun as it gains height and it's hard to keep track of it through the binoculars. Its wings are a whirr, a blur, an impossibly rapid mechanism of flight.

A lighthouse flash catches its departing form, makes the little bird blaze, the whirring wings incandesce: it looks for the briefest instant like a tiny angel. Soon the goldcrest turns into a speck and then devolves into nothingness. The tiny pilgrim, intent on returning to Europe's northern rim, has simply become as one with the widening sky.

6.

SHEARWATER ISLANDS

Of all the world's eleven thousand or so bird species the Manx shearwater is my absolute favourite. No, it's more than that. This is my animal familiar. Just as the witches in *Macbeth* had cat, so this seabird is mine: it's a totemic species, with all grace in its flight. It is a marvellous global wanderer to boot. It spends summers in Wales before wintering the other side of the South Atlantic, off the coast of South America. We share this pattern too, as I've spent a lot of time in Latin America, peregrinating there as if by mad compulsion, from wartime Nicaragua to the communal tango halls of Buenos Aires, from the thorn forests of Paraguay to the blinding snow-peaks of the Patagonian Andes. Manx shearwaters, too, divide their time: summers in Wales and the austral summer off the coasts of Brazil, Uruguay and Argentina.

Flight is the thing. The aeronautic aptitude of the shearwater is a joy to behold. As its name implies, it shears the waves, barely flapping its wings, needing the merest hint of breeze to sally forth over the brine, in sheer mastery of an element. There is a tale told about a bird that managed to fly through the tunnel at the heart of an enormous wave. This might well be just oceanic hyperbole, but watching shearwaters, as they wheel and turn over the sea, one can easily believe in such feats. They turn as if on sparkling sixpences, winking among the wave crests. They bank, then angle their bodies the opposite way, white underbelly turning and resolving into slate-grey upper parts, wings flickering now, shearing, making light of gravity. They fly close to the surface of the swell, actually touching the water, leaving dark marks which are swiftly erased. The flight patterns mesmerise. A series of rapid flaps followed by long glides on stiff wings. And repeat.

And, being an inspiring species, they fly through many poems. The poet Derek Mahon knew them from Achill island: in the poem simply named after the bird a 'shearwater skims the ridge of an incoming wave' while Simon Ó Faoláin in his 'Cánóg Dhubh' (the Irish name for Manx shearwater, meaning 'black bird') sees the bird 'mar chros dhubh thanaí ar an storim Ghemidridh,' looking like a thin black cross on a winter storm.

The Welsh islands of the Irish Sea such as Skomer, Skokholm, Bardsey and Ramsey support half the world's population of Manx shearwaters: there are 1.5 million individuals present just in the Pembrokeshire area in the summer. Taxonomically they're tubenoses, seabirds of the order Procellariiformes, which name refers to the tube-like structures that cover the nostrils, which possibly help them channel smells and thus find their prey. They can live a very long time, with one individual on Bardsey Island living into his fifties. And they are the very definition of long-distance migrants. Flying back and forth from South America to the Irish Sea each year really racks up the avian air miles: a Manxie might fly 5 million miles in a lifetime, or ten times to the moon and back. They can cross an ocean in double-quick time: a Skokholm fledgling proved precisely this when it travelled to Brazil in sixteen days. I have seen them over the Patagonian Shelf – tiny flickers in the distance, admittedly, but sufficient to make me feel curiously at home despite being on quite another continent.

After a day out at sea, the shearwaters bring back food for their young, settling in chattering flocks on the sea's surface, waiting for nightfall. These congregations, called rafts, are reminders that while we often imagine seabirds as they are when seen on land their true habitat – their real element – is the sea, and most pelagic, or oceanic, species become vulnerable on land.

If a shearwater seems to own the air, to subjugate breeze and sea-breath to its own devices, on land it's quite another matter. Land is danger. They nest underground, like puffins. Indeed, Manx shearwaters used to be called Manks puffins back in the seventeenth century. Puffin is an Anglo-Norman word – the Middle English is *pophyn* – and was used to describe the cured carcasses of nestling shearwaters. The puffin itself acquired the name much later, possibly because of its similar nesting habits.

Land is *so* perilous for the shearwater, and not just because of rats. Ungainly, able only to shuffle most inelegantly, the bird's legs are set too far back on the body. They may paddle super-efficiently in the sea but on land they can only waddle in an ungainly fashion, giving little forward propulsion. To even say they waddle is a kindness. But it's not just a matter of inelegance. If a bird returning to its nesting burrow doesn't disappear pretty damn quick then marauding gulls will snaffle it up. On moonlit nights, in particular, ravenous great or lesser black-backed gulls stand sentinel at the mouths of burrows, waiting as if for a Deliveroo. They're gobbled up quickly, and pretty much devoured whole, crammed into a goitre-like bulge in the seagull's extended crop. In the morning all that will be left of the midnight feast will be the indigestible wings and a sternum stripped completely clean of flesh. They strip and tear and gulp with avidity.

* * *

The Manx shearwater is the only bird to be named after the Isle of Man and the connection between the two goes way back. The thirteenth century *Njall's Saga* describes how a Viking fleet, achored off the Calf of Man – a smaller island to the south of the main island – came under 'attack' from legions of shearwaters as they swarmed back to their huge colony there at night. The warriors defended themselves with sword and shield as the iron-billed ravens hurled at them under cloak of darkness. The Vikings also gave one of the hills on the Scottish island of Rhum the name 'Trollaval', the 'hill of trolls', because they thought the shearwaters' cries were the sounds of these creatures roaming the bare hilltops.

* * *

The cry of the shearwater is out-and-out extraordinary – a catcall and cockcrow uttered at one and the same time. It helps explain some of its local names – 'baakie craa' in Shetland and 'cocklolly' in Pembrokeshire. R.M. Lockley once played a party game with some of his friends, encouraging them to write down a simile for the nocturnal scream of an individual Manx shearwater. The winning entry, described in the monograph *Shearwaters*, said it was 'Like the crow of a throaty rooster whose head is chopped off before the last long note has fairly begun.' He himself had described the sound of a colony at night as 'a bedlam of weird screaming. There seemed at first no intelligence in that wild howling – it was the crying of insane spirits wandering without aim or restraint over the rough rocks and the bare pasture,' but even after that fine attempt Lockley admitted that, in truth, he struggled to describe the sound at all.

By the time Francis Willughby wrote his *Ornithology* the bird was known as 'The Puffin of the Isle of Man'. They were already well known to non-ornithologists, with records from the early sixteenth century of young birds being harvested to be packed and cured in firkins or small casks of salt water. Their feathers were sold, too, and there was even a reference in 1599 to 'Puffin Oil', which could be used to treat wool and make it waterproof, a bit like making an oilskin jacket.

The birds were sometimes gathered on the Calf of Man on a near-industrial scale. The Welsh naturalist Thomas Pennant, writing in 1776, said that 'great numbers are killed by the person who farms the isle; they are salted and barreled, and when they are boiled they are eaten with potatoes'. He was so right about the numbers: in the 1700s parties of men could spend a few weeks on the island and hunt '822 dozen and two'. To save you looking for a calculator that adds up to 9,866 birds. Yet the fortunes of a bird that was so numerous could yet change very quickly. The wreck of a Russian ship on the Calf of Man in 1788 brought with it a consignment of rats, which jumped ship and wreaked havoc with the shearwaters, which are defenceless against their predations. By 1812 all the birds had gone, and despite attempts to eradicate the rats the population is nowadays minuscule. The island is now connected to the species in name alone.

Braving the gulls, the arriving birds, burdened with their oily gifts of sardines, sprat and squid, do not arrive quietly. The colony is a cacophony, as the birds, whirling in, announce late supper for their chicks with an astonishing, gurgling cry.

* * *

I came to know Manx shearwaters through the writing of Lockley, whose books I devoured from the age of twelve onwards. His evocations of life on the Welsh islands, and in particular the old red sandstone island of Skokholm, really got under my skin, and I started reading all of his books. By now I have them all, meriting their own bookcase. If you scan the titles you can easily see his preoccupations: *Dream Island. Dream Island Days. Flight of the Storm Petrel. Birds and Islands. The Saga of the Grey Seal.* Lockley considered himself to have always been an escapist and after reading Henry Thoreau's *Walden* he thought this was everything he wanted in life – to get away, to live simply. Chance smiled on him when at the age of 27 he discovered the island of Skokholm and a reason to live there, as the tenancy of the island was up for grabs.

For me there is one volume that stands proud in the Lockley library, a monograph called simply *Shearwaters* – mine has a well-thumbed maroon cover, slightly foxed pages, is printed on thin, wartime-rationing paper. Here's his description, in prose both clear and beautiful, of birds gathering on the water of an evening: 'The flocks would swing as one being, their white breasts now a silver flash in the sun's last rays, and then, as their dark upper parts were simultaneously presented, they showed velvet-black on the grey-blue sea. They would settle on the water again, so that from the island cliffs a mile distant we could barely discern the united host – it was merely a cloud shadow, a black streak like a puff of wind or a vein of the tide on calm water.'*

I soon became transfixed by Lockley and intrigued by shearwaters, the black and white flicker of their wings creating a sort of silent film

---

* R.M. Lockley, *Shearwaters*, London, 1947.

in my young mind. That countershading plumage acts as a kind of camouflage. In flight it's a rapid, wing-flick *chiaroscuro*. The birds flash white breasts that seem to disappear as they reveal the back and under-wing. The black plumage can thus be quickly lost against the darkness of the water, but, when swimming, the white breast seems to hide the bird from its underwater prey, hidden in the light from above. Underwater, they use their wings as oars, diving down up to 55 metres to hunt for fish and jellyfish.

A fellow Lockley enthusiast is seabird expert David Saunders, who knew Lockley back in the 1960s. I met the gentle-voiced David at his home in Haverfordwest, where he assessed Lockley's contribution, not least the sixty books he produced in his lifetime. 'He was one of the great amateur naturalists,' Saunders averred, 'and not only studying but also writing, enthralling people in his popular books and in arti-cles and in scientific papers. He spanned both.' Some of Lockley's experiments as he studied bird migration were pioneering, arranging for a bird to be taken by land to be released at Start Point, the south-erly finger of Devon, to see how quickly they would return to Pembrokeshire, 225 miles away. It took the bird, named Caroline, less than ten hours. Lockley then sent birds to France, and his shearwaters returned as surely as homing pigeons. Emboldened, he then arranged for birds to be taken to Venice, Istanbul, to land-locked Switzerland, and on ships bound for South Africa, learning all the time about the birds' speed and navigational certainties. In one of his boldest experi-ments, a bird taken to the eastern seaboard of the US returned to Skokholm before the telegram announcing their Stateside release in Boston airport arrived.

One of Lockley's more scientific books was *The Private Life of the Rabbit*, a monograph which was a major source for Richard Adams's bestselling rabbit saga *Watership Down*. I met Adams not long before he died in 2016, by then an amenable man of advanced age who woke briefly in the afternoons to nibble at Victoria sponge. His Hampshire cottage was chock-full of rabbits – soft toy bunnies, porcelain ones, miniaturised conies. He agreed that Lockley's book about rabbits was 'Enormously valuable in writing the novel. There isn't much to be said about rabbits apart from what's in that book.' The two of them corresponded following the success of *Watership Down* and they became firm friends, even venturing to Antarctica together. In one of Adams's later books, *The Plague Dogs*, there is a character actually called Ronald Lockley who makes a brief, heroic appearance, as if a small debt is somehow being repaid.

When I was fourteen I was fortunate enough to get a job as a 'shearwater slave' on Skokholm, which basically involved losing a lot of sleep in order to help the warden ring, weigh and generally survey birds at night. It's a hoary old chestnut to say that the experience was magical but it was, the hurtling birds seeming to conjure themselves up from nothing before hurtling towards you. They were feathery wraps of darkness.

As you can imagine, everything about that trip was an adventure. My childhood home was a Monty Pythonesque existence, like the classic 'Four Yorkshiremen' sketch in which the four Northerners compete with their recollections of a deprived upbringing. In our case four members of the family crammed into one room and we had to bathe in a zinc bath in front of a coal fire. If anyone happened to call at the wrong time we'd end up naked in the hall, waiting for them to leave. The toilet was outside – although we had two outside toilets, which must have made us posh, even if one was halfway up the garden behind my grandfather's canary shed. My father was an ill-tempered cider-drinker who could go off on one at any time, so coming to this island – to the boundlessness of sky, the candyfloss banks of thrift, the scything excitement of a peregrine falcon chasing the wind like the fletch of some enormous arrow – was a great escape. Everything seemed new, explosive to the senses, as if the world was newly minted, its colours freshly mixed. The Pantone orange of the puffin's bill. The muted browns of meadow pipits as they chinked overhead. Green swathes of bracken, enlivened by whitethroats. The ultramarine window panes of calm sea.

So much about the Manx shearwaters of the Irish Sea entranced and intrigued me. The way they lived. How far they flew to feed. It used to be believed that Pembrokeshire birds flew to the Bay of Biscay to catch sardines and the like, but work with radio trackers in the early 2000s found that the birds flew well north, foraging in the Irish Sea up as far as Galloway while their southern feeding zones included fecund waters in Dublin Bay and concentrations of food also in Cardigan Bay. When the chicks are being fed on islands such as Skokholm, Skomer and, nowadays, rat-free Ramsey, the Manx shearwaters – very appropriately given their name – forage in the waters surrounding the Isle of Man, a sea zone known as the Western Irish Sea Front. This is an area superabundant with sea life and therefore attractive to anything from shearwaters through Dublin Bay prawns to Irish inshore trawler boats. There is also a plenitude of food to be had in the more southerly Celtic Sea Front, which stretches between the northern tip of St Bride's Bay and Rosslare. Here similarly stratified waters break down at the entrance to the Irish Sea, sea currents meet and converge to create a place of marine fecundity.

Little wonder there's a matching abundance of seabirds. Skomer island alone plays host to a third of the world's population of Manxies, and is indubitably the biggest colony in the world. A day visitor to this jewel of an island would have no inkling of this, unless they recognised the skull, wings or sternum of a stripped bird – all that was left after a great black-backed gull had suppered in the night. The Victorian naturalist Robert Drane, seeing such carnage, referred to the place as Golgotha, the Biblical place of skulls. Suitably, in 2015, a macabre carrion crow's nest was constructed on Skomer, made almost entirely of shearwater bones, like something from *The Blair Witch Project*, an unsettling prop from a horror film.

* * *

My next formative experience of Manx shearwaters came one paradisical summer when I went to work on Ynys Enlli, Bardsey island. I was sixteen and had just finished my 'O' levels. My parents dutifully drove me across Wales from Llanelli to catch the boat from Porth Meudwy, the Hermit's Cove, but the news wasn't good. The weather was so wild and inclement they had no idea when the island boat would be coming over to pick up visitors. Which meant my parents were faced with the prospect of driving all the way back again before returning, day unknown.

Luckily we met a rangy bird-watcher with flailing grey hair, weighted down with the sort of heavy-duty binoculars that would have been standard issue for East German spies. He offered to let me stay with him, and his dog-collar was enough of a reassurance for my parents, who took up the offer with alacrity, even though I'm sure my mother would have had her qualms.

Even luckier for me, the bird-watching vicar was R. S. Thomas, a fine poet and equally talented bird-watcher. Indeed, in the very spot where we met there is a record of the first red-eyed vireo to be spotted in Wales, and behind the details are the initials of the man who spotted it: RST.

The weather proved stormy for days, so I had to make conversation with the great man. Full of the arrogance of someone who expected to pass his exams with flying colours I found myself discussing Wordsworth, cockily informing R.S. that he was a pantheist poet, before patronisingly asking if he knew what that meant. The finest pantheist poet of his generation must have nodded or something, sparing my blushes.

But that stay was the beginning of a friendship that hinged on birdwatching. We hardly ever talked about poetry – that was, until I has the good idea of taking a tape recorder with me on our walks. He opened up a lot, and could make me laugh like a drain, a fact which flew in the face of the public image of him as a curmudgeonly ogre, with fierce eyes like a hawk.

Over the years we saw the first goshawks nesting in Wales and the first ever appearance of a ring-billed gull on this side of the Atlantic. We visited South Stack on Anglesey to see the serried ranks of seabirds, getting pretty close to them as we climbed down the steps towards the lighthouse. And in the autumn of his days, when he had moved to live in Llanfihangel-yng-Nghornwy, again on Anglesey, we would go and look at the terns at the Cemlyn lagoon. There he would show off his range of bird calls and cries, able to mimic a splendid range of them, all delivered deadpan, although I always thought he might well have been laughing inside.

* * *

If you go birdwatching through the pages of R.S.'s *Collected Poems* you'll be sure to spot a few species. Some are spotted far away, such as the nightingales the poet spots in Burgos, Spain. Some are mythological species such as the owl of Cwm Cowlyd and Cilgwri's ousel which appear in 'The Ancients of the World', not to mention that fine eagle, Eryr Pengwern and the birds of Rhiannon out of the *Mabinogion*. And then there are the cuckoos sounding out their lilting notes and curlews, of course. His early parish in Manafon was a good place in spring to see such birds returning, 'to lay their eggs in the brown heather' and to hear the 'spring cadenza' of their piping. There are larks, too, and owls, ravens and rooks, herons and hens, buzzards and bright jays. In some poems sparrows come for crumbs of prayer and there is the occasional real eagle as opposed to the ones that flap through legends on enormous wings. And there are birds in their season, of course, such as summer's swifts that 'winnow the air' and martins that return to nest under the eaves.

* * *

When I finally left the poet and got to Ynys Enlli, to Bardsey, it was to an island where the shearwater colonies aren't as numerous as on the Pembrokeshire islands. I again spent nights with them, again catching them to be ringed, or to recapture ones that had previously been caught to see how they had grown and check the condition of their plumage. But there was one problem. One of the only defence mechanisms the Manx shearwater has when it's waddling on land is to spray fish oil out of the tubes above its bill at anything that comes within range. Harmless enough to a human, you might say, even if a tad unsalubrious and smelly. But this was the ultra hot summer of 1976, months characterised by drought, so that each day one of the things you would see was the nun who lived on the island keeping the holy wells open by digging down with a tool that looked like something used in World War I. There certainly wasn't enough water to bathe or shower that summer, and so being sprayed with the equivalent of a syringe full of cod liver oil each and every night did put one in a pickle.

You could swim in the sea, certainly, but there was no bath, shower or washing machine. Gradually I began to smell like a recently beached jellyfish before the aroma intensified to eau de deceased cetacean, the stench deepening so that my skin gave off the tang of sun-baked bladderwrack, overlaid with notes of rotten dogfish. When I finally left the island at summer's end – I wanted to stay for ever and put up a fight against returning to full-time education – I caught the train from Pwllheli to Aberystwyth, a two-carriage affair which was all the more full because it stopped at the ginormous Butlins Holiday camp along the way. Plastic bucket bearing holidaymakers squeezed in like anchovies in a tin but by some unholy miracle I ended up with a carriage all to myself, travelling like some young potentate on his own royal train. It was only at journey's end, when my brother Alun picked me up in the car and then had to get out pretty damn quick to be sick, that I realised just how pungent I'd become. The romance of shearwaters, eh? Needless to say the journey back to south Wales seemed to him to last a century, and despite all the windows being open I gave him a horrible fug for company, being the very epitome of ocean rot, an experience like riding shotgun with a dead dolphin.

*　*　*

My most recent experience of shearwaters was more salubrious. I was staying in the lighthouse on Skokholm, which is set in the middle of what might be the most densely packed colony on earth. The stroboscope of light strafed the low heath perforated with thousands of burrows. The illuminated, incoming shearwaters might have been Macbeth's witches, screaming as they tumbled towards the safety of their holes. There was the silent film-flicker of their disembodied wings, caught in my torchlight, as they whirred overhead like big, wildly displaced nightjars.

On such rare nights I am content to a fault and profoundly so. When I am with *my* birds.

PART TWO

FACING COASTS

'The sea fits the coast precisely from moment to century'

Steve Griffiths, Backward Glances

7.

SHERAWEES AND SEA-SWALLOWS

A tern colony in high summer is a seabird bedlam, a screeching cacophony as birds fly madly back and forth to feed, or scythe back to their nests with shivering silver bounty. Lady's Island Lake in County Wexford is the largest tern colony in Ireland, which means the decibel level is raucously high.

Four kinds of tern add their calls to the soundscape hereabouts. Flick through the bird books which variously describe tern sounds and you get an array of approximations of the excited chatter. The larger sandwich tern's cry is a loud, rasping, raucous 'kirrick' or a striding, rasping 'keer-reck' along with a sharp 'tripp' or 'kirr-kit'. The smaller, common tern's voice can be 'noisy and varied' with a 'long, grating "kree-errr" with a downward inflection', kirri-kirri' and a chattering 'kikikikik'. The Arctic tern, easily confused visually with the common tern, also sounds similar 'but with a whistled "kee-kee", with rising inflection'. The books tell us that the roseate tern, meanwhile, has a 'long, rasping aaak', a soft, very characteristic 'chu-ick' and a 'long angry chattering "kekekekek"'. The roseates can give their presence away by their cries, a long drawn-out 'aach-aach' and a softer, gentler 'tchu-ik' or 'chik-ik' note. Straightforward stuff.

There is also a noisy roseate tern phenomenon known as 'gakkering'. Threatening each other by crouching down with body and tail elevated, the roseates raise their back feathers and pump their heads up and down in unison, emitting loud, guttural, cackling calls, hence the gackering. At the ternery all of these loud sounds meld and jumble, the shrieks marrying with the chatter, the crackling cries, the swooping sounds. The cries are present, too, in the names for terns found in the local but now defunct Yola dialect, a mix of Anglo-Saxon with borrowings from Irish and French: 'Skirr', 'Skers', 'Sherawee' and 'Skeerane'.

But it's noisy visually, too. As the poet Roland Mathias put it:

Air itself has bravado
Leaping bare
From such wings
To fresh platforms of height,
The terns banking, cruising,
Occasional raucous
Blasts on their intercom

Intercomming, outgoing and incoming terns are a veritable whirlwind of grey, black and white as they lift and swoop, their primary feathers slashing the air into razor shards, a mad orchestration of forms in dizzying flight, cutting across each other. Sea-swallows some call them, because of the long tail feathers that trail behind, while others such as Roland Mathias note also their slit eyes, the 'hooked, arrogant beaks … a blade-bone/Cleaving the wavelets' interface'.

I remember once visiting the Skerries, off the coast of Anglesey, and having to walk warily through the ternery. Those fish-spearing bills became little stabbing dirks or daggers as the birds strafed and dive-bombed, defending by attacking, quite without fear. The air was frenzied by them, a bombardment of wings accompanied by screeches like toy ambulance horns as you ducked and weaved to avoid the swooping stabbers. The two wardens who lived on the islet during the summer must have lived on their nerves. Or worn hard hats to go to work.

Sadly a lack of wardens during the Covid lockdowns led to peregrine falcons, well, peregrinating to the Skerries, which meant all 3,000 pairs of Arctic terns deserted. Some of them moved to other colonies such as the nearby Cemlyn lagoon, where the number of Arctic terns duly swelled by 1,000 pairs. Individuals were also spotted at Hodbarrow lagoon in Cumbria and at Dalkey Island near Dún Laoghaire, underlining the way in which the Irish Sea population is full of swapping colonies and interchange. The wider sea area is very important for the roseate tern, in particular. Luckily 2021 was a very good year, especially at its main stronghold on Rockabill, north of Dublin, as over 1,700 pairs nested on this lonely rock, along with some 200 pairs at Lady's Island Lake.

*   *   *

The tern mayhem at Lady's Island Lake is a mere sherawee's swoop away from the busy Europort at Rosslare. Here a naturalist arriving in Ireland might well enjoy the sight of black guillemots that nest in the harbour walls. They are unusual for County Wexford because its coast is generally soft and therefore unsuitable for the species. Sadly, the population of this very sedentary species has fallen here in recent years, and is now down to four or five pairs. They are very handsome birds, with black plumage the colour of pitch along with white flashes pure as a nun's whimple. It's a striking mix, especially if you happen to see the bright scarlet of the bird's gape as well, the colour of Boots No. 7 lipstick.

One of the other inhabitants of the harbour is less conspicuous but no less interesting. The Irish stoat is attracted here because any port infrastructure is synonymous with rats. This inquisitive and ferocious muscelid is a sub-species found only in Ireland and likes nothing better than a fine rat supper. With extra rat. I keep my eyes peeled as I cycle up the hill towards Kilrane but know that I would be fortunate indeed to see one, although one doubts if one could get close enough to note the neurasthenic smile of the Hollywood killer.

All of the principal harbours around the Irish Sea happen to be very close to superb nature sites, and thus many wildlife experiences are very easily accessible. How accessible? Well, thinking of my own experience, an overweight man in his early sixties who has two kinds of arthritis, I can easily go by bicycle from the Rosslare Europort to Lady's Island in just over half an hour. You pedal quiet country lanes out to the sandbanks near the great vanes of the windfarm at Carnsore point. These separate the brackish lagoon from the sea and, sitting there, I had the whole, long stretch of beach all to myself. On the shingle I watched black and red Burnet Moths feeding on the lavender-coloured flowering heads of sea holly and small squadrons of cormorant which seemed to come in threes, flying in trident formation.

We know that the tern colony here is especially important because of the roseate tern. Why? Well, this primarily tropical species is the rarest seabird in Europe, and this is one of the best places to see them in Ireland. Breeding birds skitter over the barrier beach to feed and plunge-dive along the southern shore around Carnsore Point, trailing their long tail streamers. The birds feed in open clear water on small schooling fish, diving as deep as 1.2 metres and staying submerged for as long as two seconds. Sandeels form 60–92 per cent of the bird's diet on Lady's Island, with sprat and herring also featuring prominently, along with very small amounts of pollack and snaithe. Inish Island, one of two little islets set in Lady's Island Lake, is the second largest colony of roseates in Britain and Ireland, and is host to important numbers of sandwich, common, and a few Arctic terns.

It's worth dwelling a moment on the last of these. The Arctic tern is a bird that sees more daylight than any other, as it can breed as far north as the Arctic circle and then migrate to the longer light of the south polar summer in the Antarctic Ocean. Conservative estimates of the journey reckon on its being 40,000 km a year. As one bird can live three decades it can travel the equivalent of three round-trips to the moon in its lifetime, all the more remarkable when one considers that this small bird weighs little more than a garden blackbird.

The roseate is easily confused with common and Arctic terns, but it can be distinguished by its black bill, which goes red at the base for a few weeks in mid-summer, and by its enormously long tail streamers. The overall whiteness of the bird also makes it stand out a tad. That said, you do need to be a skilled birder to spot a roseate. When the bird is seen at a distance the pink breast does not show up all that markedly: it's a faint shell-pink or peachy bloom on the underparts. Think old red wine stain washed out of a starched white shirt and you'll have a fair sense of it. It makes one think that an appropriate collective noun for the species would be a blush, yes a blush of roseate terns.

Another good place to see roseates is the south side of Dublin, where large numbers – up to 1,000 birds – come in to roost alongside other tern species every evening in August and September. They feed out over the Kish Bank's sandbars and then roost raucously on the rails of the Kish lighthouse. Roseates also gather on Sandymount Strand in Dublin – occasional gatherings number as many as 645 birds, as occurred on 14 September 2010 – and another important roosting site is Maiden Rock, Dalkey, about 1km to the south, where upwards of 1,000 individuals were counted from late July to late September in the 1980s.

* * *

There was a long history of confusion surrounding the identification of the various tern species and it wasn't until 1812, when a number of them were shot by Dr Peter McDougall and his friends on the Cumbrae islands in the Firth of Clyde, that the roseate was particularised. Douglas sent the dead birds to Lord Montagu – he of Montagu's Harrier fame – so they could be identified, and in so doing earned himself the right to have the bird named after him (*Sterna dougalii*) even if the Scottish prefix of his surname was unceremoniously lopped off.

The species took a precipitous dive towards extinction in Victorian times when it was exploited by commercial collectors supplying feathers to furnish women's hats. In addition to the demands of millinery, taxidermists also went all out both to kill and stuff this newly discovered rarity. Such depradations took their toll in Ireland as elsewhere. Indeed by 1900 it was doubtful if roseates nested anywhere in the country.

There was a population rebound in the early years of the twentieth century. Roseate terns had re-established in Ireland by 1906, with several large colonies found in the 1910s and 1920s, including one with 500 pairs and another 329 pairs when it was counted in 1932 – but these precise locations were properly cloaked in secrecy.

Llanddwyn island off the coast of Anglesey had 'many' roseates in 1902 and there were 500 birds there by 1910, a number that rose steeply to 500 pairs in 1918. The species recolonised the Skerries off the coast of Wales – as opposed to the Skerries in Dublin Bay – in 1925, increasing to 200–300 pairs in 1928.

Luckily, legal protection led to a reversal in the roseate's fortunes, but then a new peril became apparent. In Africa, it was discovered that overwintering birds were trapped and eaten by locals on the coasts of Senegal, Ghana, Togo and Côte d'Ivoire, and as far south as the harbour-sides of Lagos in Nigeria. Children would throw hooks – made attractive with shiny bits of silver paper – into the surf to catch the birds, briefly turning them into struggling kites or living toys. The bedraggled birds would only last for a few days, their fates reminiscent of a time in nineteenth-century Italy when delicate black terns were similarly caught, only to have their wings torn off and be sold to 'young girls to use as playthings'.

A fickle species, the roseate tern is notorious for its habit of suddenly deserting a breeding site for no apparent reason, before setting up a new colony elsewhere.

They like to breed on sandy beaches or on shingle, and their nests are simple scrapes on the ground, usually unlined, so they are subject to human disturbance and vulnerable to mammalian predation. Immense numbers once nested at Mew Island, one of the Copeland islands, Co. Down, but this was destroyed by shooting and egg-collecting. Hundreds of roseates on Rockabill were similarly annihilated in 1844.

In Wexford the roseate terns had a forced desertion when their favourite site in the harbour, known as Tern Island, was lost in the 1970s. Before that, in the 60s, it was the largest breeding colony in Europe. It was the only place where all five British and Irish terns nested together, and had a splendid assemblage of 2,000 pairs of rose-ate terns in 1968, the largest colony ever recorded in Britain and Ireland.

Pairs of roseates often set up their nests in terneries among other species. They like dense vegetation, so that one pair may not even be able to see its neighbours. Closely packed at a colony, with landing space at a premium, there is therefore often a lot of quarrelling as a pair defends the small territory around its nest. The ground might be bare at first, but vegetation becomes lush during the tern breeding season, in great part because of the constant spray of droppings. They take very readily to nest boxes, so now the majority of those at sites such as Rockabill and Lady's Island Lake take to them readily.

*　　*　　*

Tony Murray, the conservation ranger for the Wexford coast, has been working with terns for a long time. His first tern project was on Dalkey Island in South County Dublin; the second took him to the Ynys Feurig tern colony at Rhosneigr on Anglesey. He sees the various colonies as being interconnected, forming one Irish sea unit: 'And not just with the roseate terns. We've been ringing sandwich terns on Lady's Island, which is the largest Irish colony of this species number-ing almost 2,000 pairs. The next one is terms of size is in County Down and there is one at Cemlyn to the east, on other side of the sea. The rings we use are field-readable, which has allowed to find out that most of the juvenile birds, when they leave, move north to congregate between north Wales and Merseyside.'

As he takes off his boots after a very long day's work, Tony sketches the local history of terns for me: 'Basically, from the 1960s to the 1970s the terns were all on the sandbars in Wexford harbour but in 1976, 1977 and 1978 there were winter storms and the island finally got washed away in 1979. There were thousands of pairs of roseate terns in Wexford harbour at that time and they certainly didn't all move to Lady's Island, as a significantly smaller cohort moved in. But the islands weren't really wardened at that time, so in the first few years water levels weren't ideal and terrestrial predation was a problem. The numbers of terns just dwindled until there were just eight pairs nesting on the little islands. Basically any tern colony that isn't policed effectively does not succeed.' Wooden nest boxes have to be built and deployed, placing them in the same positions as in previous years. Four-foot-high chicken wire is used to enclose the nesting area with extra enclosures to allow the gathering of biometric data about the birds. Electric fences are erected to the east and west of the roseate tern nesting sites to defend them from mammals, while trail cameras are installed on Inish and Sgarbheen islands to record the presence of any such threats. By dint of such efforts almost 200 pairs of roseates nested on the little islets in 2019.

At other sites around the Irish Sea such measures are *de rigueur*. Rats are baited on Dalkey Island and nearby Lamb Island, while six-foot bamboo canes are set in the ground at 90-degree angles to deter seagulls. Also, on Maiden Rock on Dalkey, gravel scrapes were created to encourage nesting birds. On the Welsh side, in the Anglesey Tern Special Protection Area – the Skerries, Ynys Feurig and the Cemlyn lagoon – special measures include building tern rafts and using sonic deterrents and electric fences, particularly directed at the otters that forced the complete desertion of the colony in 2017. To deter great black-backed gulls, which took many fledgling terns, laser hazing was employed. This a technique in which a laser is aimed at the ground in front of a bird, the bright spot edging towards it to scare it away. Fox patrols were mounted at Ynys Feurig, while tape lures were used to try to attract roseates to the offshore islands, although numbers on the Skerries remained stubbornly in single or double digits. It's very hard work.

At the time I met Tony in mid-August there was a huge flock of terns in and around Liverpool Bay, anything up to 5,000 birds, drawn from all points, as he told me: 'They'll be birds from Cemlyn, Lady's Island, probably the Hodbarrow colony on the site of an old iron mine in Cumbria, all concentrating in the post-breeding season – going wherever the grub is. So we can see the Irish Sea tern population as a meta-population with lots of interchange: we're getting Cemlyn ringed birds, ours are up in Cemlyn and we're getting some up in Hodbarrow. Just because they bred in Lady's Island doesn't mean they stay here.'

That interchange also means that Tony sees birds from Copeland island and the Farnes in Northumberland, 'and it's not only an Irish and British population as we also have visiting birds from Brittany. Some birds might nest with us but they might go to Cumbria next year, so it is definitely a meta-population.'

As well as rats, avian predators such as kestrels, short-eared owls and peregrines can be problematic in some years, while crows and greylag geese are deterred in various ways, the crows being trapped while the greylag nests and eggs are removed under licence.

It's a war they don't always win: brown rats completely devastated the Lady's Island Lake colony in 1970. They repeat the Man versus Rat challenge each and every year because they have to. They now place rat bait in permanent clay pipes during February and March each year, but if water levels are low rats can still cross from the mainland. Meanwhile red foxes, badgers and American mink – an unwanted and fierce cousin of the Irish stoat which escaped from fur farms – are deterred by one-inch-mesh electric fencing. A predator, possibly a hedgehog, still managed to hoover up all the eggs of the sandwich tern colony on Sgarbheen in May 2011. Oddly, otters at Lady's Island may keep the mink away.

For such a low-lying site, and given the fragile nature of lagoons, sea-level rise is another issue. A lagoon is a temporary habitat. Natural succession brings about change: a woodland becomes a bog and then becomes a woodland again – a pattern that can repeat over thousands and thousands of years. Lagoons are especially affected by transient coastal features. Maps of Lady's Island show it as an estuary in the seventeenth century; in the next century it's mapped as a lagoon; by the next century it's back to being an estuary again. Sea level rise might turn it back into an estuary, accelerated by the new weather patterns which mean once-in-a-hundred-years' storms now come every five. Hurricane Ophelia directly hit Wexford and came straight on the back of a straight southerly wind, doing a great deal of damage to the dunes, so the lagoon might not be there in ten years.

Rain and low temperatures are also factors which limit tern breeding success. Plus that roseate fickleness, I suggest. Tony agrees up to a point: 'All terns are fickle in that they're all trying to find a place where they can breed successfully. The Lady's Island colony is on small islands in a lagoon so terrestrial predation is a factor we have to deal with, whereas it's not a factor at, say, Rockabill near Dublin, which is a lighthouse several kilometres offshore. So you could argue that a tern colony is better suited or placed somewhere like Rockabill, or the Skerries, whereas the big Welsh colony at Rhosneigr is connected at low tide to the mainland and that colony was basically depleted by fox in the mid 90s, I think. So it's not that they're fickle; they're not going to come back to a site where they've had predation the previous year or years. Rather, they're going to look for locations which present them with minimal problems, be that terrestrial predation, aerial predation or disturbance. Which is one of the reasons why the LIFE project is trying to get roseates onto the Skerries off Anglesey because you can't really get onto the islands, so your disturbance issue isn't there. You're well off the coast of Anglesey, so your terrestrial predation problem isn't there. The terns are looking for sites that tick all the boxes, as it were.'

For now, one of those is right in Tony's patch, where rare birds like the roseates return each year to fully grace the summer season when he does his level best to protect them as if they are his charges.

8.

AN ISLAND THRICE OVER

Just before first light at Holyhead and Newry Beach is a still Whistler painting, the sea a dove grey wash. Sedately, a Stena Line ferry slides into view, its lights making of it a fairy castle, seemingly drifting between dimensions. The light on the breakwater rhymes quietly with the bright pulse of the lighthouse on the rocks of the Skerries, 7 miles north-east and burning much stronger today than when it was first lit in 1716. Then it was nothing more than a big coal fire kept burning in a conical grate. The two lights flash into the widening light: a visual Morse code spelling danger, beware. The Skerries flashes every fifteen seconds, visible for 20 miles. The Breakwater flashes green every ten. Meanwhile murky Whistler is replaced by bright Mondrian, Dayglo colours threading through the brightening sky – tangerine, candyfloss pinks, pale apricot amid deep indigo.

The sound increases, too. On the big roads into town lorries clatter in, air-braking near the Edinburgh Castle pub as they choose their lanes for the next sailing to Dublin. They're heading home to depots all over Ireland: Tierney International from Dunkerrin, County Offaly; Hannon Transport from Blakes Cross; Caffrey from Coolfore and Nolan Transport from New Ross in their smart red and white livery. Technically, and to my mind romantically, they are all on the E22 road, which stretches all the way from Dublin via Holyhead to Moscow and then eastwards to Ishim in western Siberia.

Nowadays 2 million passengers still arrive in Holyhead, although Brexit has had a big impact on cargo, with many exporters choosing the growing array of ferries that sail directly from Ireland to the Continent instead of sending trucks over the British 'land bridge'. As Nation.Cymru reported on 21 October 2021: 'Wales is being increasingly bypassed as a trade route ... Ireland-France sea routes have risen from 12 before the UK left the European Union to 44 now.'

*   *   *

Holyhead, the 'holy headland', lies on Holy Island, which is situated in the north-west of the island of Anglesey, and is thus an island three times over, being an island off the island of Anglesey, off the isle of Britain. The historic heart of the town is compact to a fault and overlooks the port with its cranes and the dominating height of the enormous *MPI Resolution*, looking like a gargantuan oil rig. It is actually the world's first purpose-built vessel for installing offshore wind turbines, currently at dock in Holyhead. Its six 200-ft legs are used to raise itself out of the sea when installing the turbines, and it has the impressive capacity to carry no fewer than ten at a time. It's much taller than the town's buildings. I stare down at it from the low cliff on which St Cybi's church is situated – a neat medieval building, dedicated to St Cybi, first cousin to St David, and rimmed by the walls of a Roman fortlet. Next to it is the square box of Eglwys y Bedd, Church of the Grave. The grave in question is reputedly that of an Irish leader called Sirigi who was killed in Holyhead by the Welsh leader Caswallon Law Hir. Although the historical evidence for this deadly encounter is scant, the alternative name for Eglwys y Bedd is Capel Llan y Gwyddel, which means 'Chapel of the Irishman's enclosure'.

The town itself is backed by the dramatic summit of bare rock known as Mynydd Twr or Holyhead Mountain, itself only a brisk walk from the stunning cliffs at South Stack with its dramatic lighthouse setting and, in summer, teeming colonies of auks. An early traveller, Askew Roberts, noted in his *Gossiping Guide to Wales* how

'The sea in S.W. gales often dashes over the dwellings of the lightkeepers, when the scene is truly sublime ... No-one, by order of Government, is allowed to shoot the sea birds, as in foggy weather they are invaluable to steamers and shipping, being instantly attracted round a vessel, or induced to fly up screaming, by the firing of a gun.'* The sea birds at South Stack constitute a superb spectacle in any weather, with 11,000 guillemots arrayed on the ledges in high summer, when pairs guard their single bright blue egg set precariously on mere inches of jutting ledge. The pear shape reminds me of those children's toys which use their regular centres of gravity to rock back and forth but never fall, complemented by the slogan 'Weebles wobble but they don't fall down.'

In the water the adult guillemots are superb divers, often plumbing depths of 70 metres on a single breath before high-speed chasing their prey of sprat and sand eel. The adult birds read the sea supremely well, seeing variations in colour on its surface which tell them where the currents speed up and where there are upwellings, as these are the places where the fish are often most easily found.

* * *

Holyhead's growth as both a cross-channel port and a town is in many ways a reaction to events in Ireland. London is 300 miles away, with Dublin only sixty. In the reign of Elizabeth I, Holyhead was one nerve-ending of an expanding empire, with ganglia receptive to information carried across the sea. It was essential info: a wily Irish chieftain, Shane O'Neill, The Earl of Tyrone, had capitalised on discontent first instigated by Henry VIII announcing himself King of Ireland and consequently turning Irish-owned land over to the Crown. O'Neill was soon busily fomenting an uprising. On hearing that O'Neill was writing to the Holy Roman Emperor and communicating with Spain, Elizabeth got a bit jittery and instructed Sir Henry Sidney to quell the uprising. Her new Lord Lieutenant in Ireland

---

* Askew Roberts, *The Gossiping Guide to Wales*, London, 1882.

insisted on having good lines of communication and so a new system was ushered in.

The system was cumbersome to say the least. A courier on horseback would take about twenty-nine hours in summer and a saddle-sore forty-one hours in winter to gallop from London to Holyhead, stopping at various 'posts' or lodgings along the way, through torrential rain or fording rivers sometimes in full spate. At Penmaenmawr the post 'boys' – often retired soldiers – would negotiate a hair-raising bridle path between an overhanging cliff on one side and a precipitous fall to the sea on the other. They then navigated quicksands and the dangers of the tide as they crossed Lavan Sands to Anglesey, pressing on to what was then the small village of Holyhead. From there it was a testing sea-journey to Ireland by barque – itself a hazardous proposition as the wind whipped at the rigging and, getting up, threatened to shred the sails. To improve the lines of communication a man called Mr White was given £300 by the Court in London to build and maintain a barque, being a sailing vessel to carry mail across, to be stationed at Holyhead for this purpose. The bone-weary messenger would hand over a satchel bearing royal missives from Elizabeth I and would then wait in the port for Sidney's reply, which might arrive some days later. Drinks might be served.

By late autumn 1635 new 'posts' were being established throughout Britain after Charles I legalised the use of the Royal Mail for private correspondence. At the time the cost of hiring a 'a boat with furniture to transport the packets to Ireland' was £10 per lunar month. Eventually these became known as 'packet boats' or 'packets' and a man suitably named Thomas Swift became the contractor responsible for not one but three packet boats between Holyhead and Dublin, drawing a salary of £400 a year. The passage across the sea was freighted with danger. In 1670 a packet was lost with 120 passengers on board. Soon after another two were lost. The sea was a voracious hunter of souls.

Things formalised a good deal with an Act in 1643 to establish a General Post Office in London and a responding General Letter Office in Dublin. To send a single sheet letter between the two cost sixpence, as opposed to a letter sent to an inland destination, which would cost four. The tuppence surcharge seemed fair considering the dangerous palaver of getting the mail through perilous seas.

Holyhead Customs Officer William Morris – one of four brothers – described the pace of change to his brother Richard Morris in a letter of 18 February 1742: 'We never had so much business upon our hands in this place before – occasioned by ships being cast away, others stranded, others drove in by stress of weather. We are now discharging a cargo of tobacco and going about another of rum and sugar, shipping off teas, indigo, etc.'

William Morris's brother, Lewis, was one of the most remarkable men in Holyhead's history. As George Borrow, chronicler of *Wild Wales*, described the polymath: 'Perhaps a man more accomplished never existed; he was a first-rate mechanic, an expert navigator, a great musician, both in theory and practice, and a poet of singular excellence. Of him it was said that he could build a ship and sail it, frame a harp and make it speak, write an ode and set it to music.'*

The sea coursed through Lewis's veins like fish through a channel, demonstrated in a love-ode dedicated to 'The Fishing Lass of Hakin', whose 'cheeks are as a mackerel plump/No mouth of mullet moister/ Her lips of tench would make you jump/They open like an oyster ...'†

As a young man Lewis Morris learned all about the mysteries of the sea, about fish and fishermen, about oyster beds, ships and sloops by shadowing his father, who traded wood and grain. The young Lewis – trained as a land surveyor – would take goods over to Dublin, offering opportunities for the young man to develop his navigational skills but not if the wind was westerly, as an early poem about sailing from Caernarfon to Ireland attests when it says 'I'r gorllewin troes y gwynt/ Waeth inni fynd tuag adra.' When the wind turns to the west it's best to head home.‡

---

* Alun R. Jones, *Lewis Morris*, Cardiff, 2004.

† Ibid.

‡ Ibid.

Dublin – or the 'Irish metropolis' as William Morris described it – was much closer to Holyhead even than Liverpool: as a consequence Dublin's daily newspapers and 'white bread' were part of the weave and weft of Anglesey life. Many of the books that graced the shelves of the Morris brothers' home were printed in the city, a place that also helped aspiring writer Lewis connect with the English literary scene to the extent that he penned Welsh epitaphs after the deaths of Richard Steele and William Congreve.

Lewis Morris was to work in Holyhead for thirteen years, supplementing his income with a percentage of any levies imposed on those who tried to sneak goods through the port untaxed. While a customs officer in Holyhead, Morris set up a printing press in 1735 to produce Welsh books and popularise Welsh literature. Then, between 1737 and 1742 there are frequent references in the Customs House records to his absences: he had been commissioned by the Admiralty to make a definitive coastal survey of Wales. It was both timely and necessary, not least given the myriad hazards to shipping around the coast.

Before the advent of the railways in the second half of the nineteenth century trade was facilitated through coastal ports and coves. As the trade in mineral goods increased – things such as iron, coal and, to a lesser extent, lead – so too did the level of trade between ports in Wales and elsewhere. The dangers of the sea were amplified by the deficiencies in charts, which were often out of date if not downright antiquated, a situation described by Morris as contributing to the 'melancholy account of shipwrecks and losses so frequent on the coast of Wales.' Luckily Morris had a restless intellect, and, as a child of the eighteenth-century Enlightenment, the idea of mapping both land and sea had a definite appeal.

He started on familiar ground, charting the Anglesey coast, starting in Beaumaris in July 1737 and finishing in November before moving on to Welsh coast and sea areas previously unknown to him. He worked at a Stakhanovite workrate: a man almost defined by his energy.

Lewis Morris sent *Cambria's Coasting Pilot: The First Part* as an 11-part series of folio-sized charts to the Admiralty on 5 April 1738.

He then returned to his work as Customs Officer and had to wait three long years before receiving a letter from Thomas Corbett, deputy secretary of the Admiralty, giving him the green light to continue his surveys. This time he was given permission to hire a boat. So in March 1743 he took charge of a sloop to undertake the huge task of surveying the indented west coast of Wales. During this period he wrote a lecture called 'A Specimen of the Sea-Language of Great Britain, as it now is in its purity spoken by Midshipmen and Sailors, on board his Majesty's gallant Ships of War. The Terror of Nations.' In it Lewis Morris somewhat solipsistically gives voice to an illiterate sailor describing himself, Morris the hydrographer, to a friend: 'Dam my blood, *Jerry*, I have met ashoar a confounded piece of good luck; here is a person *implored* by the King to make observations at sea. I have promised him half-a-dozen fish; and I hope he'll give me a card of the *Crow-rock*; dam that rock, the breakers run still in my head. I have forgot his title, it is some villainous hard pen-and-inkhorn word, *idrographer*, I think ...'

The 'idrographer's' work had to stop in Tenby in May 1744, as the Admiralty's attention was now fully fixed on the looming war between Britain and France. Morris then had to wait until 1748 to publish his charts, by which time the Admiralty fully appreciated the value of such work to maritime trade and safety. The economy was improving and so the Admiralty sanctioned two publications. The first, published on 30 September 1748, was a big chart of the coast of west Wales, to which 300 people subscribed. Morris was also given the Admiralty's permission to publish his plans of individual ports, showing sandbars and places where refuge could be found during bad weather. This small volume containing twenty-four maps appeared in September 1748 as *Plans of Harbours, Bays and Roads in St George's and the Bristol Channel*. The book, full of meticulous and beautifully drawn charts, also included trade statistics, as well as an account of the natural products of each place and a handy Welsh vocabulary to help those English traders who dealt with Welsh ports. It sold like hot cakes, with some 2,000 copies being bought. One Anglesey merchant alone bought twenty of them. Lewis Morris had to live in London to oversee the printing, to ensure the highest standards. As he put it: 'The exactness necessary in operations of this kind, by sea and land, demands extraordinary care and application; the many observations proper for determining justly the situations and positions of places, what regards the tides, soundings &c, require the utmost attention, and much labour and pains.'

Lewis Morris was the first to suggest improvements to Holyhead although these didn't start until the nineteenth century: constructing a pier to keep the swell out of the harbour. When Morris surveyed it, Holyhead was just seventeen dwellings and a church set along a straggling creek-fed inlet. Political changes affecting Ireland would help change all that.

* * *

When the first Royal Mail coach service began in 1785, carrying the Irish mail as well as passengers, it left the Golden Cross Inn in Charing Cross at eight in the evening, arriving at the Eagle and Child in Holyhead a bum-numbing 45 hours later. Facilities were basic, with arriving passengers at the Anglesey port ferried to shore by small wherries or some even carried on the backs of redoubtable sailors.

At the same time, at the end of the eighteenth century Wolfe Tone raised an uprising, creating the 'United Irishmen', which made George III panic somewhat. William Pitt was ordered to pass a new law, the 1801 Act of Union, which eventually required 100 Irish MPs to travel to London. These Protestant landowners often insisted their entire households be given passage on the packet boats, the wealthiest even commandeering them for their exclusive use, leaving the other MPs haplessly stranded on the quayside.

Passenger numbers through Holyhead thus increased because of a political shift, as did concomitant demands for both the comfort and safety of the politicians passing through. It could still be a fearful trip across: in 1735 an Anglesey squire, William Bulkeley, took twenty-six hours in the choppiest of seas, which he saw as ordinary. Demand also grew because of the simple growth, in the eighteenth century, of

Dublin as a city of the Enlightenment: a place of order and symmetry, not to mention the simple growth of the population. This was a golden age which saw fine work by architects such as James Gandon's Four Courts and Custom House – the latter widely regarded as the finest single classical structure in the city. Architecture matched a city's ambitions. Dublin's 'Wide Streets Commission', established in 1758, might well have been the most powerful city planning body in European history. With the help of private money from the likes of Bartholomew Mosse, the city burghers turned Enlightenment ideals into reality, with the new order of avenues and streets and buildings such as the Lying-In Hospital (the first dedicated maternity hospital in the world) and the fashionable Sackville Mall consolidating the sense that here was a fine capital indeed.

Dublin's burgeoning development, and consequent growth of population, led to more cross-channel traffic and a concomitant response by the harbour at Holyhead. Steamships, which started to come into common usage in the early 1800s, were set to speed up passenger passage. The South Stack lighthouse (1808) was built to guide packets in and out of the harbour; soon a regular connection between Holyhead and Howth enabled ships to avoid the stretch of rocky Welsh coast from the Dee estuary. John Rennie built a Pier and Graving Dock in Holyhead in 1810 so that boats could berth safely and be repaired *in situ* if need be. Which in turn led to Irish business opportunities. Within five years of the establishment in 1833 of the City of Dublin Steam Packet Company, it had amassed no fewer than seventy-nine vessels in its fleet. Full steam ahead.

* * *

The roads lagged behind somewhat. The one from London to Chester had been slowly improved but that between Chester and Holyhead was far from, well, road-worthy, yet the Royal Mail plumped for this as the shortest route. By the early part of the eighteenth century there had been three sailings each week between Dublin and Holyhead, with packets taking anything between seventeen hours and a testing two days to make the crossing. Passenger traffic increased nevertheless. Holyhead was so popular for sea arrivals and departures by the mid-eighteenth century that Lewis's brother William reported some aristocratic suffering, as 'there are so many lords and ladies in the town that the inns are full and they are compelled to put up at houses with thatched roofs.' Thatched roofs! What a frightful inconvenience.

In 1815, the self-taught Scottish engineer Thomas Telford was commissioned to survey and suggest ways to improve what he would eventually call 'The Great Holyhead Road', setting in train a series of some of the greatest engineering feats of nineteenth-century Britain. It was the first major civil engineering project in Britain to be directly funded by Parliament, with 83 miles of it running across north Wales. One of its most important features was an impressive iron construction spanning the Menai Strait, indeed the world's first ever suspension bridge, opened in 1826. Soon various companies were running trains from Holyhead to London. Travel times contracted. What had been a four-day journey from London to Dublin shrank to a relatively comfortable forty hours or so and continued to speed up. As Stephen Dedalus says in Joyce's *Ulysses*, 'the shortest way to Tara is via Holyhead,' Tara being the mythical, magical hall of the Irish Kings. To get to this Celtic nirvana, Joyce seems to suggest, you might have to leave Ireland. Leaving would be made easier as the improvements in steam technology were ushered in, alongside new rail lines connecting with the boat. The journey times would shrink even further, so that a ten or twelve-hour road journey, with a four-hour sea crossing, eventually came to be the norm.

Work on a huge breakwater at Holyhead was begun in 1848 in order to create a harbour of refuge. It was to prove the saving grace for many a ship, but it was not without its problems, as Dr Gareth Huws, deputy chair of the Anglesey Antiquarian Society, explained to me as we stood in its lee: 'A breakwater is a wall and if you're out at sea in a sailing ship at night, say, then the last thing you want to meet is a wall, and a number of these wrecks did just that, they ran into one. Even though there was a lighthouse at the end it was still a physical barrier in the middle of the water.' It's a very substantial wall and at 1.7 miles long it's the longest breakwater in Britain.

One ship which ran into the wall of the Great Breakwater was the barque *Kirkmichael*, which had been diverted there by Captain T. Jones on 22 December 1894, whilst on its way from Glasgow via Liverpool to Melbourne, Australia. A wild and whipping storm ripped away her sails. The lifeboat, despite its best efforts, couldn't battle through the surge, but a land-based crew did manage to land a rocket carrying a line, allowing them to haul seven of the crew to safety. Two mariners had tied themselves to the mast, however, and by the time the rescuers were able to get to them they had perished. On other occasions Holyhead could offer a safe haven for many vessels, with as many as 200 held windbound in the harbour when the weather was at its most testing and the wind in the wrong direction. Some days the masts of the sheltering flotilla would resemble birch thickets, so numerous were they.

Now that the breakwater arced around the harbour, the prophetic air of Thomas Jackson's jaunty *Visitor's Guide to Holyhead* (1853) seemed to be justified. 'Holyhead,' he maintained, 'was formed by Nature to become a great trading community ... The bay provides a fine spacious opening, one half sheltered by eternal rocks, and on one side of its entrance, are brilliant lights to guide the mariner. It is, moreover, centrally situated in St George's Channel, in the track of all its trade; and presents the only station from the Land's End to the Clyde, on the east side of the channel (except Milford) to which vessels can approach when the tide has considerably ebbed. No wonder then, that the various commissioners appointed by Government ... should select it as the best place on the coast for an asylum harbour, and a packet port.'

The new road to Holyhead had been completed in 1826 but just over ten years later the train was invented: an iron horse that could carry a burden of enormous change. People started asking if they could connect a railway with the mail packets and in 1851 Holyhead duly became a mail packet port, trains connecting with steam-driven ships, and this service continued until the 1950s. Such developments led to new institutions opening in Holyhead and the place had a pronounced dynamism. This was driven in part by the competition between the two companies which provided services across St George's Channel, being the London and North Western Railway (LNWR) and the City of Dublin Steam Packet Company (CODSPC) – rivals to a fault.

The mail service had actually already been put out to tender in 1849 but the Treasury accepted the lowest bid from the CODSPC which, with its own fleet of four twin-propeller driven steamships – the *Banshee*, *Llewelyn*, *St Columba* and *Prince Arthur* – was also hoping it could carry passengers as well as mail. The original bid had been made by the Chester & Holyhead Railway Company (CHRC) and was accepted only because Royal Mail officials had 'leaked' details of the bid. The rival Dublin company, feeling properly cheated, duly cried foul and went to appeal. The Royal Mail, begrudgingly, had to rescind its original decision.

There was now a clear division of labour. The LNWR carried the mail to Holyhead while the Dublin Steam Packet Company conveyed it over the sea, and they both had to do so to agreed times. Speed was not only of the essence but it was in the contract, too: trains must connect London with Holyhead in 6 hours and 40 minutes and the sea passage should take 3 hours and 45 minutes. The latter was easily achieved by new vessels, ordered in 1859 and called the *Ulster*, *Munster*, *Leinster* and *Connaught*. This quartet, named after Irish provinces, could keep up a steady 17 knots and were each given the grand prefix Royal Mail Steamer. For speed, the LNWR simply couldn't compete. Between 1850 and 1870 the LNWR ran a cargo service directly from Holyhead to Dublin North, carrying only a limited number of passengers (usually in Third Class), while CODSPC ran to Dun Laoghaire. Fully imbued with the spirit of competition the LNWR bought themselves two speedy steam vessels, the *Rose* and the *Shamrock*, and decided to improve the Inner Harbour, adding new warehouses and capstans and a splendid new railway station, complete with a five-storey Railway Hotel. New development fuelled further improvements, such as the Town Hall, opened in

1875, which took its place among 2,000 houses, 58 public houses, 12 chapels and 2 churches: this boom town trebled in size between 1845 and 1850. As the port grew, so did the town.

The Town Hall also put on entertainment, such as Maggie Morton's 'famous troupe of actors who stopped for one night only on their way to Ireland, where they performed their "thrilling" drama *Two Little Drummer Boys*.' Irish merchants and workers settled here, necessitating the building of a Roman Catholic Church, which was opened in 1858. The local Catholic graveyard is today full of their names: Keegans, Magees, Flanagans, Walshes, Bogues, Dolans, O'Neills, Sullivans, Kennedys and Kinlans. Holyhead, however, was a staunchly nonconformist town and between 1840 and 1860 some fourteen chapels were built, such as the Armenia, Ebenezer and Bethel. On the other side of the water a Welsh chapel was established in Talbot Street, Dublin by John Roberts of Hyfrydle chapel in Holyhead, with ministers travelling over to preach in Ireland of a Sunday. Welsh nonconformist chapels were often decidedly anti-Catholic, so there was a certain wariness of the Irish. That said, one of the Protestant ministers in Holyhead, William Griffith, collected money to provide a mission in Dublin, so that children could be taught through the medium of Irish: this at a time when Welsh was strong but the Irish language was weakening.

There had long been Irish folk in the Holyhead area, although some of them had not been welcome exactly. Amongst them were the 'Irish vagabonds' who were here in such numbers that a house of correction had to be built in 1741 to accommodate them. In the early nineteenth century the problem still pertained. In *The Irish in Wales*, Paul O'Leary says that 'in north Wales, the cost of removing Irish vagrants made substantial inroads into local budgets. Approximately half the expenditure on removals from the counties of Anglesey and Caernarfonshire in the years 1820–22 was absorbed in conveying vagrants to Ireland.' A small ditty in Welsh could be their riposte:

Maent yn dywedyd yn Werddon
Hob y deri dando
Fod Caergybi'n llawn o Ladron
Dyna ganu eto

They say in Ireland
Hob y deri dando
That Holyhead is full of thieves
Let's sing that again

Commercially, the tussle between the two competing companies continued. There was a surge of new developments in the Inner Harbour, and the increased fleet owned by the LNWR, not to mention the ease with which their customers could move swiftly from the station to the boat, gave them the edge over their Dublin-based competitors. But the Steam Packet Company had their own plans and the arrival of a passenger boat without paddles, the new, twin-screw *SS Ulster*, came as a shock to its rivals, especially as its construction had happened in secret. Each company had its strengths. Commentator Charles H. Harper saw the LNWR as running things like clockwork: 'Then, just as though it was an ingenious mechanical toy of a larger growth … everything begins to work furiously. Trains roll in, electric lights glare coldly from tall standards in the docks, mountains of luggage are shot out upon platforms or quay walls; porters, sailors, passengers, newsboys, and a miscellaneous crowd rush back and forth, just after the fashion of those little clock-work mannikins in the glass cases. Then the whistles of the steamer or train blow; the passengers are all aboard, the porters trundle their trucks back from whence they came, the crowd disperses, the newsboys end in the midst of their shouting, and out go all the lights.'

An interesting tradition was maintained by the 'Irish Mail' train, the first named train service in the world: before leaving Euston, the guard was handed a watch in a leather case by a Post Office messenger. When he arrived in Holyhead the guard gave the correct time to an official on the Kingstown boat. The watch was returned by the return-ing mail train in order to be readjusted at the General Post Office for its next journey. In the days of the mail coach, Greenwich and Dublin times were different, so the Irish Mail literally carried the time to Holyhead as well as letters.

The First World War took its toll on the Holyhead fleet. The Railway Company's roster of ships was reduced to two, as vessels were commandeered for military use, but this vestigial duo continued to ply pluckily back and forth to Kingstown. The contract to carry mail had come to an end in 1915; the Dublin Steam Packet Company was allowed to continue its service because of the war, but tragically lost two ships, the *Leinster* and the *Connaught*. They tendered for the mail again, but this time they lost out to their old rivals, the LNWR. Their quartet of ships – the *Anglia*, *Hibernia*, *Cambria* and *Scotia*, new vessels using traditional names – could cross the sea in 2 hours and 55 minutes. The four were twice the tonnage of their predecessors and could not be turned in the Inner Harbour, so had to be towed out stern first. But the denizens of the town-by-the-sea would surely find the sight of one of these ships driving through pounding high seas, half obscured by great washes of spray, a thrilling spectacle, especially from the safety of land.

* * *

The year 1922 saw the declaration of Irish Independence, which brought in restrictions, customs barriers and a consequent fall in trade for a town where sea-connectivity was all. A newly-arrived chapel minister once observed of Holyhead folk: 'Ask them the way to Rhosneigr and they can't tell you. But ask them the way to Hong Kong and they'll explain in detail.' That extensive maritime connec-tion was there in the pub names, which rostered as a sort of oblique atlas: The Lord Nelson, Skerries, Bardsey Island Inn, New Harbour Inn, Ship and Castle, South Stack Branch and South Stack Vaults, Hope and Anchor, Trefadog Ferry, Marine Hotel, Marine Tap, Pilot Inn, Hibernia Inn, Holland Arms, Dublin Packet, Boston Arms,

Globe Inn, California Arms, and The Travellers Inn. Many of these, by now, of course, have had to sound their very last orders.

One of the best places to appreciate Holyhead's long and complicated relationship with the sea is the town's Maritime Museum, housed in what used to be the lifeboat station on Newry Beach. It's a cross between Dickens' Old Curiosity Shop, with its 'tapestry and strange furniture that might have been designed in dreams,' and the physics-defying spaciousness of Doctor Who's Tardis. In it you'll find the jawbone of a woolly mammoth dragged up from the harbour, which journeyed to the Natural History Museum before it was returned. There's an assortment of decorated whale's ear-bones, which used to be found in many homes in the town, dating back to the dark days of the Great Depression, a period of economic misery between 1929 and 1939, when men left the town to seek a living wage on whale boats heading for Antarctica. And, of course, there are details and artefacts about wrecks, such as the *Primrose Hill*, lost near South Stack, and the *Norman Court*, rock-crashed at Rhosneigr. There's also a display dedicated to Alfred Holt's Blue Funnel Line, which recruited so many young men from Holyhead and north Wales they jocularly called his fleet, operating out of Liverpool, the 'Welsh Navy'.

One of the biggest artefacts on display is an incredibly solid-looking sailmakers' sewing machine out of the Holyhead Marine Yard, made of cast iron and attached to a drive belt. It looks as if it could stitch through the toughest canvas: only one other has been identified in the world and that one is in New Zealand. Until 1986 – when the yard closed – there was a strong tradition that ships working out of Holyhead would be repaired in the port. So, should they need new boilers, new engine room parts or whatever, there was a whole array of skills available to them locally – joiners, fitters, boilermakers, copper-smiths – all able to service their needs. Hundreds of ships might be sheltering in Holyhead, and because they were sailing ships their spars might be broken, sails ripped or shredded, so there was great call for skills that could facilitate running repairs.

One end of the museum is naturally devoted to the lifeboat service. Museum trustee Barry Hillier's mother's family is from the Amlwch and the Cemaes area, and thus his family were all at sea, as it were, going back four or five generations. Barry's father-in-law also went to sea school in Ireland at the age of 12. With so many maritime connections it's little wonder that the sea is in his blood: he is an ebullient guide to the various models, photographs and lifeboat paraphernalia on display. 'The lifeboat displays start in 1855,' he tells me, 'when Holyhead had two lifeboats, one of which would be moved around on a big carriage, while the other one was taken out to sea from a beach somewhere. This was in the days when the lifeboat had sails and oars, until a version appeared that was propelled with a steam engine.' Barry proudly shows me a display about the *Duke of Northumberland* lifeboat which he informs me 'was driven by two large water pumps. It had no propellers but rather worked on the jet ski principle – you drew water in at the front and shot it out at the back. It was the product of a competition to design a lifeboat in 1886.' He then tells me about the Gold Medal-awarded rescue of the *SS Harold*, which was carrying china clay from Teignmouth to Liverpool in 1908, 'when her engine broke in the middle of one heck of a storm. Here is a model of a lifeboat that went out to rescue nine mariners in atrocious circumstances, in a full gale which was close to being a hurricane. It took them two hours to reach them and the lifeboat crew and the coxswain William Owen was awarded the Gold Medal, which we display proudly.' Owen's obituary summed up his achievements succinctly: 'He was as fearless as a lion, and was ever in the midst of the perils which beset the vast deep.'

Barry next shows me a very fine model of the current lifeboat, the *Christopher Pearse*. 'The model was presented to a retiring coxswain and he very kindly allowed us to have it here. We almost lost the real boat in the great storm of 2018 known as "The Beast from the East", when it was on the pontoon and the whole marina was wrecked by the storm. They managed to get it on board and took it out to sea, otherwise it would have been badly damaged.'

* * *

The port for crossing to Dublin had to be an exciting place. Millions of people shared the sort of experience described by the historian Christopher Harvie in the *Irish Review*, who 'quitted the muzaked and fruit-machine intestines of the Holyhead ferry and stood on deck. Spray, white paint pustular with corrosion, grey seas crashing on either side. Caer Gybi, and Snowdonia behind it, sinking into the east.' A traveller coming in the other direction could throw on a meta-phorical cloak of anonymity on arrival, after leaving the close-knit confines and tight, gossipy grapevine of Irish village life. As the short story writer Frank O'Connor from Cork tellingly puts it: 'An Irishman's private life begins at Holyhead.'

Among the sea-borne multitudes great national figures strutted; wanted men and spies slipped through unobserved; political prisoners and silent coffins made the passage over the water. In 1891 the great Irish nationalist politician Charles Stewart Parnell's coffin was conveyed to Dublin from Hove in Sussex via Holyhead, en route to a momentous funeral which would be attended by almost 250,000 people. The poet W. B. Yeats went to meet the very same early Mail Boat, on which his friend Maud Gonne was arriving. Activist, actress and mystic Gonne was returning from Paris, shattered by the death of her two-year-old son Georges. In her drape of black mourning she might have easily been mistaken for a member of Parnell's grieving entourage. Interestingly, another frequent cross-channel traveller had been Yeats's uncle, the stockbroker Robert Corbet, who had lined his pockets selling off bankrupt estates after the Famine. In what might be seen as a demonstration of Celtic karma, Corbet ran into his own money problems before taking his own life by jumping off the Holyhead Mail Boat in 1870, in so doing making a small splash in the newspapers.

Another coffin passing through Holyhead caused much more commotion. Terence MacSwiney was an Irish playwright and politi-cian, and Sinn Féin's lord mayor of Cork during the Irish War of Independence. In 1920 he had been accused of having in his posses-sion two secret documents belonging to the police. Successfully charged with sedition by the British government, he was sentenced to two years in prison. Protesting his innocence in Brixton prison MacSwiney went on hunger strike on the very first day of his sentence, eliciting support from many quarters: dockers in New York threatened strike action and some 300,000 Catholics in Brazil asked the Pope to intervene.

MacSwiney died on 25 October 1920, seventy-four days after he started his protest. His coffin was visited by 30,000 people in Southwark Cathedral, amongst them Clement Attlee, who would one day become prime minister. The death was also noted by a man washing dishes in a London hotel at the time: a certain Ho Chi Minh.

The body was then to be taken home. Mourners gathered at the station and along the route. As the train passed Bangor one of those standing respectfully on the platform was the Reverend Lewis Valentine, one of 'the Three' Welsh Nationalists who would later set fire to the bombing school at Penyberth on the Llŷn Peninsula.

When MacSwiney's coffin arrived at Holyhead there were unseemly scenes. A last-moment decision by the government meant that the body could not be taken to Dublin as planned because of the perceived risk of political demonstrations. The mourners struggled for possession of the coffin as a number of Metropolitan Police entered the van and forcibly ejected MacSwiney's party, including family members. They were forced to walk towards the boat by the police, accompanied by 300 members of the Auxilaries and the Tans. Some people tried to form a cordon around the coffin but against such a robust show of force they reluctantly had to watch the body being lifted by crane onto a steamer, the *Rathmore*. The family and mourners refused to board, choosing rather to kneel on the harbourside and pray, led by Father Dominic, who chanted the De Profundis.

* * *

There was one set of travellers to Holyhead who were desperate not to be noticed. On 16 July 1914 the crew of the pleasure yacht, the *Asgard* – the Cambridge-educated Englishman Erskine Childers, his wife Molly, Sir Roger Casement and two sailors from Gola island, Donegal

– were on a gun-running trip, taking 1,500 Mauser rifles to the Irish Volunteers at Howth harbour in Ireland. They had managed to evade detection ever since they met a tugboat carrying the arms out of Hamburg at the Ruytigen buoy off the coast of Belgium. The guns and ammo took up most of the room in the cabin, which made the journey uncomfortable in the extreme. On their return journey they had to sail through an entire British fleet which was then conducting night manoeuvres near Devonport – one destroyer hoved perilously close to the small yacht – and the *Asgard* also faced ferocious storms. But the biggest danger came when they reached Holyhead. The sixth crew member, Mary Spring Rice, who kept a remarkable diary for the duration, recalled some heart-pounding moments when the coastguard paid them a visit: '"Erskine," I shouted. "Wake up, you're wanted; they're asking her name." But Erskine is very hard to wake and I was just meditating shaking him when he turned over and said sleepily, "What?" "Come on deck," and I dashed up, he after me. There were the coastguards in a boat close by, calling out questions: "Last port; destination; registered tonnage; owner's name." Erskine, now thoroughly awake, shouted prompt answers, some of them truth and some of them fiction and, to our immense relief, they rowed away and we breathed again. Luckily, someone had had the presence of mind to throw a sail over the ammunition boxes in the cockpit.'*

Gun-runners, as we all know, need nerves of ice. Childers, true to form, showed steely sangfroid the next day, when he went into the town of Holyhead to have himself a haircut. You need to look good for history.

Childers wasn't the only gun-runner to pass through Holyhead. In the 1860s a deal was struck in one of the town's taverns to carry almost 15,000 rifles and revolvers to the Confederate side in the American Civil War, carried on the Clyde steamer *Fingal*.

* * *

* Mary Rice Springer, 'Diaries of the Asgard,' https://www.anphoblacht.com/contents/24233.

There were dangers whatever the direction of travel. In the fourth of Anthony Trollope's Pallister novels, *Phineas Redux*, the eponymous hero returns to London and the perils of parliamentary life: 'Doubtless there is a way of riddance. There is the bare bodkin. Or a man may fall overboard between Holyhead and Kingstown in the dark, and may do it in such a cunning fashion that his friends shall think that it was an accident. But against these modes of riddance there is a canon set, which some men still fear to disobey.'

Phineas doesn't know that returning to London will see him eventually standing in the Old Bailey, accused of the murder of a friend, but leaving Ireland brings with it some trepidation. He nervously walks up and down the long harbour wall wondering, 'what might not London do for him? Would those fabled streets be paved with gold?' Travellers carried such nagging questions as certainly as they took with them bulging luggage.

As we know from the passage of MacSwiney's coffin, reaction to many events in Ireland at the beginning of the twentieth century funnelled through Holyhead: the bloody events of the Easter Rising of 1916, for instance, sent dark ripples into the port. One of the ships that regularly travelled back and forth from Dublin to Holyhead was the *Slieve Bloom*, often found carrying livestock. One day, however, it was used to transport Dubliner Jim Mooney, who had been one of those firing from the roof of the Central Post Office on the fateful Monday of the insurrection. Along with the 1,800 others who became British prisoners afterwards, Mooney was being sent to the Frongoch internment camp, in an old whisky distillery near Bala in north Wales. He had signed the Defence of the Realm Act, admitting to his revolutionary acts and membership of proscribed bodies. Another prisoner was Ambrose Byrne, also from Dublin, who recalled with bitterness being marched at bayonet point down Sackville Street and Thomas Street to the barracks at Inchicore as fellow Irish threw objects at them. A man called Joe Clarke was marched to the ship accompanied by the raucous, mocking chorus of people who jeered at the 'foolish Sinn Feiners'. Rotten apples were thrown, and worse. 'We felt very low,' he recalled, 'but others were waving green flags and singing old rebel songs. We walked to the ship with our heads held high, even if our hearts were not.'

A handful of these prisoners crossed the sea as third-class passengers, but the majority were locked away in the cattle pens, some of them having to share the space with the agitated animals. One of the prospective prisoners at Frongoch recalls arriving at the ship only to hear a British officer telling his men to stay 'where they were and to let the dirt go first.'

It was a soul-besmirching passage and a perilous one, not least because of the silent predations of German U-boats. The prisoners, unlike the soldiers who guarded them, were not given lifejackets, and neither were they given much food. A ration might be as little as one biscuit, and that a dog biscuit, per man with no water to wash it down. Then there were the animals to contend with. Michael Brennan from County Clare was one of those forced to travel with the cattle. They were goaded by the boat's slow slalom as it tried to confuse the submarines and their torpedoes which, in turn, helped drive the animals mad with confusion. Joe O'Doherty, from Derry, recalled being taken to the ship weighted down by chains and being pelted with stones by his compatriots. The cattle ship had not been cleaned at all and the hold was full of animal ordure. There was no way out and the only source of light came from a single hold door, wedged slightly open. But one of the prisoners stood in the single, wan shaft of light and started singing defiantly.

The men were greeted at the quayside in Holyhead by more soldiers, ready to transfer them to prisons in Stafford, Wakefield, Wandsworth and Woking, with rumours that some were to be sent as far away as St Helena. The ones who went to Frongoch would be staying in what was later known as the 'University of the Revolution', as there they learned under the tutelage of men such as the charismatic Michael Collins many skills which would be useful for insurgency. When prisoners were finally released from their Welsh internment in 1916, many of them travelled home to Ireland again via Holyhead; some on the *Slieve Bloom*, the self-same cattle ship that had brought them over. This time they arrived home proudly, wearing

Sinn Féin uniforms and carrying in their heads the guerrilla tactics they had learned in the peace of the green Welsh hills.

* * *

It wasn't always clear sailing across St George's Channel. The writer Kerri ní Dochartaigh was stuck in Holyhead for twenty-four hours on her way home to Derry. In her memoir, *Thin Places*, she recounts the anxiety about the trip to a place where childhood memories included being petrol-bombed out of their home: 'From that crossing,' she recalled, 'I remember the light above Holyhead Port, in the tenderly falling spring evening. How it seemed to bleed out over all the soft grey clouds, and the screeching off-white gulls, as they turned in a not-quite-empty sky. The winds – bitter, full of fragments of ice that never quite became earthbound. The waves – choppy, heaving them-selves against the well-faded paintwork of the vessel's iron.'* Fear churned in her belly during that journey 'home' to Ireland, a land she had been desperately trying to forget, and crippling anxiety 'choked me when I tried to feel positive, when I tried to convince myself that this was the end to the line of sorrow I now knew I could not simply outrun.' Such memories re-emerged like the slick black heads of cormorants in the waves, slippery and fleeting.

The trepidation the writer felt about the country had sometimes been matched by the country's suspicions about writing. The Republican newspaper *An Phoblacht* applauded the censoring efforts of the three laymen and two clergymen who made up the Orwellian-sounding Committee on Evil Literature, which tried to stem the flow of 'filthy' literature from Britain – anything from *Woman's Weekly* to *The Catcher in the Rye* and adverts for depilatory cream. The Irish State banned no fewer than 12,000 books, up to and including pop idol Madonna's *Sex* in 1992. Whilst it approved some censorship, *An Phoblacht* also berated, in no uncertain terms, the writers and artists of Dublin for having minds like sewers: 'Some will wonder that they

---

* Kerri ní Dochartaigh, *Thin Places*, Edinburgh, 2021.

have to take the Holyhead boat to look for fame. Their bright, beauteous souls love to hover around the prostitutes of Dublin, the thieves and murderers of Dublin. These writers cannot have healthy brains, cannot have brains at all but a slack mass of matter like frog-spawn where grim, filthy ideas crawl and breed like so many vermin.'

* * *

The satirist Jonathan Swift, author of *Gulliver's Travels*, was marooned in Holyhead for a week that felt like a century. This sojourn in September 1727 gave him all the ingredients he needed to stew in his own Irish misery. The strange, unhappy Irishman was desperate to get to Dublin, where his beloved Stella was perilously ill, but the weather was set against him. This was often the case for travellers to Ireland, who could be confined to port in Wales by the batter of the prevailing south-westerly winds. The arch-curmudgeon, who had left London already suffering from indigestion and scurvy, did not have an easy time of it. It was a trip he'd done before and he had written with spleen about travelling 'above 200 miles from home/O'er mountains steep, o'er dusty plains/Half choked with dust, half drown'd with rains.'

The suffering Swift was forced to stay in expensive inns in a town he describes as the 'worst spot in Wales under the very worst circumstances.' As his journal puts it, he was 'cooped in a room not half as large as one of the Deanery closets.' Misery begat misery. He was confined to a 'narrow chamber in all unwalkable hours.' The owner did not treat him 'with the least civility.' Dogs kept him awake and he yearned for a slice of bread and a glass of Deanery wine as the Irish porter he managed to procure tasted sour. Meanwhile, the weather gnawed away at Swift's fortitude, or, as the poet Austin Clarke has it in his poem 'The Hippophagi': 'Weather reports/Lay bare our soul in ancient ports.' Little wonder then that Swift's eventual poem about the testing experience is hardly couched in the language of a travel brochure:

Lo here I sit at Holy Head
With muddy ale and mouldy bread
All Christian vittals stink of fish,
I'm where my enemies would wish.
Convict of lies is every Sign,
The inn has not a drop of wine
I'm fastened both by wind and tide,
I see the ship at anchor ride.
The Captain swears the sea's too rough,
He has not passengers enough.
And thus the Dean is forc'd to stay
Till others come to help the pay.

Other more contemporary, but no less splenetic, satirists also took a pot at Holyhead, such as the critic A. A. Gill, who called it the 'town where pebbledash goes to die.' There is a lot of pebbledash, even nowadays: indeed, it can be fairly described as ubiquitous on its houses. The modern poet R. S. Thomas had very different memories of Holyhead. Thomas moved here at the end of the Second World War, and his English accent stood out 'as though some alien life form had materialised among the pebbledash.'*

R. S.'s father had found work on the ships that sailed between Wales and Ireland. His first day there started with a 'jewel of a morning. Every place gleaming and the sea a wondrous blue although the weather wasn't always like this.' In his *Autobiographies* he playfully suggests that should anyone be asked what sort of weather can be expected on Anglesey the answer should be 'Oh, normally clearing towards afternoon.' For Thomas, a sickly child, the weather was king in Holyhead, not least because his mother 'believed that enough fresh sea air would make a new man of me.' The sea provided its fair share of magical moments for a young boy, especially swimming with friends and porpoises in the bay called Porth Gof Du.

---

* R. S. Thomas, *Autobiographies*, London, 1997.

Baptismal and blessed, the sea for Thomas would be an inspiration for all of his days. One of his finest poems, 'Sea Watching', depicts the poet as a hermit of the rocks looking out to sea, waiting for a rare bird to arrive. But like God, suggests the poet, it only comes when one is not watching, when the observer isn't there.

It is easy to picture him, then, gazing out to sea at somewhere like South Stack – where he and I used to go birdwatching together. Or wandering with those heavy binoculars of his around the Cemlyn lagoons, near his last home at Llanfair-yng-Nghornwy, waiting for a rare bird to arrive, elusive as God.

Another of Thomas's early poems connects directly with Holyhead, as he imagines the poet W. B. Yeats carrying embryo poems in his skull as other travellers carry suitcases. The poem, called simply enough 'Memories of Yeats Whilst Travelling to Holyhead', evokes the metrical rhythm of the train wheels, the monosyllabic sea and the listening hilltops, whilst suggesting the diffidence of the Welsh poet travelling in the same compartment as Yeats, hurled between the white audience of the waves. It's a poem with dream and reality, sea and land, Wales and Ireland – and Holyhead all in the same breath.

9.

THE CRAFT OF THE SEA

It's a postcard image, albeit sepia tinted, the stiff paper now all hairline fractures. The strand at Rosslare, County Wexford, the line of the storm bank punctuated with small boats lying on their sides like hospital patients. The swish of small waves as they rummage though banks of pebbles.

To a landlubber these might be pleasure craft, fit only to take rod-and-reel fishermen just offshore, or to bear the clumsy weight of Sunday rowers. But in truth such boats, known as Wexford cots, are sturdy indeed. They even traversed the turbulence of the North Atlantic, going through the eye of a storm, facing waves as high as church steeples.

Boatbuilding and shipbuilding have taken many forms on the facing coasts of Wales and Ireland – harbourages busy as bees with men working wood, making sails, tempering metal and manufacturing masts.

The Wexford cot is one of the most distinctive expressions of these sea-building trades, and has been described as 'one of the longest lived and most seaworthy of all the traditional craft of north-west Europe.'*
Its seaworthiness was often sorely tested on runs to Wales at a time when Ireland needed to import coal in the middle of the sixteenth century. Trade went the other way of course, with goods coming out

---

* Robert Kee, *Ireland: A History*, London, 1981.

of Ireland such as the timber and barrel boards brought from Wexford to Milford in 1602, when fifty herring nets were also imported.

Of the fifty-five Irish ships that plied their wares to the port of Bridgewater, Somerset in 1560, thirty-five of them were probably cots. They were laden with hides, cloths, wooden boards and re-exported licks of French salt, along with barrels of 'corrupt' wine – so described for reasons of excise no doubt – and ample stocks of fish. Fish out, coal in: the trade of the day.

Various sea-going vessels drift into Irish writing from very early on. Adamnan's *Life of Columba* lists many, including several types of planked boats, dug-out boats and curraughs, while St Brendan took his second voyage to sea in something like a cot. 'Not elegant,' the aptly-named naturalist Gerald Boate wrote witheringly about cots in 1645, saying they were a 'thinge like boats but very unshapely, being nothing but square pieces of timber made hollow'.

The name of the cot derives from 'coite', the old Irish for log-boat, as simple as a dug-out canoe. It is interesting that the Welsh word for wood is 'coed' which suggests they might have a common arboreal root, if you pardon the pun. Nowadays, the name 'cot' applies to 'any flat-bottom craft without a keel, but usually having a distinct angle or chine at the junction of the bottom planking' – a natural development of simpler boats, increasing the beam, freeboard and, consequently, seaworthiness.

While the double-ended cot with stem and stern posts was used on rivers such as the Blackwater, Nore, Suir, Barrow, Ban and Slaney in the south east of the country – and exceptionally in North Derry – there was only one place where it was modified to go to sea, namely Rosslare. Its origins are lost in time's mist. There are similarities between the Somerset flatners, which in turn derived from whale-catching dories used in the Bay of Biscay, but both the cot and the flatner might go even further back – surviving evidence of the North European Celtic tradition of boatbuilding, perhaps.

What is certain is that the tradition of building the Rosslare cot goes back 200 years. One family, the Wickhams, built them through five generations. The length was important, adding to their confidence in the waves, so modern cots were hardly ever more than 26 feet long and the mode of their construction barely changed since the nineteenth century.

Traditionally the Rosslare cot went after herring, and during the 1920s there were as many as forty-six large cots registered in the port, sallying forth into the north of the Irish sea and along the south coast. Until 1926 when the sea destroyed it, Rosslare Fort was sea-cot-central, with larger craft carrying four men who would launch its flat bottom into the rollers before skilfully navigating through the shoals barring the way to open water.

The cot was not only a vessel for St George's Channel-hopping: it also traversed the wild Atlantic, with Wexford fishermen hauling in what seemed at the time to be the boundless harvest of the Grand Banks in Newfoundland. They went as crew members on craft from the West of England. As a consequence, a fifth of the Newfoundland population of Irish descent comes from Wexford, while it has been suggested that the bateaux that work the mighty St Lawrence river are modelled on the cot.*

The vast majority of Newfoundland's immigrants came from specific areas within four bordering counties of south-east Ireland, namely south Wexford, south Kilkenny, south-east Tipperary, and all of Co. Waterford. Wexford and Waterford by the late 1600s were bustling ports, heavily engaged in the provisions trade, supplying English ships that called into port with food items such as salt pork and beef.

Waterford port's success lay in part in its agricultural hinterland, producing food which could be taken by English companies to the new American colonies. However, by the mid-eighteenth century other ships began to call here, this time not looking for provisions but instead for local Irishmen willing to crew trawlers netting cod in the Newfoundland fisheries.

The majority of them were farmers' sons from the inland areas. The ironic aspect of this workforce from Ireland is that many of them had

---

* Billy Colfer, *Wexford: A Town and its Landscapes*, Cork, 2008.

absolutely no experience whatsoever of the sea, and that would be a source of constant complaint of British government officials in the Newfoundland fisheries. This seemingly insurmountable difficulty still did not deter the droves who crossed the Atlantic to work the summer fishing season. For this migration was seasonal – like modern grape pickers in Europe or the men who would man the Alaskan canneries – and many would in fact return in the winter to Waterford with wages from the fish companies, or indeed the fish itself, that could be traded for money in their home port.

The Irish weren't alone in heading for Newfoundland, of course: fishing the Grand Banks was the piscine equivalent to the Gold Rush, the Klondike of cod. The French dominated in the early years, followed by the English and the Portuguese. There were many Basques, too, but their numbers were hidden in the official Spanish statistics. And there were some Welsh, lured north by the promise of abundant cod, as 'the sea there is full of fish that can be taken not only with nets but with fishing-baskets'. Commentators at the time seemed to suggest you could catch cod as easily as catching a cold.

One of those Welshmen smitten by the idea was Sir William Vaughan, from Golden Grove near Llandeilo, who decided to establish a Welsh colony in Newfoundland, buying up land on the Avalon peninsula for the purpose and then sending along his own settlers. These included farmers from the Tywi valley who were startlingly ill-equipped to catch fish, fight off the French, or survive the bleak winters. The venture was doomed and short-lived, although Vaughan himself later celebrated the disastrous affair in a long poem called 'The Golden Fleece', which deliberately invoked the idea of Jason and the Argonauts as he tried to make of this failed adventure a heroic myth.

Irish fishermen, on the other hand, successfully crossed tempestuous seas and made a living in John Cabot's New Found Land. Indeed the Avalon peninsula, the location of the doomed Welsh settlement, became an Irish heartland, alive with fiddle music and seamen's *craic*.

Other Welsh fishermen had better luck than Vaughan's unfortunates when they sallied north, such as the crew of the bark *Perrot* of

Milford, which returned to Pembrokeshire in 1566 bearing 19,000 'Newlande fish'. Some venturers from Wales went there regularly, such as the Anglesey landowner and MP Sir Richard Bulkeley, who 'sent yearly two ships to Greenland for cod, ling and other fish,' which he then bartered in Spain for Malaga wines and sherry.

One part of the cots' story connects with the Vikings. Settling in Ireland, they introduced their clinker-planking techniques after violently laying claim to sites on both the Irish and Welsh coasts.

The Viking ships are almost the stuff of legend, or specifically of saga, taking Norsemen to plunder all over, and settling Greenland and Iceland into the bargain. One Irish annalist conjured them up in an almost cinematic image:

> Bitter is the wind tonight
> It tosses the ocean's white hair
> Tonight I fear not the fierce warriors of Norway
> Coursing on the Irish Sea

The Norsemen attacked Ireland on pretty much an annual basis from the 790s onwards, venturing from their local headquarters on the Isle of Man, where they had set up a bridgehead from the conquered Hebrides. They were on Man long enough to leave traces in the language, which consequently diverged from both Irish and Scots Gaelic: their most enduring legacy is the Tynwald, the island's assembly, which still meets and carries with it an echo of the Viking system of governance. By the 830s they were sending fleets of ships into rivers such as the Boyne, the Liffey and the Shannon. This presence grew and grew.

There were sixty longships on the Liffey between 839 and 941. A Viking captain called Thorgisl had conquered Ulster before proceeding south. He built a longport that he called Dublin, after the Irish *Dubh linn*, or 'Black Pool', where he promptly declared himself king. There followed a period when the Danes, know as the Dhubgaill, or 'dark foreigners', skirmished with the Finngaill, the Norse 'fair foreigners'. The latter prevailed, allowing two brothers, Olaf the White and

Ivar the Boneless, to establish a major slave trading centre in Dublin, while the Vikings would eventually establish other coastal centres in Wexford, Waterford and Limerick. From here they set sail to plunder Wales, which they did for over 300 years from the eighth century onwards – long enough to have given them a name, *gynt*, which means pagans. A cathedral, newly built in St Davids and consecrated in 1131, only lasted fifty years before it was wrecked by the raiders from the sea. They had already murdered a bishop there on two occasions, in 999 and 1080.

News that the pagans were coming was enough to occasion dread. The ninth-century *Anglo-Saxon Chronicle* describes the sort of paranoia they engendered, noting the appearance of a red moon that ominously coincided with their arrival, these men driven south like hungry thrushes to feed on bloody berries. They would eventually settle along the Seine and be given a dukedom called Normandia, and eventually a new chapter in the history of conquest would open.

The Viking ships, known as *dreki*, were key to their plundering success, using the sea as a highway to reach their often monastic targets. They were certainly light and flexible, often made out of a single oak, which made the craft more elastic and thus superior to the leather boats favoured by the Celts. They had a narrow draught, so could be rowed close to shore in shallow water and even up river if need be. In addition to the raiding and fighting vessels, the so-called dragon ships, the Vikings also had cargo vessels, or *knorr*, powered by sail rather than oar.

A complete Viking ship is yet to be found in Ireland but many timber pieces and nails have turned up in places such as Fishamble Street and Wood Quay in Dublin, offering evidence of the 'clinker' technique in play, whereby planks would overlap and be held together by nails to build long and narrow warships with space on board for 100 men. They were fashioned from oak in the traditonal manner, by axemen slitting the trees rather than sawing them. To make a large longship might require the timber from as many as twenty-seven oak trees to make the keel, the stem, the mast and stringers, while fifty pine trees were required for the oars and spars. Ten pliable willows would yield 1,000 wooden nails, while ash would be used to form the oarport planks.

St David's cathedral in Pembrokeshire, a prime target destination for the Northern marauders, has a carving of a boat showing an oar through a hole in the boat's side in the Viking fashion. Another twelfth-century misericord – a carving set under a seat – depicts a clinker-built ship being constructed on shore. The shipwrights are seen taking a break, an axe lying behind one of them. This ship has fore- and aftercastles and a straight stern, which suggests she may eventually have been fitted with a rudder on the stern rather than the traditional Viking location on the side.

With good sailcloth made of sheep fleece woven into yarn, and a strong, billowing wind, a simple Scandinavian ship such as this could really pick up speed. Small Viking warships, built to carry some thirty-five warriors, could keep up a constant 15 knots, or 28 kilometres an hour. The sail-wool itself came from a hardy sheep variety high in lanolin, which thus helped to repel water, while the ships would be painted in strong colours: yellow, black, blue, yellow, red and green. Interestingly, on the south Wales coast even today there's a local tradition that people should fear the raven, one of the birds that decorated the Viking sails as they scouted the coast on slave-hunting expeditions.

Viking warriors travelled in cramped conditions, with very little space between each fixed seat or thwart. Here they ate, slept and manned the oars, the metronome beat of blades cutting into the water and able to propel the ship forwards even in an absence of wind. Conditions were primitive, with no toilets, cooking facilities or beds: the weather-battered sea-travellers would have to use two-man sleeping bags, open to all weathers.

The Northmen's navigation system depended on natural aids, quite literally, as they often travelled in the near permanent sunlight of the Northern day. So they would look for birds to signal the promised land, and use cloud formations, ice-glare and the presence of drift-wood to work out where land lay relative to their sea-path. They sailed far and wide, beaching at then settling in Ireland, thereby gifting a shipbuilding tradition that would allow the Irish, in turn, to venture out. Such are the ways of the sea.

The Norse held sway in Ireland for centuries, also setting up bases on the Wirral and successfully attacking the Danes in Northumbria. But by the tenth century they were overstretched, short on the neces-sary manpower and military might to compete with the Danes, with their colonies in Argyll, Rheged – between the Mersey and the Ribble – and their outpost on Anglesey made vulnerable, even as their Irish settlements also came under attack.

The Vikings had much less impact on Wales, even though they scattered their names along the coast, creating a sort of crackly, frica-tive found poem: Sger, Skerries, Stack Rock, Goskar, Piscar, Tusker, softening around Orme's Head and Osmond's Air, Gateholm and Burry Holms.

* * *

Shipbuilding was simply transformational for some small ports in Wales. Nefyn, on the northern rim of the Llŷn peninsula, was one such place. There were two ships registered here as far back as 1293, when they had a value of twenty shillings each, in days when an ox, say, was worth five shillings. In its heyday, between the 1860s and the turn of the century, there were no fewer than five insurance offices in this busy huddle of buildings. As maritime historian Meinir Pierce Jones explained to me, 'People found that it was too expensive to insure through Lloyds of London, or one of the big Liverpool insurers, so some enterprising locals opened offices. At one point, ships valued at £2 million were insured through these small local firms.' Apart from such actuarial activity Nefyn was a veritable hive of boat-building activity, assembling no fewer than 123 sloops and schooners between the mid-eighteenth century and the end of the nineteenth century. These schooners were beautiful vessels, described as 'perhaps the finest small merchant sailing ships ever built,' accounting in part for their financial value. In the absence of local forests, some of the wood would be carried on waggons from the nearby Conwy valley, while some of the specialist timber came from further afield, places such as the Baltic, while the baulkes, or timber beams to build the masts, came from Canada and America. The building of sloops, cutters and smacks was similarly important in many ports on the west coast of Wales, not least in Cardigan, which saw the growth of such maritime industry as early as the sixteenth century: by the beginning of the nineteenth century there were no fewer than 314 registered there with local farmers, businessmen and shopkeepers all owning shares.

The men who built the ships were held in high regard and were well rewarded. John Thomas, who lived in a house called Fron Olau, won the sobriquet 'The King of Nefyn'. The grandest house in the town was owned by the area's main shipbuilder, Robert Thomas, Derwen, who employed no fewer than a hundred carpenters to build schooners, sometimes two at the same time, which cost about £2,000 apiece. They had a slip to launch the ships and also had what was known as a patent slip to haul the ships out for repairs and refurbishment. The patent slip was worked by horses that would walk around in circles to turn a big wheel which had chains on, much like a bicycle chain, to drag the ships up on to cradles. There were also two smithies on Nefyn beach and three blacksmiths working them.

The men employed in Nefyn and Porthdinllaen not only came from the immediate vicinity but also from outlying villages, as well as from the town of Pwllheli. Carpenters who came from a place such as Llaniestyn would know dawn chorus and cockcrow well as they would have had an early start to walk to Porthdinllaen to start work at 6am. It would be a long day – they would finish at 8pm. These were hard-working men, tough as old leather, with eyes hooded like turtles against the whip of the wind. In the brief daylight of winter, many of them would take pieces of wood home to shape into wedges for use the following day. Others would be down on the beach before daybreak, working around fires to keep out the chill as they prepared oakum, which was used to seal gaps in timber and made by untwisting old rope for another use. For this unravelling they would earn about 12/- to 14/- a week. Sails were also made locally, and men such as David Rice Hughes sewed and shaped them for a living.

Captains' houses were therefore *fel chwain traeth*, as common as sand fleas, as they say hereabouts. House names often connected with the sea – places such as Angorfa, anchorage, or Gorffwysfa, a resting place – and locally there was a tradition of naming domiciles after ships – Portia, Ewenny, Alistair and Mont Claire. There was even a shop called Zebra after a ship of the same name.

* * *

Close to Nefyn, the village of Porthdinllaen is a nowadays a National Trust property, picture-postcard-complete with its fish crates and trailers, a lifeboat station, an offshore beacon at Carreg y Chwislan and a white snaggle-toothed strand of old cottages known as Hen Borth. The picturesque Red House pub sits right on the beach with its name painted on the roof slates in huge letters, as if encouraging passing paragliders down for a lager.

Porthdinllaen's pub on the beach used to be run by a redoubtable landlady, Jane Ellen Jones, who doubled up as harbour master. In its heyday it was a very busy harbourage and centre of boat building, with fifty-seven craft built there between 1760 and 1889. It was also the focus of a dream fuelled by real ambition. It belonged to William Alexander Madocks, the man who created the Cob, a great sea-wall at Porthmadog, reclaiming huge slabs of land from the sea. He had a dream of turning this busy anchorage on north Llŷn into the main trading port with Ireland. A turnpike road running all the way to London had been proposed, allowing fresh herring to be taken swiftly to market. Madocks established a Turnpike Trust to build a road to connect with Porthdinllaen, as well as a harbour company of the same name, but in open competition with the port of Holyhead it lost out, a matter of failing to secure just a few more Parliamentary votes.

This stretch of coast is punctuated by many coves and harbours such as Porthdinllaen, Porth Llanllawen, Port Ferin, Porth Iago, Porth Ysgaden, Porth Oer and Porth Widlin: every cove an anchorage, pretty much. A survey of 1524 listed no fewer than eighteen ports, small though they were. The sea trades hereabouts took bricks, barley and salt out to Swansea and brought in culm from Llanelli and limestone from Cork. Goods were various. The *Speedwell*, for instance, sailing to Llŷn in 1624, had a cargo which included fishing line, tobacco pipes, ferrous sulphate, hops, pepper, and American logwood for dyeing cloth. Other ships at the time carried anything from wooden heels to treacle, fire grates to vinegar.

Such ships were built to last and to travel far. The record of the Victorian schooner *Theda*, built in Pwllheli, more than confirms the sturdiness of such vessels. In March 1888 she took a cargo of slates from Porthmadog to Hamburg, then proceeded to Cádiz, where her hold was filled with salt, before heading for Canada's east coast and the island of Newfoundland. The next stop was Labrador, beladen with general goods that were then exchanged for salted cod to transport back across the breadth of the Atlantic.

Propelled by strong winds, she arrived in Gibraltar in a record-breaking twelve days. From there she pressed on to Patras in Greece, where the cargo of cod was particularly savoured, as indeed it was right around the rim of the Mediterranean. Think of *bacalao* in Spain and *bacalhau* in Portugal. She then picked up corn in Casablanca, a supply bound for South Shields in Northumberland. No idling, no tarrying. There she stocked up on coal to take to Waterford in Ireland and then, after fourteen long months at sea, her weary crew, under Captain G. E. Dedwith, made finally for home. There would have been a real welcome for the wind-stained, battered seamen who had finished this enormous journey and had to rest, exhaustedly, before the next voyage took them out of port, once again sailing out into the markets of the world.

The sheer industry of Welsh shipbuilding centres such as Nefyn and Porthdinllaen was replicated right around the coast. In Aberaeron they built around 300 ships and there was a plethora of jobs represented in the local workforce – carpenters, blacksmiths, foundry workers, riggers, block-makers, rope-makers and so many sailmakers that they had their own brass band.

* * *

Modern ship-building was never big in Dublin – mainly the Liffey yard and later Vickers, and Ross & Walpole – but it was huge in other ports on the Irish Sea. The author David Brett in *A Book Around the Irish Sea: History Without Nations* suggests that it makes 'good sense to see the great conurbations of Liverpool, Glasgow and Belfast not as being Scottish, English or Irish, but as the three great products of the Irish Sea, which were symbiotically linked by the great enterprises of canals, ships and heavy industry,' so that they were, in fact 'one great undivided organisation.' In the case of Belfast its genesis lay in an invitation by the Belfast Ballast Board to William Ritchie of Saltcoats near Ayr to open a shipbuilding yard in the city in the 1790s, in furtherance of the aim to develop the city as an oceanic port. Duly created at the Auld Lime Kiln Dock, it wasn't that long before the first cross-channel steamer of any significance, the *Rob Roy*, rolled down into the water and started a tradition that would help define a city.

Meanwhile, the Mersey saw shipbuilding thrive on the Wirral shore, in particular the mighty Cammell Laird yard, which grew out of an alliance between two metal producers, being Laird's iron foundry and the Charles Cammell steel works in Sheffield, a city synonymous of course with this alloy. Their first boats were steam paddlers for the Irish Steam Navigation Company, employing a design that would lead to such ships being sold to countries the world over, from Egypt to China and many of the countries in South America. Armed versions, too, were bought by the East India Company for use patrolling rivers such as the Ganges and the Irrawaddy. Soon the order books of Cammell Laird were full, with entire fleets commissioned by the Confederates in the US Civil War, the Portuguese government and of course the British. As trade changed so too did the ships they manufactured, feeding a production line that included refrigerated ships for the United Fruit Company in the 1910s, oil tankers after the Second World War, nuclear facility barges from the mid-1960s onwards, and a nuclear submarine, the *HMS Unicorn*, being the last of its vessels, finished in 1993.

* * *

Belfast's position halfway between the Mersey and the Clyde led to a ready interchange of both labour and capital, and Harland & Woolff soon became synonymous with the city's growth, building passenger vessels for the world. In the century between the 1810s and 1910s the travel time across the Atlantic shrank enormously: a trip that used to take a month now took a week, and the big companies started to compete apace for elegance as well as speed.

Fishguard was one of the ports that benefited hugely from such increased traffic in ocean-going liners, as it was the closest British port to New York. The visionary engineer Isambard Kingdom Brunel harboured an ambition, if you'll again pardon the pun, to create what he called a 'public highway' from London to New York. The 27-year-old was commissioned by the Great Western Railway to build a railway line from Paddington to Bristol, where passengers could then board the steam-powered vessel he had built, the *Great Western*. He was just as keen to develop trade with Ireland and proposed a jetty at Abermawr, 8 miles west of Fishguard. Indeed, work started on it but the famine and its economic ravages in Ireland prompted him to shelve the plans.

Connecting Fishguard to the world by rail was seen as a key component of its development and early on a small spaghetti junction of railways formed in the area. The South Wales Railway Company started looking for investors in 1884, with Irish names on the board to underline the opportunities for connecting with Ireland. Ultimately Brunel would engineer a route across the Severn Estuary, through south Wales, to Fishguard.

I can add a very small footnote to the history of this railway line. When I was a teenager I went birdwatching near my home village of Pwll, walking alongside the main London-to-Fishguard railway. A winter storm had washed part of the seawall away, the rails hanging in the air. I duly raised the alarm and the next train was stopped just in the nick of time. I was later given an award from British Rail – the *Collins Field Guide to the Birds of Britain and Europe*, which I still use to this day. Presented, appropriately enough, in engine sheds Brunel had himself designed.

The creation of a new harbour at Fishguard was driven by the Chief Engineer of the GWR, James Inglis, who commissioned 100 contractors and 400 men. It involved constructing a 27-acre platform at the foot of a near-vertical cliff. Men dangled like monkeys on ropes bearing the weight of pneumatic drills, before cutting holes up to 50 feet deep in the rock face. Ten tons of high explosives were then packed into the holes, as if they were going to war against geology itself. As much as 100,000 tons of rock would be shattered by the resulting blast, which could be heard as far away as Newcastle Emlyn, where they wished someone had invented ear-protectors.

The north breakwater similarly took some making, requiring 650 tons of stone and rubble for every foot of its 3,000-foot length. Almost 2.5 million tons of rock were blown to smithereens. A mighty crane called Titan helped move concrete blocks weighing up to 40 tons each as if they were made of Lego, shoring up the northern side of the breakwater. This was considered necessary to ensure that ships were protected as they approached in northerly winds, adding to the natural shelter to the west of Crincoed Point and to the north by lumpy Dinas Head.

Passengers now had ample waiting rooms and refreshment facilities for all three classes of travellers, and 100 staff were employed to look after their needs. A private house overlooking the bay was developed as the Wyncliff Hotel, which would become the Fishguard Bay Hotel, complete with sub-tropical plants in the grounds as well as croquet, tennis and fishing on the nearby Cleddau. Passenger numbers to the port increased year on year, including special services taking Irish pilgrims to Lourdes via Fishguard and Folkestone.

Facilities for livestock were included in the development. Cattle would disembark on a level below the passengers and be led along a subway to the lairages, which could house 1,000 animals.

The GWR then started to market the route, publishing *Southern Ireland: Its Lakes and Landscapes* in the summer of 1906. Not only did this trumpet the Irish attractions, it suggested the new Fishguard route would 'mark a new epoch in the history of travel in Southern Ireland'.

Duly connected by rail and with excellent facilities, Fishguard's transatlantic trade also flourished. Booth Lines' *Lanfranc* berthed here in April 1908, so that the route listed was Brazil – connecting with Northern Brazil and the Amazon – Lisbon-Oporto-Fishguard. The record-breaking Cunard liner *Mauretania* called here after it had crossed the Atlantic from New York, thus creating the shortest route to London, which passengers reached by train after they'd been greeted at the quayside by young girls in Welsh costume, who handed them sprigs of heather. In 1910 Cunard carried no fewer than 14,300 passengers into Fishguard, including some coming in from Boston. That decade saw the *Lusitania* visit on multiple occasions, while the Blue Funnel Line started advertising trips to Australia departing from the port, calling en route at Las Palmas and Cape Town. Competition for speed and luxury among the rival companies continued to grow apace.

Over dinner one summer's evening in 1907 the managing director of White Star Line, Bruce Ismay, and the chairman of the shipyard Harland & Wolff, Lord Pirrie, conspired to build a ship bigger and better than any owned by the rival Cunard Line. Indeed, the two men aspired to create a trio of the most luxurious ships on the sea, ambition and scale embedded in their very names: *Olympic*, *Titanic* and *Gigantic*.

In December 1907 work began on the first of these mammoth vessels, the *Olympic*. It required the largest gantry ever constructed, also employed when work later began on the *Titanic*, in March 1909. The Belfast workforce swelled apace. At the peak of construction, the Harland & Wolff shipyard employed approximately 14,000 men, building these dauntingly enormous ships.

It took over a year to build the gargantuan frame for the *Titanic*. Large steel plates were then riveted to the frame, needing more than 3 million rivets to hold them in place. By October 1910, the shell plating on the enormous vessel was ready.

Within the hull, the *Titanic* housed no fewer than twenty-nine boilers, containing 159 furnaces, which powered two reciprocating engines, each nearly 40 feet tall and 9 feet in diameter. The boilers were also a massive two storeys tall. Simply put, in 1912, when the ship was completed, it was the largest man-made object ever built.

The *Titanic* was claimed to be 'virtually unsinkable' due to its watertight construction. It had fifteen watertight bulkheads that divided the ship into sixteen compartments. The designers believed that even should four compartments be flooded, the boat could still float. But there was a fault. The bulkheads only reached about 10 feet above the waterline, thus allowing water to reach from one compartment to another, and defeating the purpose of the bulkheads. It was to prove a disastrous design fault.

As was customary for the White Star Line, the *Titanic* was christened with neither champagne nor wine when it left its dry dock on 31 May 1911. Nevertheless, an excited crowd numbering nearly 100,000 watched the great ship glide into the water. On 2 April 1912 the mighty ship completed its sea trials and was certified to be seaworthy. Eight short days later she would set sail on what was to prove to be both her maiden and her last voyage, from Southampton to New York. The *Titanic* had taken a long time to build but an encounter with an iceberg soon sent her down into shivering waters, with the tragic loss of some 1,500 lives.

But let me end with one relatively unknown name, Harold Lowe, a seaman born in Llandrillo yn Rhos and brought up in Barmouth. He took charge of a lifeboat and has been described by survivors of the disaster as 'the real hero of the Titanic.' He was played by Ioan Gruffudd in the movie, mimicing what Lowe did, ensuring the rule of 'women and children first' and being the only person who went back into the wreckage and floating bodies to rescue more survivors, before playing the long waiting game to be rescued by the Cunard Line's *Carpathia*. A hero of the sea, mainly unsung, who deserves his own small fanfare for saving lives in a freezing sea.

10.

AND THEN THE NORMANS CAME

On a headland at a place called Baginbun on a coastal promontory in County Wexford can be found a small metal plaque, which reads: 'In 1170 CE a Norman knight Raymond Le Gros landed here with 100 men. The fortification they subsequently built, and which still survives, enabled them to defeat an army of 3,000 from the city of Waterford.'

The plaque summarises the story of how, on 1 May 1170, a small party of Normans sailed across the sea from Pembrokeshire and landed here on the south-western tip of County Wexford, about 2 miles south of Fethard, in the old Barony of Shelburne. They proceeded to build a substantial rampart across the promontory, strong enough to withstand centuries of attrition by wind and rain. The idea was to seal off this neck of land so that these new invaders could use it as a bridgehead into the country. And as Robert Kee put it, 'What a bridgehead into Irish history it was to prove. Eight centuries of conflict were to flow from it – a conflict that is still not over.' The conquest of Ireland was described as being on a par with the coming of Christianity, triggering as it did waves of foreign settlement and the coming of an alien culture. It was a landmark moment, such that one authority averred that 'No event except the preaching of the gospel of St Patrick has so changed the destinies of Ireland.' Or as a medieval couplet put it, 'At the creek of Baginbun, Ireland was lost and won.'

These Norman soldiers-cum-mercenaries were not in the pay of the English king but rather of one of his barons, Richard Fitz Gilbert, the earl of Pembroke, known as Strongbow. They were in Ireland at the invitation of the Irish King of Leinster, Dermot MacMurrough, to help him fight to restore his kingdom. Strongbow, however, was not in the business of doing something for nothing, especially when that something involved lending the vastly superior Norman military technology. In place of the slings and stones used by the Irish in battle the Normans used archers, often Welsh archers, while their warriors themselves strode into battle fully clad in clanking armour.

There was a logistical hurdle, of course, namely the Irish Sea, which they had to cross carrying armour, weapons, supplies and horses. To get a sense of the craft they used it's useful to consult the Bayeux tapestry, where we find Viking-style longships. As these were the most successful craft to date, they were enthusiastically emulated by Norman boat-builders. They would have been some 80 feet in length and 15 feet across, and their shape would taper into two sharp ends, each decorated with dragon figureheads. There would be a single mast and a single painted sail which would mean that the craft wasn't especially manoeuvrable, although the vessel would also be powered by oars, with between twelve and sixteen on each side. The ones with soldiers on board might be accompanied by smaller, rounded craft which carried supplies – salted bacon, beef, cheese, dried beans, hard-baked bread and biscuits, not to mention water and fodder such as corn or oats for the knights' horses.

Crossing the sea to invade meant carrying mail shirts, swords, lances and helmets held by their noseguards, although no-one wore any armour on the crossing: falling in would have led to certain death. An extra danger was posed by the horses, which would be wearing bridles to stop them stampeding, especially in such a cramped and confined situation. Taking animals to sea was a risky endeavour at the best of times; doing so in an open boat where the men were fixed on rowing was riskier still.

The invasion, if you can call it that, happened in incremental stages. Firstly Robert de Barry landed in Bannow Bay in 1169, accompanied by Maurice de Prendergast, in three shiploads carrying a force of forty knights, eighty esquires, and around 400 infantry and archers. They were joined by Dermot MacMurrough and his followers and together they marched on Wexford. The town surrendered, but not without a fight, as Geraldus Cambrensis, who later travelled through an Ireland which had newly been conquered by the Normans, duly chronicled in his *Expugnatio Hibernica*: 'The citizens, very quick to defend themselves, straightaway hurled down heavy pieces of wood and stone and hurled them back some little distance, inflicting severe wounds on many. Among these invaders a knight, Robert de Barry, exuberant with youthful hot-headedness and bravely scorning the risk of death, had crept up to the walls in front of everyone else, when he was struck by a stone on his helmeted head. He fell from a height into the bottom of a steep ditch, and in the end just managed to escape being pulled out by his fellow soldiers. After an interval of sixteen years his molar teeth fell out as a result of this blow, and even more amazing, new ones grew immediately in their place.'*

According to Giraldus, the 2,000 Hiberno-Norse inhabitants of Wexford had started off feeling confident about their ability, but seeing the calibre of the attacking army they strategically burnt the suburbs and made of the town a citadel, protected by the same ditch into which de Barry fell. The Anglo-Normans were originally repulsed, so they set fire to ships in the harbour (this act perhaps the origin of the town's crest, which shows a trio of burning ships accompanied by the motto *Per Aquam et Ignem*, by water and by fire). The next morning peace negotiations were set in train, the surrender being overseen by two bishops who happened to be in the town. As they offered up the town to Diarmaid, and offered hostages by way of future reassurance, he promptly gave the town and all its land, equivalent to nothing less than the Barony of Forth, to Robert FitzStephen and Maurice FitzGerald. To Strongbow's uncle, Hervey de Montmorency, he gifted two cantreds, subdivisions of land abutting the sea between Wexford and Waterford, being the baronies of Bargy and Shelburne. These

---

* Cited in Billy Colfer, *Wexford: A Town and its Landscapes*, Cork, 2008.

were the first land grants to Anglo-Norman knights in Ireland and would lead to the establishment of the Wexford Pale, one of the most Anglicised parts of Ireland, just as Norman-held south Pembrokeshire would be a 'Little England beyond Wales'.

* * *

In May 1170 Strongbow's advanced guard arrived on the Irish coast, still more of an incursion than an invasion. It was led by Raymond Carew 'le Gros', younger son of the Lord of Carew Castle and a nephew of both Robert FitzStephen and Maurice FitzGerald. Having little hope of inheritance from his father's estate he had become a knight under Strongbow in Chepstow. Like his master, Raymond was desperate to win renown and wealth in Ireland but might not have imagined that in 1170, with only a small army at his side, he would have the opportunity to display a talent for fighting. The main source about him is Giraldus Cambrensis. His books about the island are shot through with cold, colonialist descriptions which are yet animated with the flair for language that would typify his later writings. He describes Raymond as 'very stout and slightly above the middle height, his hair was yellow and curly, and he had large, grey, round eyes. His nose was rather prominent, his countenance high-coloured, cheerful and pleasant. Although he was somewhat corpulent he was so active and lively that the encumbrance was not a blemish or inconvenience.'

So, on or about 1 May 1170, fat Raymond and his small army of about 100 men landed and set about preparing the place for defence. He knew that Strongbow was to follow but did not know exactly when. In the meantime, he had to wait and secure his bridgehead. Giraldus again tells us that he was joined shortly afterwards by Hervey de Marisco, with three knights and perhaps a small body of men. Still, all told, the little army at Baginbun numbered no more than a hundred men.

Raymond and his men now started the erection of the double embankment, with a deep trench between – 40 feet wide at the top, spanning the entire width of the 200-yard-wide headland. It was built of stone and clay and, except for an overgrowth of furze and an odd gap here and there, it is much the same today as it was in 1170.

It must have been a formidable hurdle to stem the flow of any attack, especially when it was overseen by archers. When the work of constructing the ramparts was finished, the Normans commandeered as many cows and bullocks as they could in the area and drove them within the two-acre stockade.

Raymond de Carew's cattle-rustling and stockade-raising presence at Baginbun was a palpable threat, so the Irish assembled an army of some 3,000 warriors to destroy the new fort. Statistically the invaders were really up against it as the Normans were outnumbered by at least twenty to one. 'Their small band of soldiers was unable to resist the attack of the multitudes to which they were opposed. Retreating to their camp, they were so hotly pursued by the enemy that some of them entered pell-mell with the fugitives before the barricade could be closed,' Giraldus wrote of the battle by the creek. Raymond, meanwhile: 'Perceiving the strait to which his party was reduced, and that the peril was imminent, faced about bravely and cut down with his sword on the very threshold the foremost of the enemy who were forcing an entrance. Thus nobly retracing his steps while he dealt a terrible blow and shouted his war cry, he encouraged his followers to stand on their defence and struck terror into his enemy's ranks. The enemy took to flight and, dispersing themselves over the country, were pursued and slaughtered in such numbers that upwards of five hundred quickly fell by the sword.'*

The place where Raymond and his men met the advance guard of the Norse-Irish army is still called Battlestown, about 2 miles beyond Fethard in the direction of Ballyhack. Seeing that they were outnumbered, Raymond ordered his followers back to the defences in Baginbun. They were so hotly pursued by the Irish that some of them got inside the barricade with the Normans before the rampart could be closed. The situation was now obviously critical and Raymond,

---

* https://www.yorku.ca/inpar/conquest_ireland.pdf.

realising the dire straits his men were in, according to Giraldus showed his qualities as a leader and a soldier. He faced about boldly and cut down with his own sword on the very threshold of the rampart the foremost of the enemy who were forcing an entry. Then the gap was closed.

The main force of the army was now pushing its way up the narrow peninsula towards the rampart, the substantial force crammed shoulder to shoulder as they marched along land that seemed to tighten around them. With martial cunning Raymond waited for his moment, when he opened a gap in the rampart. His men goaded the herd of confused cattle right into the middle of the tightly mustered force so that at least 1,000 of them were pushed over the cliffs into the sea and drowned. Those who could, turned and fled, hotly pursued by Raymond and his men. About 500 of them were slaughtered by sword or arrow and a large number of prisoners captured and taken inside the stockade. Captives had their legs broken and a camp follower called Alice of Abergavenny carried out many decapitations in a bloody mop-up operation that was far removed from the rules of the Geneva Convention. Raymond did not suffer the loss of even one man during this mad Norman rodeo.

The local historian Tom Walsh told the *New Ross Standard* that the key to the victory, or victories, was that 'The tribal structure of the Irish at the time made the numerous tribes incapable of unified resistance to an invader and strangely enough, it was that failing that saved the Irish from total defeat. There was no big national army to defeat, so the whole country had to be attacked and there was no capital city that, if captured, would bring about the downfall of the native government.' Whatever the reason, a new age had arrived.

Giraldus was not an eyewitness to any part of the 'invasion'. He visited Ireland some fifteen years after the events at Baginbun and would have heard the story perhaps from some of those who had fought there. He did not mention part of the story which appeared in *The Song of Dermot and the Earl,* a later narrative from the early thirteenth century, which described how that herd of cattle was driven into the Waterford army by the Normans. Stunned by the impact of the stampeding mass of animals, it was this that allowed Raymond to set the enemy to flight more than good soldiery.

Strongbow himself followed Raymond and the advance guard across the sea, arriving on 23 August 1170 to claim his reward from the King of Leinster. He brought with him reinforcements, more knights, and went into battle, ironically enough, employing the war cry 'Sainte Davide!' With the eagle-eyed back-up of his archers he aimed to lay claim to the city of Waterford.

The man who would become synonymous with the conquest of Ireland decided not to land at Baginbun. Instead, he made straight for Waterford, alighting at Passage East on the far side of the River Barrow. Gerald of Wales listed his contingent of soldiers as containing Normans from England, Normans who had come directly from France, and 'nostri', Normans from Wales, many of whom had inter-married among the natives, along with an array of south Walian archers and some Flemings who came to avail themselves of any booty. Strongbow marched to the walls of the city and put it under siege, joined in the effort by some locals, loyal to Dermot and therefore happy to take arms against the Vikings of the city. As Gerald described it: 'The people of the city came out, about two thousand strong, hith-erto unvanquished and with great faith in their long-standing good fortune ... But when they saw the lines of troops drawn up in an unfamiliar manner, and the squadrons of knights resplendent with breastplates, swords and helmets all gleaming, they immediately with-drew within the walls.'

The siege was succinct, the city yielding to unfamiliar military tactics, those lines and squadrons. Many citizens were slaughtered in the streets. The hard-nosed conquest of Ireland had been firmly set in train, Strongbow quickly seizing great swathes of south-central Ireland, and within a year they had managed to seize Dublin for Macmurrough, whose daughter Strongbow then married. On Macmurrough's death Strongbow became the new King of Leinster.

Soon an emblematic chain of castles would encircle the Irish Sea, connecting Wexford with Dublin, Trim, Drogheda, Greencastle, Dundrum, Killyleagh and Carrickfergus and mirrored by those in

Pembrokeshire such as Carew, Cilgerran, Manorbier and the huge fortifications of Pembroke Castle. New landowners would be accompanied by a new language, Norman-French. Buildings were made of stone and a market economy came to be. Ireland would soon be looking a lot like Norman Wales.

Henry II, meanwhile, watched Strongbow's coronation as King of Leinster with envy and decided to assert his own authority, setting sail from Milford Haven with 400 ships, to consolidate what would be a long and wretched conquest.

*   *   *

It's interesting that about the time of the Norman invasion of Ireland, one of the creation myths of Ireland came into being, or at least written down. The monk-written pseudo-history that is the *Leabhar Gabála Éireann*, 'The Book of the Taking of Ireland', or *The Invasions of Ireland*, describes the first people of Ireland – predominantly women with a sprinkling of men, who had as their leader the granddaughter of Noah – and the various adventures they had before being washed away by a great big Biblical flood. Just before the familiar deluge of an ending we have the appearance of the Fomoire, a darkly malevolent gathering of beings, and with that comes the appearance of an antagonism 'which did not exist before the land emerged from the waters, and existence defines itself increasingly in terms of oppositions and dualities'. The scholar John Carey described this foundational text, a mixture of poems and prose fragments, as a 'framework of successive occupations.' The *Leabhar Gabála Éireann* carried pagan myth into Christian times and was taken as history for a long time. Then history itself intervened, overturning this narrative, just as boatloads of chain-mail-clad soldiers occupied the land of the Irish, cutting away the continuities and unities of the past, as if slashing it with a newly-sharpened sword.

11.

THE DOCKERS OF DUBLIN

They gathered in hope. Each and every day, for a period of some 170 years, dock workers would assemble around platforms set on Dublin's waterfront, hoping to be selected for a day's graft and a day's pay. The selection, or 'read', would pull in thousands of men, clustered at landmarks such as the big gasometer, or at smaller reads outside the offices of individual coal-importing companies. And because this was Ireland, they often waited in seven species of rain, from pelting hail to miserably insistent mist and drizzle: Dublin gets rained on for a third of the year. The playwright and Dublin docker's son Gary Brown has depicted in verse what could be a disheartening or even degrading ritual:

Blowing on your hands as the wind blows through you
Stamping your feet to keep yourself warm
There's a lumber ship in from Takoradi
It's to be back on the tide before early morn.
There's two coal yanks in from New Orleans
A banana boat in to be discharged by noon
Should get a call for a day or a mi mi
Depends on the foreman and the mood he's in
Shape up here he is fuck it's the Finger O Reilly
The bastard ignores me cause I'm not a Southsider
The width of a river can often decide.

Docker John 'Miley' Walsh would be one of those waiting to be chosen, telling me that the 'foreman was working from memory, remembering what happened on the previous ship but always remembering to choose family, neighbours and friends.' As John, who started at the docks when he was sixteen and worked there for forty-seven years, also recalls: 'One of the foremen might sneeze and turn his head in a new direction and as a consequence 200 men would shuffle over to make sure they were still standing in front of him.' He remembers the work 'being dangerous, especially in the early days, when they were slinging stuff around,' before summing up in a saying that was prevalent: 'Nothing falls up.'

Some cargoes brought with them their own problems, such as fish meal, where the smell clung to one's clothes. Travelling to meet a date one night 'Miley' travelled on a bus where everyone moved off the top deck when he sat down. But some cargo was memorable for other reasons. John explains that 'As hard as we worked some people worked much harder.' One time a Russian ship came in with timber. When they opened the hatch the wood was covered in a layer of snow and in it was imprinted the marks of women's and children's feet, who had been working barefoot in cold weather to get the cargo on board. And, of course, the cargoes were many and various, leading to ways of describing them in dockers' parlance – perhaps the best was a 'Dana', a boat bearing a broad variety of shipments, inspired by the Irish winner of Eurovision who won with the song 'All Kinds of Everything'.

The 'read' was made easier, or at least a little more palatable, by the habit of many dockers being given nicknames by the others. Seal. Oko. Billy the Greek. Big Bob.

Then there was a small harvest of fruity monikers – Big Apple, Little Apple and Crabapple. Remy Martin worked alongside The Bombadier. The man they called Two Thumbs Murphy wasn't clumsy: he literally had two thumbs on one hand. Standing there in the wan light of early morning would be The Man from Laramie, Buckets of Blood, The Gannet and Saltbox O'Connor.

Some names were easy to work out, describing how men looked or what they did: Spit in Pint, Boxer Elliott, 'Fatser Curry', Baldo

McAuley. A man called 'The Bleeder' was the whitest man who ever lived, though there is no easy explanation of the somewhat poetical 'The Flight Careless'. Then there were names that were simply historical: Bendeyo was a name given to anyone who had broken the 1913 Lockout, a reference presumably to a scab of the same name. A docker who held down another job as an undertaker had the macabre moniker 'Chase the Corpse'.

Then there was the almost classical name 'Diesel Fitter', a name found in other ports such as Liverpool, which referred to a kleptomaniacal docker who would steal something for the wife saying 'Diesel fitter'. And goods did go missing on the Dublin quays: in one year ammunition, lead ingots, liquid mercury, 81 rolls of wallpaper, 15 suits and 25 lamb carcasses deftly disappeared, and you have to wonder about where that quicksilver went so quickly. Such acts of theft were known as 'strokes', and so you might have small strokes, such as smuggling tea out in your pockets, and big strokes, which were more involved and wily.

* * *

Standing at the 'read' could be a long and leg-wearying let-down, as Willie Murphy Junior found out in the early 1950s. He had spent the first day on a job unloading coal, only to find that there wasn't going to be another: 'Me mother bought me a pair of boots, out of that first job … and I never done another day's work! I wore the boots going up and down the docks looking for work, but I never got another day's work … They were big hobnailed boots for the next coal boat I was going to get. Jaysus. There was over 1,000 people down at the docks that time, so they had plenty to choose from … Every day, we would go to the different yards to see if there was a bit of work, see if the boats were up, but you were usually left standing there.'*

---

* In Aileen O'Carroll and Don Bennett, *The Dublin Docker: the Working Lives of Dublin's Deep-Sea Port*, Newbridge, 2017. A marvellous book on which this chapter draws heavily.

There was certainly no room for laziness or what the dockers themselves dubbed 'Irish rheumatism'. The waterfront cure for blistered hands was to urinate on them. Time was money and there was always pressure to discharge goods and get the ship out to sea again. John 'Miley' Walsh explained that the foreman's job was to maximise the amount of cargo taken out of the ship in the least amount of time. If he looked into the hold and saw some men working and others malarkeying around then the slackers would not be picked again.

* * *

The port itself had grown considerably over two centuries, although Dublin had been a centre for the sea-trades since 841, when the Vikings built their *longphort*, a defensible dock in what is now the Wood Quay area. In medieval times Dublin was a busy hub of North Atlantic commerce, but it wasn't always an easy port to navigate. Silts brought down by the rivers Dodder and Liffey settled on sandy beds to create what could be dangerous shallows, while the habit of emptying ballast into the bay led to the emergence and consolidation of two huge sand humps called the South Bull and the North Bull. In 1707 an Act of Parliament allowed the city of Dublin to create a Ballast Office, and gave it powers over the conservation of the port, thus giving birth to Dublin Port as a legal entity. The sand bar that had made life very difficult for captains was soon scoured away after the construction of the Bull Wall, initially drawn by a Captain William Bligh – he of Mutiny of the Bounty fame.

In the early days the sailors disgorged the cargo themselves but over the years, as sail gave way to steam, the need to turn ships around more quickly led to new specialisms and the birth of the Dublin Docker. Previously, men called 'hobblers' would row out to ships from various parts of the city to settle on a price for their work before much of the work moved onshore.

Offloading work remained casual for a very long time, awarded on a whim or as a favour, and therefore never guaranteed. In 1947 a system of giving lapel buttons to men gave them preference when it came to jobs. A man might inherit his father's button after he retired, or became too ill to work, so it was a way of keeping work in the family, as it were.

One way of dealing with the dockside inequities, when men might only get work by offering bribes to a foreman, was to stick together. Tight-knit docker communities made up the 'Real Dublin'. Ringsend and City Quay on the Southside and the area around Sheriff Street on the Northside – these were areas where family ties and a sense of belonging were strong. But men still had to work for a range of stevedores, with all the attendant uncertainties, until Dublin Cargo Handling was created in 1982 and became the only stevedore outfit allowed to work the deep-sea section of the port.

The dockers who were lucky enough to be picked for work divided into two specialisms: those who worked the cross-channel ships, plying the routes between Dublin and Bristol, Glasgow, Liverpool, London and other British ports; and the deep-sea dockers, who handled cargo from further afield and exported goods such as cattle and leather, peat, colts, porter and Irish larch. Handling livestock attracted extra payments for the dockers. In one famous photograph they're seen winching an adult elephant onto the quayside; on another occasion they had to handle a tiger bound for Dublin Zoo – mercifully secured behind bars, its long incisors glistening at the prospect of fresh dockers' fingers hors d'oeuvres.

As with all such docklands there was much more than safe harbourage. There were shipyards where vessels were built and repaired. There were flour mills and fertiliser companies, coal heaps and cattle pens. Five glassworks operated in the Ringsend area alone, one manufacturing bottles to hold the increasingly popular Guinness stout. The brewery was located a mile up-river at St James's Gate, near where the Vikings built the original Dublin settlement. Back down along the quays, the Guinness family moored ships for decades, to deliver barrels of stout to Great Britain and beyond. Indeed, one of these vessels, the *M. V. Miranda Guinness* was converted into the one of world's first beer tankers, with a capacity of 205,000 gallons, or 1.87 million pints – a stout vessel indeed.

Coal was another key black commodity, and the men who unloaded this fossil fuel duplicated the back-breaking work of the miners who had dug it out of the earth in the first place – working in the pitch-dark, breathing lung-clogging dust, backs bent by hard labour. And just as the colliers had an array of specialist tools, so too did the Dublin dockers. Coal was shifted with the aid of a heart-shaped, graceful, pointed spade – the number seven shovel – which could nevertheless lift up to four stone of 'black diamonds' at a time, a load weighing a spine-bending fifty-six pounds. A hard-grafting man could move 50 tons of slack coal by himself in a single day, hands blistering to something that resembled toad-skin, often working against the clock as shipowners wanted an an empty ship to leave on the next high tide. Some of the best coal, particularly anthracite, came from the seams of Pembrokeshire. This product was highly regarded, and the county produced 150,000 tons a year, although it was mined by pit children and women working 'harder than slaves'. Queen Victoria herself demanded that no other coal should heat the boilers of the royal yachts. It was also considered particularly suitable for drying salt and heating malthouses, so much of it went directly to the Guinness brewery in the city. But working coal on the docks led to the same perils as those who hewed it underground: those dockers who chose to work with coal would suffer from lung conditions such as pneumoconiosis, just as the colliers did.

One of those who worked the coal boats was William Deans, from Dublin's Foley Street. He liked working them because of the regular wage, and because of his skill he was often given the job as winch driver. Positioned on the deck, he manoeuvred the winch to lift the heavy steel tubs of coal. As a winch man, he also earned an extra few bob.

William was jobbed on 12 November 1947 to an American coal-boat, the *S.S. Amaso Delano*, berthed at Sir John Rogerson's Quay. Deans was delighted to be told by the foreman that he was manning the winch. This kept him away from some of the dirt and grime involved in the unloading of loose coal. He could breathe clean air compared to the dockers working in groups of four shovelling coal into enormous steel buckets.

At approximately 4pm, word came from No. 1 Hatch that gas was escaping from the ballast tank. The Captain, John Munro, went into the hatch to investigate. He removed the lid from the tank and was immediately overcome by gas. The engineers, Andrew Smart and Bosun Antonio Lima, then went down into the hatch to rescue the captain; but they also collapsed, overcome by the methane. The mate, Francis DeRosa, duly raised the alarm. Enter William Deans, who promptly tied his hanky around his mouth, descended the ladder, found a rope and tied it around the first seaman. He climbed the ship's ladder to the deck and hauled the man onto the deck. He put his life at risk twice more to repeat this action for the other two men. Thanks to his outstanding bravery, the three lives were saved, and he duly received a bronze medal and a certificate for his heroics.

But the story does not end there, because on 19 May 1958 he was passing roughly the same spot when he saw a man fall into the Liffey. Without hesitation, Deans jumped in and saved the man's life. From reports in the Irish press, it seems he made a habit of such heroics. In 1939 he jumped off Ballybough Bridge into the Tolka River to save a boy from drowning. Three times the hero.

* * *

There were heavy and difficult commodities to handle. Metal ore at Dublin Port was shifted with the use of a narrow number five shovel and the men who carried out this work ran the risk of their tongues turning green. Grain would be shovelled into sacks, under the rapacious gaze of fat harbourside rats. Big, bulky cargo such as calcium, timber and 16-stone bags of cement were physically humped around on shoulders that would soon be rubbed raw during a punishing twelve-hour shift. Frozen sand was another difficult cargo to handle while dust from various materials such as flour or, worse still, phosphorus and potash could cause a range of respiratory conditions, some of the men bleeding from the nose. Grain workers, or porters, often died in their forties because of the dust that had settled in their lungs.

So dock work could be injurious to health and sometimes fatal. James Brown, known as Jimmy, worked as a docker and checker for about ten years. A spirited man, he had been a former bus driver in Birmingham, England, and a Teddy Boy, with a reputation for being a brilliant dancer, jiving with the best of them.

Jimmy had initially lived with his growing family in a tenement house in the inner city, which they shared with seven other families, before they moved to Cabra West, a housing estate some 4 miles from the docks. As Jimmy's work tended to be casual, he also drove a truck for a timber company, tending to work in the deep-sea area of the docks around what is known as Alexandra Basin. In 1971 he was collecting mahogany wood that had just arrived from Africa. He drove into the yard of the Merchants' Warehousing Company and was unloading timber from high stacks when one of them collapsed and he was crushed beneath. He was alive when taken by ambulance to hospital but he had multiple injuries that ultimately proved fatal. Jimmy left four children – three young sons and a daughter – and his wife, Anna, who was thirty-three at the time.

The dockers rallied round, making a few collections, but it wasn't enough in the long term. There was a compensation claim made against Merchants Warehousing Company and Anna received £1,990, but no pension. She did receive a contribution from the state, which in truth wasn't much – more a widow's mite than a widow's pension. The family then got by mainly by dint of support from Anna's family, especially her own mother, May Kenny. To make ends meet Anna got a job as a waitress in a city centre cafe at night while the oldest boy, Gary, looked after his siblings. He eventually got a job as a part-time lounge boy at the age of thirteen in a local bar in Cabra West and then his mother got a job in the local fish and chip shop. Scraping by.

Jimmy's son Gary has listed the deprivations of the wives and families of dockers, which largely went unnoticed. Because of the dangerous nature of the work accidents were common: 'Almost on a daily basis, men were hospitalised, disabled, and often killed as they went about their work. Men were crushed under loads, buried under cargoes of coal, tipped from their boats and squeezed against large barrels and storage vats. Accidents were so common on the docks that the ambulances frequenting the quays were christened "the dockers' taxis"'.

Death visited the docks too. Should a docker perish, as Declan Byrne explained to me, his coffin would be carried some distance to the doors of the church. 'Work would stop and crane drivers would turn their jibs away as a sign of respect. It was a tradition carried on for years on either side of the Liffey and which continues to this day in Ringsend, maintained by a group of individuals for whom tradition is important.' Declan himself proudly remembers being asked to carry a coffin and describes it as 'the greatest honour of my life.'

Despite the dangers, the range of goods being imported could make some of the work both various and interesting. There might be citrus fruit from Spain and Cyprus, gifts and wedding presents to supply Hector Grey's shop on Upper Liffey Street, or crates of tea, then growing in popularity.

Ireland's 'second drink' has an interesting history. Part of the reason for its prohibitive price, early on, was the simple fact that the tea was grown far away, while a small clique of firms, including the East India Company, closely controlled the movement of this and other goods. Shipping costs for products such as Indian Assam – a key ingredient in the Irish breakfast tea blend – were made worse by hefty tariffs. These were reduced in the late eighteenth century, making the product more affordable. The Irish entrepreneur and merchant Samuel Bewley made the brave move to cut out the middleman, thus reducing costs, and tea became much more widely available. In 1935, Samuel and his son Charles decided to challenge the status quo by importing over 2,000 chests of tea directly to Ireland aboard the *Hellas*, the first ship to be chartered directly from Canton to Dublin.

Directly imported tea was soon taking its place alongside the vast range of products shipping into Dublin – steel, coffee, beer, and brandy, newsprint and machinery emerged from the various holds. Ships came in from all compass points: from Persia, Newfoundland,

Mexico and Finland. One of the least salubrious cargos was guano, which came from South America, made of seabird droppings and used for fertiliser. This had a God-awful stench; as one docker put it, 'it had an awful smell out of it – nobody robbed it!' Some of the goods were for export, such as Irish sugar beet bound for the USA, while cane sugar from Cuba and demerara sugar travelled the other way. The docks were a moving hub of global exchange, the workers oiling the wheels with the very sweat of their brows.

A report in the *Waterfront* from the 1960s captures the colour and commotion of the waterfront scene: 'Hear the clatter as the hatch covers are mechanically folded up, just like a concertina. Watch the crane as she lowers the hook to the hold, and dips her jib as if in salute. Listen to the creak and the groan of the winch as she takes the strain. See the full "bogies." Half a gross or more of 12-pound trays pulled by the brawny one, and shoved by his mates into the shed by the ship. Watch them being sorted and stacked in their separate marks, in coloured wrappings, blue and white, red and gold, green and orange, giving a gay and festive air to the toil and clamour of discharging. What a bustle! What confusion!'

Over the years the river channel had been scoured and deepened; wooden jetties had been built and later replaced by more permanent piers. By the 1960s the port's infrastructure and quays had extended so that it was now 5 miles long, with two-thirds of that being deep water berthage. It had both a north quay and a south quay as well as the Alexandra Dock and Custom House Docks. But the same decade saw the advent of container ships, when men would no longer unload individual items or loads of cargo material but rather transfer individual containers onto land. This sounded a death knell for the dockers' trade. In the 1960s there were 1,000 men on the register; by 1990 only 135 remained. That continued to dwindle year on year, as technology continued to triumph over human labour.

Dockers had tended to increasingly specialise, so that some would concentrate on deep-sea cargo – maybe grain coming in on a Liberty Ship from Norfolk, Virginia, or a small car park's worth of second-hand vehicles from Japan. But mechanisation was set to change all that: witness ships bringing in their own forklifts to work the cargo. But when containerised cargo fully came in, the contents hidden from sight, technology made manual work redundant and the proud docker a historical artefact. Today Dublin Port handles three-quarters of the trade entering and leaving Ireland, but most of it is handled mechanically, without a single docker's help. The docker, that is, who habitually put in hard shifts to feed his family and helped shape a proud and maritime city. After a bright morning of conversation Declan Byrne, John 'Miley' Walsh and myself strolled around the docklands, now all plexiglass and shiny buildings. We saw the tiny Liffey ferry which would shepherd workers across the river, then followed the remnant iron tracks embedded in the quaysides. In the mind's eye it is still possible to imagine the ant-hive of dockers on busy quays as the ships from all over the world disgorged. Dock workers such as Miley and Declan keep that busy story safe, for now, in their ready recollections and fine stories. And, besides, there may not be such a thing as history, just histories, which still exist here in entertaining profusion.

12.

URBAN GEESE

Daybreak reveals Dublin Bay. I've caught the 130 bus from the city centre with local guide and bird enthusiast Niall Keogh, and we're off to find out why Dublin is not only the capital of Ireland but also of urban brent geese. We leave this January morning's bleary-eyed commuters and walk into a peach of a day, the unblemished skies having the blush of soft summer fruit.

As we walk along the edge of Clontarf Road the light increases enough to illumine some black-headed gulls, part of a substantial roost that can be thousands strong in February. Be they rare or commonplace species, Niall has a palpable and infectious excitement about birds. He traces it back to 5 June 1995, when his father Noel took him out of school and they 'went on the hop' to see a hobby (a fast-flying falcon) in Kilcoole, County Wicklow. In truth it was not the perfect day for seeing them, what with the sideways rain resulting in a lack of dragonflies, but the weather drove down swifts and swallows for the little falcon to hunt. Father and son, he tells me, still go out together as often as they can.

Niall sets up his scope at the end of the wooden bridge that crosses the south lagoon at North Bull Island, where the ebbing tide reveals excellent feeding grounds for substantial flocks of knot and plump little waders which huddle close together on the sands just as they stick close in flight, as if one amorphous animal. The island was formed as a consequence of building the North Bull Wall to Dublin

Port two centuries ago, and it is still growing: a place of golfers, marram grass and, as we find before we don our gloves, of biting wind chill. In the distance we can see the expensive houses on Howth Head and beyond that, directly north of Howth village and harbour, the outline of Ireland's Eye, an island uninhabited other than by gannets and other seabirds.

Underneath the bridge some feeding widgeon and teal are close enough to show off the exotica of their plumage, colours often lost or indiscernible when the birds are far away. You can see the wigeon's rich mix of chestnut, yellow, powder-puff pink, and the teal's grey wine-bottle-green eye patches and chestnut-brown head. It's a diminutive dabbling duck which can take off explosively, explaining the collective noun 'a spring of teal'.

In the distance we can see the brents, just charcoal smudges in the still-widening light that seems to pour overhead. Niall hopes they'll come our way rather than disperse to the north. Our luck's in: they rise in great numbers heading our way. Maybe 2,000 birds, now on the wing. It's an uplifting sight. They disperse and unfurl as extended lines, skeins over the city skyline, dotting the air like punctuation marks, while stragglers feed in irregular rows on the tide-lines of the bay. The birds fan out in the sky like fronds of eel grass, streaming in the winter air with resolve and determined purpose in each steady beat of a wing. Some birds arrange in chevrons, making extending Vs as they gain height before arrowing away out of sight. Some stay low, passing so close over our heads that we can hear the siss of their wings, feathers parting air.

Niall Keogh thoroughly enjoys searching and sifting through flocks of wintering brents and what he playfully describes as 'fifty shades of brent'. There are various sub-species that run through the spectrum from the black brant (the brent are called brant in the New World just to stir up the confusion) to the pale light-bellied brent, and there is also the grey-bellied brant which normally winters around places such as Puget Sound near Seattle in north-western USA. He and his dad Noel have seen all four species, but never all of them in the same place, so the quest continues.

The pale-breasted sub-species has white underparts, unlike the dark-breasted race, seen in Britain, which has slate-grey underparts. *Branta* comes from the same linguistic root as 'burned', and there is something of that about the brent, with its charcoal-black neck and bill and matching wingtips. In the case of pale-bellied brents the black of the neck ends abruptly at the top of the bird's breast. It may seem numerous to the good people of Dublin but it's considered to be one of the most endangered species of goose in the world.

As geese go, they are not the silent type, and their guttural calls, taken collectively, can make for a low-pitched babble. Up close, it's a sound not dissimilar to heavy breathing, which probably accounts for one of its Scots names, *ratgas* – snoring goose, derived from the Norse. But this goose is a multi-vocalist, able to produce an evocative murmur as it drifts across marsh or sea-edge. At short range it can also generate a deafening clamour to the extent that an observer, or rather a listener, once compared them with a pack of hounds in full cry, although that might have been a bit of hunter's hyperbole. Niall agrees that it's not that good an analogy, suggesting it's more of a croaky yodel. Listening to the fly-past I suggest we amend that to 'quietly croaking yodel', and soon we're like two sommeliers of sound, replacing 'yodel' with 'gurgle' and then qualifying that to 'liquid gurgle' before jumbling them all up in various permutations. A Joycean quietly croaking liquid gurgle-yodel. Then Niall helpfully thinks of something new to add to the mix, pointing out that the full Latin name for the species ends in *hrota*, denoting the sub-species, *Branta bernicla hrota*, possibly suggesting that might be the sound of the bird as well. So, here we are, comparing the finer notes of goose call as they gurgle and honk above us.

The dispersing birds, now dwindled in number, fly so close that we can see the charcoal necks and heads of these mallard-sized geese and note the distinctive white neck patches. They will have been here since August and early September, when they wing in to places such as this. Bull Island has long been a favoured location: it is also the first designated bird sanctuary in Ireland. It was so classified by the minister for justice in 1931, in great part due to relentless championing by Father

Patrick Kennedy, a Jesuit priest and teacher from Belvedere College in Dublin. He argued that 'Birds know the difference between a man with a gun and a man with a pair of field glasses; where there is no shooting they are not easily frightened.'*

To get to the safety of their winter haunts these small dark geese have certainly racked up the air miles, leaving the wild wildernesses of northern, Arctic Canada, arrowing over Iceland, and gathering groups from Greenland as they go. Many of them stop to feed in large estuaries such as Strangford Lough and Lough Foyle after they arrive on the island of Ireland, before dispersing further afield, many then heading for Dublin.

For Niall there is a special excitement that belongs to the arrival of the brents: 'It's the opposite side of the year to the first swallows, when people remark that seeing them heralds in a new season. We may lament the loss of summer but one of the things you can certainly enjoy about the winter is the arrival of the brents. In Dublin they're so obvious and there are so many of them that they are clear indicators of the change of season.' Niall thinks that Dubliners have adapted to brents in the same way that brents have adapted to Dubliners. 'Many locals incorrectly call them Canadian geese – not to be confused with the Canada goose – because they know they've come from Canada and many people feel very proud of them. Some of them take on the role of unofficial goose warden, or brent goose vigilante, and you'll seeing them giving out – telling people off – should they leave their dogs go after them or get too near the birds on their bikes.' Another aspect of local pride in the birds can be found in the fact that the Killbarrack Coast Community Programme – which helps drug users in recovery – has adopted the brent goose as its logo. When President of Ireland Mary McAleese visited the scheme in April 2003 she cited the example of brent geese looking after injured members of the flock and suggested this community-led scheme to help those who have become involved with heavy drugs was very similar.

---

* Richard Nairn, David Jeffrey and Rob Goodbody, *Dublin Bay: Nature and History*, Cork, 2017.

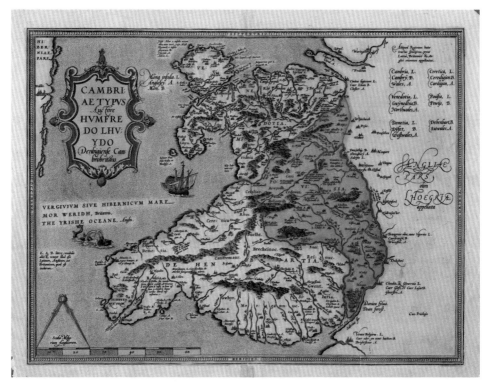

1. Cambriae typus, map of Wales by Humphrey Llwyd, c. 1570. Note use of Yrishe Ocean. Held in the National Library of Wales, Wikimedia Commons

2. Dún Laoghaire Sign, Kenneth Allen / CC BY-SA 2.0 Wikimedia Commons

3. Holyhead pebbledash © Robert Law

4. RMS Leinster (1897), postcard c. 1910, Wikimedia Commons

5. An engraving of Smalls Lighthouse near Pembrokeshire, Wales being struck by a wave during a storm with a ship visible in the distance. Engraving by Souchal, from the book *Lighthouses and Lightships* (1870), Wikimedia Commons

6. The Diving Bell, Dublin, Ireland by Giuseppe Milo, Wikimedia Commons

7. Carngwasted & Ebewalin. French soldiers being rowed ashore from ships at anchor and setting a camp, James Baker (1798), held in the National Library of Wales, Wikimedia Commons

8. A Northern Gannet, Andreas Trepte, Wikimedia Commons

9. A Manx Shearwater, Skomer Island, Pembrokeshire, Wales, Martin Reith, Wikimedia Commons

10. Dublin Dock Workers, with thanks to the Dublin Dock Workers Preservation Society

11. Roseate Terns, U.S. Fish and Wildlife Service Southeast Region, Wikimedia Commons

12. Blue Whale, Natural History Museum, London, Wikimedia Commons

13. A boat transporting cattle during a pilgrimage to Bardsey Island, 11 August 1950, held in the National Library of Wales, Wikimedia Commons

14. Hook Lighthouse, Michael J Foley, Wikimedia Commons

15. Greenland white-fronted geese winging in to the Wexford Slobs © Graham Murphy

16. Storm Petrel from *Birds of America* by John James Audubon, held by the University of Pittsburgh, Wikimedia Commons

URBAN GEESE

*   *   *

The Dublin birds have adapted to feeding in the green spaces of the city, have learned to exploit parklands, even lawn verges as replacement food sources since the mudflats have been lost to them as urban areas have expanded. You can see them all over town, sauntering around Macauley and Santry parks, plump as turkeys on the grounds of Chanel College in Coolock or at the junction of Alfie Byrne and Clontarf Roads. In such places they crop the grass to a billiard-table smoothness, as efficient as lawn mowers. It's moot perhaps to remember that the brent goose is a grazing animal, a herbivore like a domestic cow, a snail or a limpet in that they all consume different kinds of plant. Studies have shown that brent geese have a particular approach to grazing itself as they'll start with the topmost part of the grass and then return to the same patch some days later when the grass has had a chance to grow and thus avail themselves of the extra nutrients in the new green growth.

The birds still have to be wary in city locations, but the dangers are very different to those they face in the summer in the northern tundra, where foxes' pelts run white, not red like their Irish cousins, and they even have to contend with the predations of polar bears. It's quite a thing to see these wild birds roaming around the new estates at Red Arches or hoovering the turf at Foxfield Green. But they must give the AstroTurf of Donnybrook stadium short shrift, leaving it to the rugby studs and choosing, rather, to give a short-back-and-sides to park land at Malahide with the blunt razors of their bills.

It's a perfect picture as they skein down over the rooftops, skirting around the skylines. When the birds land they are said to be 'whiffling', an evocative word which derives from wind movements and describes the way the birds seem to go all topsy-turvy, sometimes coming to ground pretty much upside down. It's an ungainly act, most certainly, the wings acting both as parachute and aileron as they use air resistance to slow as the bird touches down.

On some inland sites in the Dublin area they are present in sufficient numbers for such places technically to be designated as Special

Protection Areas under EU directives. Of course, they would need to be using such sites consistently, to be core sites necessary for the survival of the species, before that would happen, but it's an interesting thought nevertheless, underlining how important this network of parks and greens is for the species. So too in Dublin Port, where spills of soya meal and messes of maize offer alfresco dining for the birds. The brent geese graze diligently all winter, not only gathering enough energy to keep them going but also putting on weight – plumping, plumping as they graze in head-down sweeps, ready for spring's long-haul flight. To reach their ultimate destinations the birds will need to eat enough excess food to convert into yellow fat, a source of necessary migration calories stored just under the skin. Then, come the lengthening days, the inner clock within each bird triggers a cue for departure for Arctic Canada or northern Greenland, to far-off Franz Josef Land and Spitzbergen, between Norway and the North Pole.

* * *

Dublin Bay is big – it covers 296 square kilometres – and the amount of water entering or leaving the bay on a single spring high tide has been calculated to be sufficient to fill 123,000 Olympic-size swimming pools. Water rotates clockwise around the bay, owing to the fact that in general the flow of water around the Irish Sea is south to north. It's nature always in flux and motion. The brent geese gather here in substantial numbers, their behaviour dictated by the patterns of such tides, with a dramatic swell in numbers from 10,000 in the 1960s to almost 50,000 in the winter of 2011/12. There have been some declines since then due to what Niall describes as the 'junk food hypothesis'. This suggests that this is an adaptation on the part of the birds to an increasingly human-mediated landscape – but the food they eat isn't as good, a bit like gannets eating blue whiting as the by-catch to trawler fishing instead of catching more nutritious mackerel. So in the case of brent geese, as Niall explains, some of them adopt a year-on, year-off strategy, so they get a brood away one year, but because they've been eating so much city grass they're not quite as healthy as they should be, so they may wait another year to have another brood. But the long-term trend shows them increasing; they're on the up-and-up because their survival rates are higher because they can get onto this ready source of grass. Some evidence for this productivity drifts by us on the channel where a family party of six is swimming by: a productive brood and thus a good breeding season.

The brent used to be thought of as a true sea-goose, suspicious of land, although it's impossible to think that now when the birds have taken so readily to urban spaces around the Irish capital. By reputation it was not considered a delicacy: quite the opposite, the flesh was considered incredibly leathery. Indeed, one old wildfowling recipe suggested that the best way to cook a brent goose was to boil it with an old boot, then after three days to throw away the goose and eat the boot. That tough.

Their favourite food source is eelgrass, also known as Zostera, much of which has been lost, though there is still a remnant patch growing on the beach near Merrion Gates on the bay's southern side. Here you might see them upending, much as mallard and other ducks do, picking at the underwater roots. Eelgrass suffered a parlous decline in the 1930s, perhaps because of the effects of a fungal disease. It's a species of interest to botanists as well as to brents since they are perennial plants, related to the pondweeds commonly found in areas of standing water. Indeed, they are important for fish species, offering cover and sanctuary in southern temperate zones below the tideline where different species can feed and breed; eelgrass is also an important component of the brent goose's diet when they return to Dublin Bay in late August and September.

On the facing coast, near Porthdinllaen on the north Llŷn peninsula, there's a substantial underwater meadow of eelgrass which acts as an important nursery for fish, including sea sticklebacks, corkwing wrasse, plaice, and a real and rare oddity, the snake pipefish, which most resembles a little dragon. A project to move millions of seeds 150 miles south to the Dale Peninsula in Pembrokeshire is the biggest seagrass restoration project in the UK and involves cultivating the plants and then dropping them to the sea-bed in small hessian sacks produced by local people. It might be a scheme worth trying out in Dublin. The links between eelgrass and brents was the subject of detailed research in the 1980s by Micheál Ó Briain, who measured the biomass of eelgrass where it was available before and after the geese arrived. He noted how the small patch at Merrion Gates was depleted by mid-November, when the birds were forced to look for another food supply. The birds now use over 100 sites around the city and, as the naturalist Richard Nairn puts it, 'nowhere is the adaptation to urban living so complete as in Dublin'.

This way of living and feeding is ingrained in them by now, a learned behaviour that sees most of the geese flying to the safety of the Bull Island saltmarshes at night, or swimming on sheltered waters in the bay itself, safe from the predations of foxes which are, of course, also urban animals hereabouts. Experienced adult birds lead younger birds on these daily feeding flights, individuals learning the routes just as surely as Dublin bus drivers know the way to Talbot Street.

The brents of Dublin bay are much studied, with many caught and ringed. In the early 2000s six individual birds were fitted with radio trackers to learn more about their long migrations, each named after significant ornithologists from Ireland, Britain, Canada and Iceland. Thus Austin, Arnthor, Hugh, Kerry, Oscar and Major Ruttledge were caught in Iceland during their journey to Arctic Canada to be satellite-tracked by scientists from the Wildlife and Wetlands Trust. They lost track of Austin and Arnthor very early on, while Oscar and Hugh were eaten by Arctic foxes in Iceland. Kerry, meanwhile, was discovered in its final resting place, being the larder of an Inuit hunter's cottage on Bathurst Island where his sad fate was recorded in a cartoon in the *Sun*.

By the eight-month mark the study group of geese had been reduced to just a single bird, aptly named after Major Robert Ruttledge, one of the great figures of Irish ornithology: a redoubtable man who studied birds for six decades and lived to the ripe age of 102. The fate of the other five birds underlined the dangers brents face when they travel. The migratory journey of the brent is the longest migration of any goose species: 4,735 miles (7,000km), which includes a non-stop leg of 1,800 miles (3,000km), not to mention beating a wing path over the emptiness of the Greenland ice-cap with its 10,000-metre peaks rising jaggedly below.

* * *

By now Niall and I have walked out to the Marian statue overlooking the long stretch of Dollymount Strand where we watch significant flocks of waders pick at the glistening acres of mud which stretch like an enormous taut animal hide towards the now defunct red-and-white-hooped chimneys of Poolbeg Generating Station. Here peregrine falcons nest each year, and these mudflats must be like a smorgasbord for the falcon equivalent to jet fighters – if you forgive the mixed metaphor. On our way back to the bus, Niall stops at one of the shelters where you can pause awhile, remembering one electrifying day when a Ross's gull, a pink Arctic species, made an unexpected appearance: 'We could only scream at each other,' he recalls, the excitement for once threatening to well and truly burst its banks. Our day together was quieter, but no less rewarding; a bright day of wild geese on the muddy rim of a city.

13.

A TRINITY
OF LIGHTS

The life of a lighthousekeeper – often stranded on a rock, sometimes in the middle of a churning sea – was seldom an easy one, but events at the Smalls Lighthouse, located 25 miles from the Pembrokeshire mainland, offer dramatic proof of just how punishing it could get.

The sea can pound mercilessly here. In 1831 the tower was assaulted by a wave of such proportions that the floor of the keepers' room was torn up and slammed against the ceiling, injuring all the keepers – one so severely that he died.

Building a lighthouse on an exposed rock, far from land, was anything but easy. A Liverpool engineer and maker of harpsichords called Henry Whiteside was the man responsible for this dangerous task, completed in 1776. Its tall lead-weighted wooden legs were placed in holes cut deep into the rock, and designer Whiteside had enough faith in his wooden tower that he stayed there himself, along with the keepers.

The days were long and the nights longer. The marooned keepers would augment their diet by spinning for mackerel, often attaching hooks and spinners to the tail of a kite they would fly from the platform of the lantern – real fly fishing. But one day Whiteside found himself, along with his workers, stranded on the Smalls. Out of desperation they put a series of messages in bottles, which were then placed inside casks before being dropped into the sea. One read:

The Smalls, February 1st 1777
Sir, – Being now in a most dangerous and distressed condition
upon the Smalls, do hereby trust Providence will bring to your
hand this, which prayeth for your immediate assistance to fetch
us off the Smalls before the next spring tide, or we fear we shall
perish; our water near all gone, our fire quite gone, and our
house in a most melancholy manner. I doubt not but you will
fetch us from here as fast as possible; we can be got off at some
part of the tide in almost any weather. I need say no more, but
remain your distressed humble servant.
H. Whiteside*

One message-in-a-bottle was washed up in Galway, another on the
pebble strand at Newgale and, providentially, the third found its way
to a creek near a house belonging to a Mr Williams, who promptly
summoned help.

The lucky owner of The Smalls, the clerical businessman Revd A.
B. Buchanan, was set to make lots of money. Indeed, the Smalls
became the most profitable lighthouse in the world, just as similar
lights such as The Skerries off the coast of Anglesey made a fortune
from charging ships for their bright services at the rate of a penny a
ton of cargo. It was little wonder, then, that the owners of both lights
put up a battle to stop them eventually being taken over by Trinity
House (the Corporation of Trinity House of Deptford Strond, also
known as Trinity House, is the official authority for lighthouses in
England, Wales, the Channel Islands and Gibraltar). Buchanan
entrenched stubbornly enough to ensure that Trinity House paid him
£170,000 in 1836, equivalent to tens of millions today, while to the
north The Skerries sold for a startling £445,000 in 1841.

There were two keepers on The Smalls to begin with, living a
confined, crabbed life in an octagonal wooden cabin suspended 40
feet (c. 12m) above the crash of the waves on nine solid oak columns

* https://trinityhousehistory.wordpress.com/2013/06/12/a-rock-and-a-hard-
place-storms-death-and-madness-at-the-smalls-lighthouse/.

strengthened by wooden buttresses, which helped the rickety structure resist the churn and hurl of the wild Atlantic. The lashing storms of 1801 kept Thomas Griffith and Thomas Howell confined to their cabin for four desperate months. It must have been a living hell. Then things got worse: Griffiths died and his co-worker began to lose his mind from having to live with the corpse, unwilling to dispose of the man's body lest he be accused of murder.

As Griffith's body began to decompose, Howell made a makeshift coffin for the corpse and lashed it to an outside shelf. Stiff winds blew the box apart, and the body's arm fell within view of the hut's window. As the winds blew, gusts would catch hold of the arm and move it in a way that it look as if it was beckoning. In spite of his former partner's decaying corpse, and working the lighthouse alone, Howell was able to resolutely keep the lamp lit. When Howell was finally relieved of duty, the impact of the situation had been so emotionally taxing that his friends did not recognise him. It also led to a decision by Trinity House that every lighthouse should henceforth be manned by three keepers at any one time.

This was the basis of *The Lighthouse*, a 2016 feature film by Chris Crow, made on a budget as lean as a lemon sole. It starred Michael Jibson as the doomed Griffiths and Mark Lewis Jones as the increasingly demented Howell. Mark told me how they managed to recreate the lighthouse on an industrial estate in Splott, east Cardiff, where he was duly drenched during pretty much every day of filming: 'They spent all the money on the set, on the lighthouse itself, while everything else was shot in green screen, so everything other than the scenes on the light were computer generated: the sea, the storm and everything. Three or four people with hosepipes were a sort of rain men and they had this aircraft engine which generated the wind. So there we were, literally in souwesters, in Splott.'

Mark Lewis Jones thought they did a fantastic job creating the lighthouse interior, which showed how the two men lived on top of each other. He and fellow actor Michael Jibson filmed there twelve hours a day over the course of a month: 'You could easily see how if you were there with someone you didn't get on with it would have been infernal. And even if you did get on with them it would have been difficult to be in such a claustrophobic, testing place for so long, especially after this death and the keeper left all alone.'

*　*　*

While The Smalls is infamous because of these two keepers – one dead, one mad – it has recently spawned another fascinating story. Despite the presence of the light, many ships were wrecked here. Indeed, any vessels wishing to travel to Ireland from the south coast of Wales were advised to steer a course well to the south of the 'Hats and Barrels' to be sure of clearing these hazardous rocks. The area is a veritable maritime scrap yard, its waters much beloved by sports divers for this reason.

One of them was searching the wreck of the steam ship *Rhiwabon*, which sundered here in 1884, when he chanced upon a small object sticking out of the twisted metal of the sunken vessel. It turned out to be the most remarkable example of late Viking art ever to be found in Wales: the lower guard of a Viking sword, dating to about 1100 CE. It was probably from a capsized vessel, on one of the long-distance sea-routes used for frequent attacks by the Dublin Viking fleet on wealthy centres such as St David's and Bristol, or gathering slaves from the coast.

The sword guard itself is cast in brass and inlaid with silver wire, each side finely decorated with a pair of stylised animals in profile, interwoven with thin, snake-like beasts. It might well have been crafted for a rich secular patron in Ireland. It offers proof aplenty that the Vikings were not only pirates and raiders, but also craftsmen and creators of art who were full of vigour and vitality. You can see similar decoration in Irish metalwork, clearly showing how it caught the native imagination: two prime examples are the twelfth century processional Cross of Cong and Saint Manchan's Shrine, the tent-shaped reliquary now housed in Boher Catholic Church in Co. Offaly.

The waters near The Smalls are not just a remarkable place to find archaeological items; they are also the haunt of blue sharks, which congregate here in large numbers during the warmer summer months, most of them females. With their saw-edged dentition, metallic navy-blue backs and pointed snouts, they attract increasing numbers of people who want to both swim with them and study them in the 100-metre, cold-water upwellings. One such is marine biologist Emma Williams, a member of the Celtic Deep and Marine Research and Conservation Foundation team, which actively looks for sharks. In an article for *Oceanographic* magazine she described how 'The first sign of a fin or shimmer of their bodies swimming through the water sends waves of excitement through my body. Rather than running from the ocean at the word "shark", I now find myself running towards it, hoping to get a glimpse of these amazing animals as they go about their business.'

* * *

Some 60 miles away from the sea-wash and shark-blessed waters of The Smalls stands The Hook lighthouse, on Hook Head in Co. Wexford. It's widely acknowledged as the oldest established light in Britain and Ireland. Indeed, it claims to be the world's oldest operational lighthouse, having been shining brightly for 800 years, though it has a rival in the Torre de Hércules in Galicia, northern Spain.

A light was first lit here as far back as the fifth century by St Dubhán, now the Patron Saint of the Irish Lighthouse Service. By a curious accident of etymology his name in Irish means 'hook', and to put a finer point on it, means a *fishing* hook. The well-known phrase 'by hook or by crook' is said to have originated from Oliver Cromwell's vow to take Waterford by Hook (on the Wexford side of Waterford Estuary) or by the village of Crooke, on the Waterford side.

Dubhán, the uncle of St David, crossed the sea in search of solitude and found it on this windswept, flat and treeless promontory, choosing to create a tiny cell and oratory here. It would have been impossible for him not to appreciate the myriad dangers of this jagged coast with its powerful currents and so, to help sea-travellers, he 'kept' a primitive light. He invited a local blacksmith to forge an outsized iron basket or chauffer, which he hung from a mast on a cliff edge. Each and every night Dubhán would climb the ladder to his simple beacon, burdened with enough fuel to keep the flame burning, using anything from tar to wood, charcoal to coal. Ironically enough, the one material that was never in short supply was driftwood from the splintering of wrecked ships that would drift into nearby coves and land on shelves of rock.

The eremitic monk managed to survive on this wind-assaulted headland, but he saw plenty of evidence of those who had not, when ships bound for Waterford were wrecked on the rocky reaches of the coast. The waves often carried in a grim harvest of the floating dead and sometimes sailors, barely alive, whom he would nurse back to health, thus turning his simple monastery into both a hospital and mortuary. Over the years the steely grey waters hereabouts have wrapped their cruel wet jaws around many unfortunate vessels, and so a graveyard of 1,000 ships includes the last resting place of Cromwell's flagship *Great Lewis*, which sank in the seventeenth century.

It was the Norman invader Strongbow's son-in-law William Marshal – lauded with the title 'the greatest knight that ever lived' – who built the existing lighthouse tower in the thirteenth century, in order to guide shipping to the port at New Ross, Wexford. The massive tower has weathered centuries of wind and storm and looks set to last another millennium. But The Hook is just one bright link in a chain of lights that extend along the Irish edge of St George's Channel. Going north they include Barrels, Coningbeg, Tuskar Rock, Wicklow Head, Mugins, Kish Bank, Dún Laoghaire Lights, Poolbeg, Baily, Howth Pier and Rockabill. An observer in the International Space Station might look down to see such lighthouses braiding their coast, sparkling bracelets of tiny lights.

Of these The Kish is perhaps the most familiar, as it's on the route to Dublin Port and therefore seen by many travellers. An eponymous poem describes

A lone tower, the lighthouse
Rises out of the sandy ocean bed.

When it was built in 1965 The Kish was meant to be the first of several such lights arranged along the east coast of Ireland, but the idea of erecting such expensive structures was subsequently rethought. Before then, from as far back as 1811, a lightship had been moored here, where twice a day the crew would fire two shots from a twelve-pounder gun to mark and aid the passage of the packet ship from Dún Laoghaire to Holyhead. The passing vessel would reply with a single shot to signal it had safely passed the dangers of the Kish Bank.

The new-fangled design might have offered some creature comforts to the keepers, but it also made access to the world difficult, with just a balcony, or murette, to walk around:

> The man who walks the balcony
> In prescribed circuit, round and round,
> Counts the railing's uprights, cross-pieces,
> To pass his hours of watch away.
> With never room to make a change,
> But pace and stop, retrace and pace
> Along a single narrow track.
> Not side to side, or to and fro,
> Confined within the murette's range,
> A type of roofless iron cage.
> While here and there, with beady eyes,
> The grey gulls watch him move around;
> In disdain spread their wings, or swim
> Free as the tidal currents run.
> The choice is theirs; he has no choice,
> Impounded by the catwalk's rim.*

That penultimate word puts me in mind of a snow leopard I once saw in La Ménagerie, the small zoo in Paris's Jardin des Plantes. It had a dreadful routine, pacing back and forth behind the glass, a heart-

* Cited in Bill Long, *Bright Light, White Water: The Story of Irish Lighthouses and their People*, Dublin, 1993.

163

clawing image of a wild, wild animal in suffocating confinement. The keeper in D. J. O'Sullivan's well-paced poem would have probably known exactly how the big cat felt.

The Kish light, like that on Enlli and many others, would attract migrant birds. The keepers here helped a man called Richard Barrington, from Fassaroe in County Wicklow, to learn more about the phenomenon by sending him the skins of birds that had died by flying into the light or the tower. Barrington eventually collected and measured about 1,600 wings over the period 1881–97, resulting in his ground-breaking *The Migrations of Birds at Irish Lighthouses and Lightships*, published in 1900. Keepers took to logging with alacrity. A report from the Kish Bank Lightship on 17 March 1890, for instance, noted 'a skylark killed by striking the light at 11pm going NW'. The following night 'several skylarks were about the lantern at 11pm'.

The systematic study of bird migration at night was relatively new at the time, and Barrington's study in Ireland was quite simply pioneering. He sent out blank schedules to keepers of lighthouses and lightships right around the coast, as well as a request for sample legs and wings to be sent to him for identification and measurement. This new task must have appealed to men who were normally mired in mundane events, because he got a huge amount of information, with macabre deliveries of body parts arriving every day. There were some-times rare birds, such as the first woodchat shrike seen in Ireland, on the Blackwater Bank lightship, off Country Wexford on the night of 16 August 1893; or the male hobby that sat on board the Lucifer Shoals lightship off the Wexford coast on 23 May 1890. Autumn saw occasional periods of wholesale slaughter at the lights, such as the 500 or 600 thrushes and blackbirds killed each night on Tuskar Rock over the course of three nights in October 1897. Unsurprisingly, birds of prey, such as long-eared owls, followed such an 'extraordinary rush of birds' to hunt down tired individuals.

The lightships of the east coast furnish interesting records of corn-crakes occurring 'in large numbers' about the lanterns in spring. On 5 May 1888, Mr Wall (at South Arklow lightship) reported 'hundreds of Corn-crakes about light 10.20pm to 12.20am; large numbers killed against the glass, two fell dead on deck, several fell overboard; one caught alive and let go; went off N.W. flying low; weather clear, light breeze S.W.' On 16 May 1893 Mr Wall observed a similar rush of corncrakes on the North Arklow Light Vessel during rain; but though many were about the light from 9pm to midnight, none on this occasion were killed. Barrington suggests that Mr Wall's observations show that the corncrake 'migrates at that season in flocks of its own kind.'

On land the corncrake's flight looks very weak – its pattering wings look as if even getting from one hedge to another was a tall order, explaining why it chooses to hide rather than fly. Yet this was not the experience of keepers: 'Notwithstanding the doubts which are commonly expressed as to this bird's ability to migrate, it would appear to be an exceptionally powerful flier, for though it has repeatedly been killed or caught striking the lanterns, it has only once been reported as seeming "exhausted" which was a bird of Tuskar rock in May 1883.'

The corncrake, in truth, does fly very far. Birds from, say, Coll in the Hebrides fly to the Democratic Republic of the Congo in Central Africa, even though, when they're in Scotland, they do seem hugely reluctant to take wing. Amy Liptrot, who studied them on her native Orkney and wrote marvellously about them in *The Outrun*, refers to local beliefs that the birds don't leave the islands at all, instead 'going underground', turning into moorhens, or even catching a piggyback on other birds' backs.

The corncrake is now an extremely rare bird in Ireland, down to just 151 calling males in Donegal and West Connaught in 2018, so the idea of hundreds of birds hitting the lights on a single night is remarkable. The corncrake, or land rail, was one of the most familiar signs of the Irish summer, its rasping call – very much apparent in its Latin name *Crex Crex* – as ubiquitous at night as the sight of stars. Smallholder farming, where swards were cut by scythe, suited this secretive, skulking summer migrant, which likes to nest in the high grass of hay meadows. As William Thompson put it in *The Natural History of Ireland*, published in 1850: 'Everywhere that we go in this island in the months of May, June, and early in July (irrespective of the vicinity of rivers, which are considered to influence its distribution in Great Britain), except to the mountain top, or to stony and heath-covered tracts, the call of the corncrake is heard, not only at its favourite times, in the evening and during the night, but throughout the day. From its frequenting the meadows or pastures nearest towns, and even those within them – as the grounds of the Royal Academical Institution, Belfast – the corncrake makes itself heard through the night over a great portion of the towns in Ireland.'

The corncrake is archetypically a land bird, one connected with quietly farmed land, the smallholder's patch, which formed part of the quilted landscape of so much of Ireland. There's an affecting vignette of a bird kept as a pet for six years in the 1820s in the house of a Mr Spear in Carrickfergus: 'It became quite tame, and partook of food very various in kind, such as groats, raw meat, bread and milk … yolk of boiled eggs, and butter, which last was especially relished. This bird was very clean, and washed every morning in a basin of water set apart for the purpose. It was accustomed to be taken upstairs at night … and of its own accord habitually went out of the cage into a basket containing moss, where the night was passed … When allowed to go about the house, the persons to whom it was attached were sought for, and followed everywhere … Every spring it called with the usual crake, often … quite impudently in the parlour, when brought there to be shown of … At pairing time, this bird was very comical, coming up with its wings spread, and neck stretched out, after the manner of a turkey-cock, and uttering a peculiar croaking note. It would then make a sort of nest in the cage, croaking all the while, and carry a worm or piece of meat about in its bill.'

Corncrakes used to be found in every single parish in Ireland, but its parlous decline started in the early 1900s, when it began to disappear in the south east, followed by a steady retreat in its range to the north and west. In places the disappearing act was swift indeed. In 1938 it was estimated that there was a breeding density of a pair per acre in Kilkenny: this was reduced by half the following year. Its strongholds nowadays are islands such as Tory Island, Co. Donegal, which makes the records from the lighthouse keepers all the more fascinating: those feathery beats, the dull thuds of the birds against the glass, the determined corpse-collecting by dozens of lighthouse keepers that shed so much light on patterns of bird migration along these shores.

14.

A FRENZY OF SHIPBUILDING

In Sir Edwin Landseer's 1864 painting *Man Proposes, God Disposes*, two sleekly muscular polar bears face off against each other either side of what looks like a jagged piece of iceberg. One of the animals, its huge paws splayed out to give stability and extra strength, is tearing at a piece of a flag, the red ensign, which resembles a big ribbon of flesh. The other bear has just snapped off a bone from a meat-stripped rib cage, which it is raising aloft, trophy-like, between its massive incisors. Between the two powerful animals lies the mast of a ship, its sails ragged and reddened. There are other scraps and shards of rigging scattered about, along with a mariner's brass telescope. This is nature red in tooth and claw, the drama playing out against dark tones of ice.

The ship in question is the ironclad icebreaker HMS *Erebus*, one of hundreds built in Pembroke Dock. It, along with its sister vessel the HMS *Terror*, was smithereened by the very ice they were meant to break. The *Erebus* undertook not one but two of the most ambitious naval expeditions of all time. During the first she ventured further south than any ship had ever been. The second was a voyage to find the Northwest Passage, which proved to be her doom: she vanished in the wastes of Arctic Canada along with 129 members of crew, including those of her sister vessel.

No fewer than 260 ships were built in Pembroke Dock over the course of 112 years, including HMS *Erebus*. It took two years to build her; she was a special kind of warship known as a bomb vessel, able to carry mortars that could hurl shells high over coastal defences – very much in keeping with her classical name, a sower of destruction, a bringer of havoc.

The yards of Pembroke Dock were almost built in nearby Milford, where a man called Charles Francis Greville established a private shipyard to take advantage of the Navy's urgent need for new vessels in light of the Revolutionary Wars in France. A contract was issued to build three ships there, even though it was a long way from any source of timber. In other ways, too, Milford didn't make sense, but it may also be that the developers had influential friends. Horatio, Lord Nelson visited the town on the last leg of his triumphant tour of Wales, and stayed in a hotel that is still named after him. As he was in a *ménage à trois* with Emma Hamilton and her cuckold of a husband, he might well have done some high-level lobbying of the Navy Board, and this trip to Milford could have helped consolidate matters.

Charles Greville passed away while the Navy Board was in the process of buying the Milford yard. The Board found one 6 miles upriver. The site, at a place called Pater, had both the physical features and water access they needed, although the necessary labour wasn't available locally. A decommissioned frigate, the *Lapwing*, was beached deliberately as a temporary accommodation for workers. Without further ado, work started in earnest, and the Pater Dockyard, later renamed the Pembroke Dockyard, was established in 1814.

Orders were placed for the construction of seventy-four-gun battleship, and four frigates, and honoured even after Napoleon's defeat at Waterloo in June 1815, which meant a smaller navy would be required. The willingness of the Navy Board to spend money in a seemingly cavalier manner was curious in the extreme. It took the work away from Milford, too, and the last ship to be built there, the *Rochefort*, was launched in April 1814.

To supply the necessary manpower, some men had to row over from Milford to Pater, 6 miles away. Conditions when they got there were far from comfortable. Shipwrights and carpenters might have to splash around up to their waists in muddy water, only shielded from the rain and wind by drapes of sack or wraps of ship's canvas hung over their shoulders as they were pelted by the small artillery of Atlantic rain. In February 1816 the first ships to be constructed there, two 28-gun frigates, the *Ariadne* and the *Valorous*, slipped into the water for their maiden voyages. The *Ariadne* became the last sea command of Captain Frederick Marryat, famous for children's novels such as *Midshipman Easy* and *Masterman Ready*, which drew on his experiences at sea during the Napoleonic Wars.

With the work pouring in, the shipyards at Pembroke Dock expanded at a lick. The eastern section of the yards was added and Royal Marines were drafted in to guard the establishment, living in an old wooden ship called the *Dragon*, which was dragged up onto a shingle bank nearby.

The first houses in the town, on Front Street, were initially occupied by officials such as storemen and shipwrights. Living conditions there were less than salubrious, with streets such as Pigs Parade earning this swinish sobriquet because the shacks and sheds were squalid in the extreme. But house construction proceeded apace and soon there was a public house, too, the first of many: in its heyday the town would have no fewer than 200 pubs to slake the thirst of thousands of workers. Houses accreted around the twelve-foot-thick dockyard walls, streets arrayed like ribcages around the beating, clanging heart of the town, the shipyard.

A report published in 1843 offers a snapshot of the yards' busyness: 'Slips 1 and 2 are presently vacant and have no roofs over them. On slip 3 the frame of the *Lion*, 80 guns, is now complete. On slip 4 is more than half the frame for the *Victoria*, 110 guns; but the building has been stopped by order of Admiralty, dated the 18th December last. On slip 5 the 50-gun frigate *Constance* is about three-eighths completed. On slip 6 is laid the *Colossus*, with frame completed. On slip 7 the steam frigate *Dragon* is being built, and is half completed. All of the above slips are fit for building first-rates. Slips 8 and 9 are vacant; they are fit for two-deck line of battle ships. On slip 10 the 36-gun *Sybille* is about three-eighths completed. On slip 11 the *Inflexible* steam sloop is laid down, and is half built. On slip 12 the brig *Kingfisher* is about five-eighths advanced.'

But the technology of shipbuilding was changing apace and a dock-yard established in relatively short order after Nelson's October 1805 victory at Trafalgar was soon out of step, even though it was producing fine ships, including the Royal Yacht the *Victoria and Albert* – the first of four Royal Yachts to be built in Pembroke Dock. Then there was the enormous three-decker wooden battleship, the *Howe*, twice the size of Nelson's *Victory*. Meanwhile, the construction of the largest wooden battleship ever constructed, the *Duke of Wellington*, was paused halfway in order to extend her length. Like a magician's assistant she was cut in two and then a middle section inserted even as she floated: no mean trick.

By 1850 the roster of workers at the yard had grown to 500. Pembroke Dock gained a reputation as one of the most modern ship-yards in the Navy. A frigate would be launched every year and battleships every three or four, so that some years saw a series of launches: there were four in 1820, for instance. In the boom years of Victoria's reign, it was the most important site in the world for building warships.

Consequently, Pembroke Dock, and indeed the whole of Milford Haven, became very well defended. A series of thirteen forts was erected, even though Europe was experiencing an unusual period of peace. Little wonder, then, that the sea-forts were dubbed the Palmerston Follies, after Lord Palmerston, who had commissioned them (there is no truth in the rumour that nearby Folly Farm, the children's fun park in Kilgetty, was also named after him). Defences were also strengthened around Pembroke Dock itself, with a battery of twenty-three guns and two large Martello gun towers. Unfortunately, the latter were soon obsolete, as high-explosive shells from warships could easily outmatch their smooth-bore cannon to blast them into rubble and dust.

To provide more permanent accommodation for the Marines, the Defensible Barracks were built in record speed. Twelve months after being commissioned, the huge stone edifice – still standing very solidly to this day – was ready in November 1845. It was ringed by a proper moat, which sadly claimed the lives of a local GP who'd had one too many, and Private John Harding, who also made a fatal splash.

Sometimes things didn't go to plan: the launch of the *Caesar*, a two-decked wooden screw ship, was scuppered when she refused to budge into the water. Some penny-pinching had resulted in fir being used instead of oak for the launch-ways, and the weight of the ship had bedded her into the soft wood. Some of the locals blamed something more supernatural. A local woman called Betty Foggy – reputedly a witch – had been denied access to the launch and on being refused entry through the dock dates had muttered, 'Very well, then there'll be no launch today!'

Of course, superstition and a belief in ghosts were very much part of the Victorian age. The most famous local story concerns a survey vessel, HMS *Asp*, which was brought into the yard for repairs and refitting. A letter from her commander, Captain Aldridge, appeared in the *Pembroke County Guardian* in September 1869: 'On taking possession of her, the Captain Superintendent remarked to me, "Do you know, sir, your ship is said to be haunted, and I don't know if you will get any of the Dockyard men to work on her." I, of course, smiled, and I said "I don't care for ghosts and I dare say I shall get her all to right fast enough."'

The *Asp* sailed away to the River Dee and odd things started to happen: the unsettling sound of drawers being opened and closed, a percussion cap being snapped close to the captain's head as he lay down on his bunk; but these were just small augurs of the uncanny events yet to come: 'One night, when the vessel was at anchor … I was woken by the quartermaster begging me to come on deck as the look-out man had rushed to the lower deck, saying that the figure of a lady was standing on the paddle-box pointing with her finger to Heaven.'

The Captain's reaction was to send the look-out man back on deck but when the order was given to him the man was seized by violent convulsions and so the Captain himself had to stand on duty for the rest of the watch.

The apparition made herself known many times after that, her finger always directed skywards and the sight of her was enough to send men screaming. Indeed, many categorically refused to serve on board the *Asp*. When she returned to Pembroke Dock for repairs in 1857 a sentry on the dockside spotted a lady mount the paddle box, her hand pointing towards the skies. As Aldridge's letter explained: 'She then stepped ashore and came along a path towards him when he brought his musket to charge. "Who goes there?" But the figure walked through the musket, upon which he dropped it and ran for the guardhouse.'

The ghostly vision was never explained, although Captain Aldrige recounted a story which might have served as a clue. The *Asp* had formerly been used as a packet ship, plying back and forth between Port Patrick and Donaghadee. One night the body of a young lady had been found with her throat cut, lying on the bunk. It was a grisly if not entirely satisfactory explanation of the spectral apparition.

* * *

Steam and iron replaced wood and sail and Pembroke Dock valiantly tried to keep up with the times. James Anderson Findlay depicted an imposing scene: 'Building sheds rise majestically and barrier-like along the very water's edge. There are joiners, millwrights, black-smiths, plumbers, coppersmiths, coopers, wheelwrights, painters, pattern-makers and armour plating shops … near to the docks lie numberless armour plates, varying in thickness from two to eighteen inches, destined to cover the sides of the powerful ships of war, which are being constructed in the neighbouring sheds.'

The noise, bustle and crash of metal surrounded you on all sides where 'is heard the din, clang and clash of hammers and machinery forging and manufacturing the various kinds of heavy iron work now so requisite in the present advance state of shipbuilding. Here, also, are three immense steam hammers, beneath whose ponderous heads masses of red-hot iron are continually becoming subject to their will.'

The blacksmiths alone employed nearly 200 men and by 1900 there were 2,500 hands employed in the yards. But work on the iron armour-clad *Ajax* took far too long, at seven long years. By 1875 the

Dockyard itself extended over 80 acres and employed 1,500 men, a figure destined to swell to 2,500 at the end of the century. By then it had become the single largest employer of labour in Wales, outpacing the collieries and iron works of the south east of the country.

Some of the ships were very impressive, including the *Inconstant*, the fastest ship on the seas at the time, and the *Shannon*, built in 1875, which was the first British armoured cruiser. Meanwhile the *Renown* was the first British battleship to be built with all-steel armour plating, while the diminutive *Iris* and *Mercury* made history in 1877 and 1878 by being the first Royal Navy ships to be built entirely of steel. These two despatch vessels were small and fast and were the antitheses of the *Hannibal*, a gigantic, elephantine craft and the biggest to be constructed at Pembroke Dock. Other ships won fame a long way away, such as the *Starling*, which surveyed the waters around Hong Kong, and has an Asian inlet named after her. The *Alert*, built in 1856, managed to winter at Floeberg Beach in the Arctic, which, at that point, was the highest point of latitude in these frozen wastes to have been reached by explorers.

Presiding over the shipbuilding endeavours in Pembroke Dock was the admiral or captain superintendent, who had supreme authority over everything that went on, and there was a succession of thirty-five of these powerful local figures between 1832 and 1926. Some were real characters, even if they weren't exactly loved by the workforce. Sir Watkin Owen Pell, for instance, got around the problem of only having one leg by training his pony Jack to climb onto gangways and gantries, helping him to surprise any laggardly workers. Theft was a problem, too. With so many things to steal, not least a plentiful supply of wood, the police had their work cut out, especially when one way of getting timber out of the yards was to simply throw it in the water and wait until it was washed up on Front Street.

One man who singlehandedly changed the course of Pembroke Dock's fortunes was the massively energetic First Sea Lord Jackie Fisher, who was determined to modernise the Navy, bringing in turbine-driven battleships because gunships were 'too weak to fight, too slow to run away'. The advent of the battlecruisers was a serious blow to the dockyards, one of many as technologies advanced and Pembroke Dock's seeming remoteness was exposed.

In September 1925 came the news that the dockyard was to close, with 1,000 men being discharged by the end of the month. The news was expected but no less cataclysmic for that, not least because some 16,000 people in the area depended on the yards for their livelihoods. By May the following year the yards were closed and 1,400 were on the dole. The following year Lawrence Phillips chronicled the change by saying that the town is now 'almost entirely a town of unemployed and pensioners'. Some people moved away in search of work and the statistics show that between 1921 and 1931 a quarter of the entire population of Pembroke Dock migrated, some finding work in other shipyards in places as far-flung as Malta and Bermuda. But the Depression still cast a dark shadow over the area. By 1937 over half of the insured population of the borough were unemployed.

There had been some good news in the early 1930s when the RAF established a flying boat base there, the deep waters of the Haven being ideal for sea planes and the like. During the Second World War, Catalinas and Sunderlands, roaring off from the calm waters, helped wrest control of the seas from the convoy-raiding U-boats. The base was to remain in operation for almost thirty years, with the graceful, elegant planes becoming a familiar sight over the town.

All of this military concentration naturally made the area an obvious target for German bombers. Soon after the dockyard was opened up again in 1940 the first bombs were dropping. Three Junkers Ju 88s, escorted by two fighters, flew over and managed to drop their loads on the oil tanks at Pennar above the town: an important strategic hit as they contained thousands of gallons of fuel for use in the Battle of the Atlantic. Luckily, two farming brothers who were working near the tanks survived an almighty blast that threw one of them off his feet, landing 20 feet away. The Celtic gods smiled on the pair of them.

One burning tank ignited another, and soon more than 600 firefighters were involved in fighting flames that roared like the Great Fire of London. In all some 38 million gallons of fuel – so necessary for the war effort – were lost. It took over two weeks to bring the fire under control.

On the night of 12 May 1941 the bombers struck again, and this time with even deadlier effect, damaging 2,000 houses and killing thirty-two people – like the London Blitz transposed to the west. Meanwhile, the Sunderlands continued to make their long-range sorties, seeking out submarines in the wild Atlantic. But by 1957 even those were obsolete, so the flying boat station was shut down, followed in 1966 by the closure of the Llanion army barracks. Hammer blow after hammer blow after hammer blow to a town that connected with the wide world.

* * *

In July 2020 the sapling of a gingko tree was planted in the grounds of the Kure Naval Base in Japan, gifted to the city by the people of Pembroke Dock. This happened with much ceremony as it commemorated the links between the west Wales town and Admiral Togo Heihachiro, who once lodged there, and with a 2,200-ton armoured corvette called the *Hi-ei*, constructed in its shipyards for the Japanese Navy. To thank the people of the town Lieutenant Togo had given them a gingko tree, to be planted in his lodgings at the master shipwright's house. Lieutenant Togo went on to become one of the country's most fêted and decorated war heroes: he took on the Chinese navy before defeating the Russian Baltic Fleet, so saving Japan from invasion. Little wonder that this connection with Wales is taken seriously.

Milford Haven meanwhile had a resurgence, importing oil and latterly liquid gas. Oil tankers entered the frame in the 1960s when jetties and plants were built by companies such as Esso, Regent (later Texaco), BP, Amoco and Gulf Oil. Some local firms offered specialist help with things such as rope running – carrying ropes from the giant tankers to dolphins, being protective pilings on the piers. In 1979 a Ro-Ro (roll on – roll off) ferry terminal was created, and in May that year the B & I Ferry *Connaught* travelled between Pembroke Dock and Rosslare for the first time, opening up a service that lasted until 1986. Two years later, Irish Ferries reopened the service to the Republic.

I travelled back to Pembroke Dock with Irish Ferries on a trip from Rosslare whilst researching this book. I shared the stowing space on one of the lower decks with a Chopper Squad, a gathering of Harley Davison hogs ridden by men in studded leather. Their 'President' led them down the ramp and I duly followed on my pushbike, as if re-entering Wales with a processional escort of modern-day Hells Angels. It must have made quite a sight as I struggled to keep up with in the fug of fumes and the collective roar. Of such moments are memories made.

15.

THE LAST INVASION
OF BRITAIN

It's hard to imagine it as the scene of a historic military incursion. Carreg Wastad Point, a rocky lip of land with a dolmen, a megalithic tomb, sat atop, a couple of miles out of the town of Fishguard. It overlooks what is today the aquamarine bowl of Aberfelin Bay and is set within a quietly quilted land, shot through with cadmium yellow threads of gorse. They, in turn, bind together a tight patchwork of fields belonging to old farms such as Bristgarn, Tre Howel and Pontiago. Stand on this hump of rock and you can see the frayed edges of this landscape-tapestry – the other promontories and fingers of rock that reach out to the sea along this busily serrated coastline: Carn Helen, Trwyn Llwyd, Y Globa Fawr, Capel Degan and the intriguingly named Maen Jaspis. Who was Jaspis that he should have a rock named after him?

Today the wind is quietly sibilant, whispering through the thin grasses, only the electric chirp of swallows interrupting the soughing lilt of the gentle south westerly. The little hirundines zip along like tight, blue bullets, keeping low to the ground as they trawl insects into their small gapes. A raven passes overhead, its cry a hoarse kronk like that of a heavy smoker.

To underline the utter peacefulness of the place you can approach it from Llanwnda, where the ancient well has recently been cleaned up, and the watercress runs in a stone-built channel recently unchoked of weeds. It's such a special place, this, one of those liminal spaces where the line or veil of separation between the physical world and another is impossibly thin, or even rent asunder. Pause awhile at the well as I did and you'll soon be quite pleasantly unsettled by the palpable sense of the past taking hold. Or maybe it's something else. Alastair Moffat certainly got the specialness of the place when he visited, remarking in *The Sea Kingdoms* how the dolmen at Llanwnda 'looks as though it is a door to the underworld which stands permanently ajar. And, indeed, that may have been what the makers intended. The Celts believed that holy wells were portals to the Otherworld, and if they lifted their heads to look up the hill at Carreg Wastad, they may have seen another way in.' It's certainly a place where, as Moffat avers, the old gods seem very close.

Llanwnda and the Carreg Wastad all seems too peaceful and undisturbedly ancient for the setting of an invasion, but the same cliffs where fulmars wheel today on stiff wings once had French soldiers scaling them, an invading force hell bent on destabilising Britain. This wasn't war as noises off. They saw and heard the guns here. Soldiers added blurts of scarlet tunic to the dark gorse green of the land. There's a simple rocky monument erected during the centenary of the landing that crowns the hump of hill as if to prove it all actually happened. This edge of land was the unexpected backdrop to 'The Last Invasion of Britain' which still sends ripples of excitement through gossipy local history. Despite the local naysayers of Nayland, the sceptics of Solva and the doubters of Dale. Invasion! Yes. At this Pembrokeshire version of Finisterre, of Land's End. Yes, here. Just imagine.*

* * *

In the last decade of the eighteenth century warfare and political upheaval spread like wildfire across the continent of Europe, as the French Revolution set the old order ablaze. In Paris the five-man revolutionary council – The Directory – retaliated in kind to British

---

* J. E. Thomas, *Britain's Last Invasion: Fishguard 1797*, Stroud, 2007 was invaluable in compiling this chapter.

interference in Brittany and La Vendée, where they tried to enlist angry Catholics against the new state. The French set out to appeal to Britain's poor to join the struggle and thus improve their lot. Such a liberating plan might appeal in west Wales, where the disparity between the rich and the poor was pretty much a chasm. Here a small group of landowners had accrued considerable wealth and expanded their estates – in stark contrast to the peasantry, whose lives were blighted by poverty. It was no coincidence perhaps that eleven of the nineteen workhouses in Wales were in Pembrokeshire, making it destitution central. Travellers' accounts of the area describe wretched living conditions, where poverty bred despair. It was fertile ground for people's anger, a sterling place to seed insurrection.

France had seen chaos spawn institutional change, with the end of monarchy, experiments in government, and the brutal regime of repression known as 'The Terror'. Robespierre, its brutal poster boy, had himself been executed before the newly-formed Directory took control. One of its aims was the invasion of Ireland, and later events at Fishguard unfolded as an expression of this desire. Why Ireland? In July 1795 Wolfe Tone, the so-called 'Prophet of Irish independence', had held meetings in Paris, intimating support in Ireland, which promoted a French fleet to set sail for Ireland at the end of 1796, only to be thwarted by stormy weather.

Much later than planned, the French fleet set sail from Brest on 16 December 1796, numbering seventeen ships of the line carrying 15,000 men – not to mention ample supplies of arms to place in the ready hands of Irish rebels. Frightful weather proved fateful, dividing the fleet on the open seas, although some of the ships did manage to make it to Bantry Bay in West Cork. However, eleven vessels were lost, along with 500 hands, and even the ships that made it through the storm were properly pummelled. It was the mere shadow of a fleet that made it back to Brest. Undeterred, the French made plans to land men on the shores of England itself, aiming to attack Newcastle and Bristol as diversions from an Irish mission.

Yet Wolfe Tone's dream held firm, shored up by the notion that tens of thousands of Irish members of the British navy could be convinced to mutiny. He argued: 'Ireland is now at war with England in defence of her liberties; France is the ally of Ireland, and England is the common enemy of both nations. You are aboard the British navy. You will probably be called upon to turn your arms against your native land and I hope and rely that you will act as becomes honest Seamen and honest Irishmen.'

The French had showed willing but had been slow to act. Wolfe Tone believed crucial time had been lost, not least because English sailors were feeling mutinous: 'Damn it, damn it, damn it! … There seems to be a fate in This Business. Five weeks, I believe six weeks, the English fleet was paralysed by the mutinies at Portsmouth, Plymouth and the Nore. The sea was open, and nothing to prevent both the French Fleets to put to sea. Well nothing was ready; that precious opportunity, which we can never expect to return was lost.'

By now the French were heartily sick of war but also sick of England, their old *bête noire*. Ireland was key to military success, as the Directory explained in a letter to General Hoche, the man in charge of the Revolutionary Army: 'We intend, Citizen General, to restore the people ripe for revolution the independence and liberty for which it clamours. Ireland has groaned under the hated English yoke for centuries … Detach Ireland from England, and she will be reduced to a second-rate power and deprived of most of her superiority over the seas.'

These revolutionaries, as they so often are, were also evangelists, desperately keen to sell their message of change to others. Having failed in Ireland they would now march on Bristol.

Fishguard at the time had a population of some 2,800. Isolated in large part from the rest of Pembrokeshire, let alone the rest of the world, it was still an important point of export for corn, coal, culm, and produce harvested from the sea. Although the bulk of the population were overwhelmingly loyal to King George and the British state, some radical folk in places such as west Wales knew about the French Revolution and were sympathetic to its ideals. Food was scarce, life expectancy in the low 30s, and the political mood could be defiant, as demonstrated by the strike by coal miners of Hook, Pembrokeshire.

Fishguard was not a town without its defences. A fort, built in 1781, guarded the Bay – erected in part as a response to an attack on the town two years earlier when a privateer called the *Black Prince* shelled the town and took seventeen vessels for ransom. But the fort was not well provisioned in terms of supplies of gunpowder: the governor, Gwynne Vaughan, had to write to London to plead for more, especially as 'the bay and harbour of Fishguard is extremely well calculated to afford shelter to all vessels navigating the Irish Channel.'

Fear of invasion by the French had also led to major fortifications in places such as Milford Haven, which had a level of protection second only to the coastal strip of southern England facing the Channel. You'll see all of them on the ferry out of Pembroke Dock, a sort of open-air museum of military might. Two blockhouses complete with half a dozen cannon had been previously designed by Henry VIII to defend the mouth of the Cleddau estuary. Charles I followed suit seventy years later and erected a fort at Pill. There are two solid forts at Thorne Island and Stack Rock, making a dozen fortifications in all.

All of these defences were irrelevant on 22 February 1797. A small force of French soldiers, augmented by a few Irish and a few American troops and led by an American, William Tate, landed near a largely undefended Fishguard to kickstart what was to be the very last invasion of British soil.

Colonel Tate's invasion force was transported on board four ships – two frigates, *Le Vengeance* and *La Resistance*, a corvette called *La Constance*, and a lugger called *La Vautour*. They were spotted several times as they sped along. The master of a sloop near Lundy Island sent anxious word to the collector of the port of Swansea. People in the Barnstaple area were 'greatly alarmed by the Appearance of three French Frigates and a Lugger … their Appearance had greatly agitated the minds of all Ranks and brought forth the Volunteer companies from all the neighbourhoods.' At mid-morning on 22 February a local landowner, Thomas Williams of Trelethin, trained his telescope on three ships of war passing North Bishop rock. The French captain Commodore Jean Joseph Castagnier left the Bristol Channel and made for Cardigan Bay, exchanging the ship's colours for the British ensign in order to confuse. Then, at noon on Wednesday 22 February 1797 Castagnier spotted St David's Head and at four he dropped anchor. An hour later the troops were landing, sixteen small boats taking their contingents of men to Carreg Wastad Bay along with all their equipment.

Indubitably, they had caught the British government napping, as they believed that any attack had to be on the east coast of England. Indeed, the secretary of war, Henry Dundas's *Memorandum on the Coasts and Bays of Great Britain and Ireland and their General Defence*, stated that 'The coast of the Bristol Channel, St George's Channel & the North of Scotland demand such peculiar and great arrangements to attack them, that they probably do not enter into the contemplation of an Enemy, who has greater objects to aim at nearer at hand.'

There is some doubt whether or not the French landing force was made up of proper, trained soldiers. Hoche had promised Tate 1,500 'resolute and determined' men, 'armed and equipped with provisions for four days, and a double ration of wine and brandy, to recruit them after the fatigues of the journey.' Letters from the time, however, suggest they were irregulars, recruited from prisons, and numbering only 600, all aggrandised with the title of *Deuxième Legion des Frances*, or the Légion noire. Wolfe Tone estimated there were more of them, 1,800 'banditti intended for England and sad blackguards they are.' This idea of a criminal army took hold in the retelling of the story, even though less fanciful accounts, such as J. E. Thomas's *Britain's Last Invasion*, suggests that half of the invading force were in fact grenadiers, thus professional soldiers.

General Hoche's instructions were clear, listing three main objectives: 'The first is, if possible, to raise an insurrection in the country; the second is to interrupt and embarrass the commerce of the country; and the third is to prepare and facilitate the way for a descent. In all countries the poor are the class most prone to insurrection, and this disposition is to be forwarded by distributing money and drink, by inveighing against the government as the cause of the public distress, by facilitating a rising to plunder the public stores and magazines and the property of the rich, whose affluence is the natural subject of envy to the poor.'*

Hoche further encouraged guerrilla warfare: 'The commerce of the enemy in the country is to be interrupted by breaking down bridges, cutting of dykes, and ruining causeways ... plundering all convoys of subsistence, the public stages and wagons, and even the public carriages ... the cutting off of supplies of provisions from the principal towns, burning all vessels and boats in the rivers and canals, destroying magazines, setting fire to docks and coal yards, rope-walks, great manufactories, etc.'

Discipline was strictly imposed, a deadly serious business whereby 'any denunciations against those who join the legion are to be punished by death'.

The weather was kind to the French and so they scaled the cliffs, rolling casks of ammunition with them. This was no mean feat and they incurred their first fatalities. An Irishman, Lieutenant Barry St Leger, headed the advance guard, entrusted to set up headquarters, which they duly did at Trehowel Farm, a mile inland. The farmer, John Mortimer, had already fled along with his family and staff. The unlucky Mortimer had been planning for his wedding and so the house was well provisioned, including his share of wine from the recent wreck of a Portuguese ship. The French 'grenadiers' promptly got drunk and with each glass they raised the invasion plan began to unravel. Or as Mike Parker put it in his typically lively travelogue *Coast to Coast*, 'The would-be conquerors set to the supplies with such relish that they were pissed as newts within hours and unable to threaten anything more than a dormouse. In their drunken confusion, they did manage to raid the church at Llanwnda, nicking a few pewter plates as they went.' There was a rape and two fatalities. A historian who was alive at the time of the invasion, Richard Fenton, reckoned that had they not found the wine the repercussions would have been serious: 'Fishguard, a place totally incompetent to oppose such a force, with all its wealth,

---

* *Bye-gones: Relating to Wales and the Border Counties*, Volume 6, Oswestry, 1882.

its shipping shut up at the time benepped in the harbour, was in sight, and might have become an easy prey: nay, all the county, even to the opulent town of Haverfordwest, might have felt the force of their arms before they could have received any material check.'*

But sozzled soldiers do not an invasion force make: little wonder the historian Gwyn Alf Williams described the whole débâcle as a 'comic-opera landing'. At the time of what might have been the invasion operetta's overture, Colonel Thomas Knox, the man in charge of the Fishguard Volunteers, was, suitably, attending a dinner dance at a splendid farmhouse called Tregwynt, some 4 miles from the landing site. It was the home of the Harries family and fortuitously there is a chatty eyewitness account of how quickly the farmhouse came to resemble the *Marie Celeste*: 'Miss Mary Gwynne Harries ... knew a Mrs Bird who was a niece of an old servant of the family who was a lady's maid to Mrs George Harries and in the house on the night of the ball in 1797. This servant told Mrs Bird that she was serving tea in an ante-room on the news of the French landing and that the hostess and their guests at once took to their carriages and horses, leaving the lights all burning and the supper laid on the table.'

Knox headed straight for Trehowel, encountering folk fleeing the French along the way. News was travelling fast. Britain had been at war with Revolutionary France for four years and so talk of invasion had often been febrile. But it was now a reality and it was time to act. The commanding officer of the Pembrokeshire Militia, Lieutenant Colby, moved the Cardiganshire Militia from Pembroke, where they had been tasked with guarding prisoners of war. Further news flashed around. The Pembroke Volunteers were summoned, as were the Pembrokeshire Yeomanry, thus entrusting the task of repelling the invasion to volunteers as well as a sprinkling of conscripts. Even more locally, the military reservists known as the Fishguard Volunteers or Fishguard Fencibles were called upon, as was the Pembrokeshire Company of Gentlemen and Yeomanry Cavalry. In total these various units added up to 5,000 men. The exact strength of the invading force

---

* Richard Fenton, *A Historical Tour Through Pembrokeshire*, 1811.

wasn't known but it was somewhere between Knox's estimate of 800 to 900 men and the French official figure of 1,229.

Colby gave instructions to Knox to send men in civilian dress to scout out the strength of the enemy, while those in uniform were to make themselves obvious by stationing themselves visibly on vantage points. Knox thought he had insufficient manpower to take on the French so decided to retreat to Haverfordwest to join the main body of men. Under the command of Lord Cawdor, a column was soon on its way to Fishguard.

The French had prepared an ambush at Carn Gelli on the main Haverfordwest to Fishguard road while others were told by Tate to place themselves on high ground at Carnwnda, and make themselves as visible as possible. There was sporadic action across the county. A group of seamen marched from Solva and encountered a group of five Frenchmen, while two men at Llanwnda lost their lives in a skirmish that left one of the French dead as well. Tension rose throughout Pembrokeshire as groups of men marched to the coast from many directions to defend not only a county but a country, civilians hiding for their lives.

The local troops had all gathered in Fishguard by the night of 23 February. Tate was now in a quandary. The intelligence reaching him was that he was outnumbered and to compound his problems those soldiers he could muster had sore heads from too much drinking. A military leader does all he can to avoid defeat, but Tate knew that eventually he must surrender to the inevitable and expose himself to a loser's ignominy.

He despatched his second in command, Baron de Rochemure, to deliver a letter which reads:

Cardigan Bay,
5th of Ventôse, 5th year of the Republic
Sir,
The circumstances under which the Body of the French troops under my command were landed at this place renders it unnecessary to attempt any military operations, as they would tend

only to Bloodshed and Pillage. The Officers of the Whole Corps have therefore intimated their desire of entering into a Negociation upon Principles of Humanity for a surrender. If you are influenced by similar Considerations you may signify the same by the Bearer, and, in the mean Time, Hostilities shall cease.

Health and Respect,

Tate,

Chef de Brigade.

To the officer commanding His Britannick Majesty's Troops*

This offer was summarily rejected and a letter from Cawdor set out his position.

Fishguard

February 23rd 1797

Sir,

The Superiority of the Force under my Command, which is hourly increasing, must prevent my treating upon any Terms short of your surrendering your whole Force Prisoners of war. I enter fully into your Wish of preventing an unnecessary Effusion of Blood, which your speedy Surrender can alone prevent, and which will entitle you to that Consideration it is ever the Wish of British Troops to show an Enemy whose numbers are inferior.

My Major will deliver you this letter and I shall expect your Determination by Ten o'clock, by your Officer, whom I have furnished with an Escort, that will conduct him to me without Molestation.

I am &c.,

Cawdor

To the Officer Commanding the French Troops

---

* Quoted in J.E. Thomas, *Britain's Last Invasion: Fishguard 1797*, Stroud, 2007.

Surrender was inevitable. It took place on Goodwick Sands, where Tate gave up his sword to Cawdor while the bedraggled prisoners waited for a boat to take them round to Fishguard. This took some time to organise, not least because it was hard to muster the Frenchmen, and no doubt to rouse some of them from their wine-steeped slumbers. The men were separated from the officers before they all marched to Haverfordwest – the men on foot, the officers on horseback. The latter were housed in the town's Castle Inn and the next night at the Ivy Bush Hotel in Carmarthen, such accommodation being consonant with the codes of military conduct of the day.

Local legend, meanwhile, has it that the French gave up because they saw Welsh women in traditional dress and believed them to be soldiers: 'In their accustomed Habits, and with the kind of Weapons that several Thousand People appeared with near Fishguard Feby 24th 1797 the Day the French surrendered to Ld. Cawdor & Colonel Colbey's [sic] Troops. The wonderful Effect that the Scarlet Flannel had that Day should never be forgotten … Lord Cawdor very Judiciously placed a considerable number of Women in that Dress, in the rear of his Army, who being considered by the French as regular Troops, contributed in no small degree to that happy and unexpected Surrender.'

There were letters galore about this event while historians, print-makers and writers helped embed the story, and although it is unlikely women were dragooned into helping in this way there would have undoubtedly been some around in traditional blue cloaks, wrapped in red shawls, those being the same colour as a soldier's tunic.

One woman stands proud in local esteem: the cobbler Jemima Nicholas, who is said to have taken soldiers prisoner all by herself. Her memorial stone describes her as 'The Welsh Heroine who boldly marched out to meet the French invaders.' When she died in 1832 the Vicar of Fishguard set down in the parish register an account of 'The woman … called Jemima Vawr, i.e. Jemima the Great, from her heroic acts, she having marched against the French who landed hereabouts in 1797, and being of such personal powers as to be able to overcome most men in a fight. I recollect her well.'

Much of the writing about the invasion casts the Welsh efforts in heroic terms, each sentence pretty much a building block for a local legend. An anonymous Welsh language ballad with the catchy title 'Praise to the Welsh, the men of Pembrokeshire, for seizing the voracious, fiendish enemies, savage plunderers, the French, when they landed in Fishguard,' made the fiends sound even more fiendish:

The French men, sour dregs
Were teeming with steel weapons
Oh! Irascible, furious host
Merciless men

The merciless men had been completely thwarted, The Last Invasion of Britain undone. In Ireland, however, a brief rebellion was successfully fomented in 1798 and bolstered by further invasions, with 11,000 Frenchmen landing in County Mayo and managing to get to within 80 miles of Dublin. Tone's brother was taken, followed by Wolfe Tone himself when a third wave of invasion was dashed by an intercepting English squadron.

* * *

In the Town Hall in Fishguard there's a superb tapestry illustrating the events surrounding the last invasion of British soil. It depicts the invasion force sailing in, the French troops clambering up cliffs, the locals mounting their defence, and the Pembrokeshire militia amassing to face the foreign troops. It was created on the 200th anniversary of the landing in 1992 by three friends, Audrey Walker, Eirian Short and Rozanne Hawksley, who had all been lecturers in the Embroidery Department at Goldsmiths College in London. They, in turn, were assisted by local artist Elizabeth Cramp, who sketched out the dramatic events. The women sourced unbleached cotton fabric from Greece; local builders' merchants donated wood. It's a modern-day equivalent to the Bayeux Tapestry, following the same format and indeed the approach of the medieval embroiderers. In total, seventy-seven people helped make it, using 178 shades of crewel wool, which allowed them to introduce subtle shades to suggest late winter days, candle light and events at night-time into the dramatic tableaux, all telling an extraordinary tale of an invasion and defeat.

16.

WILD GEESE WINTERS

The most exciting sound of my childhood arrived with winter's grip, when wild geese flew over the house at night. We lived on the south coast of Wales, on the rim of the Loughor estuary. On hearing the nocturnal fly-past I would go out to the small back yard to listen to a sound that was, for me, the very distillation of wildness. Honking their way through skies of ink-swirl clouds were small flocks of European White-fronted Geese, flying from their daytime feeding areas on the riverine meadows of the river Tywi to settle at night-time roosts at Whiteford Burrows on the north Gower coast.

At Whiteford stands a disused iron lighthouse and if I was really lucky I would see the small skeins of geese pass in front of a plump moon, their imprinting silhouettes making a Chinese silk lantern of the scene.

Sadly, the numbers of the geese fell, year on year. There were just over a hundred present in the winter of 1992/93, which halved the following year; the last small flock that was present in 1996/7 numbered just a dozen birds. With that the winter skies above my childhood home seemingly fell silent, but the birds still fly on in memory, together with that simple, haunting soundtrack of excited calls.

Nowadays the white-fronted goose is only really found in Wales on the marshes of the Dyfi estuary, and even there the flock is small and unstable in number, mixed occasionally with ones that fly in from

Greenland. Meanwhile the European stronghold of the Greenland white-fronted goose is Ireland, especially the Wexford Slobs. It's therefore an important place, globally speaking, for this is Europe's rarest goose and the Slobs are key winter haunts. Today, Wexford Wildfowl Reserve hosts about two-thirds of Ireland's approximately 12,000 white-fronts, which themselves make up half the world population.

If you come here at either dawn or dusk in winter you can relish a real wildlife spectacle. The skeins fan out in pulsing, dotted ribbons against the grey sky and the musical honking is like that of a ghostly vintage car rally. As the *Irish Times* journalist Paddy Woodworth once described it, 'You are likely to be astounded by the sight of huge flocks of geese shifting, in vast patterns alive with kinetic energy, to and from the sandbanks in the harbour where they roost at night.'*

I decide to walk to the Slobs from Wexford, where, out on the mud in front of the Quays, redshank are the pipers at the gates of dawn, so often they are the early warning system of marsh and estuary – much as blackbirds function on land – as they alert all to intruders and disturbance. The first few miles of wintry trek are mainly past car salesrooms, although I am very impressed by the drive-by launderette on a garage forecourt: a first for me. A farmer is doing his smalls. I have seen the future. But once I leave the main road and saunter down a country lane the landscape looks far more promising, and soon I see my first party of Greenland white-fronted geese, landing without sound in a field of cut beet. It's a food source they apparently adore, and these birds start grazing with avidity only seconds after landing. One bird raises a long neck like a periscope, scanning over hedge-tops for signs of danger while its fellows take brunch, heads to the ground.

The Greenland white-fronted goose was only identified as a sub-species in the middle of the twentieth century, courtesy of one of the pre-eminent naturalists of the day, Sir Peter Scott. He tells the

---

* Paddy Woodworth, 'An utter slob: Wexford's unique wildfowl reserve', *Irish Times*, 9 November 2019, https://www.irishtimes.com/news/environment/an-utter-slob-wexford-s-unique-wildfowl-reserve-1.4073208.

story thus: 'In the 1930s and 1940s the taxonomy of the Palaearctic White-fronted Geese was very confused, especially on those birds breeding in Greenland, whose wintering grounds were then unknown. I had received live hand-raised Whitefronts from West Greenland which had predominantly yellow bills and rather dark plumage. I had also noticed a description in a book by no less an authority than Payne-Galway, a normally reliable source, that the Whitefronts in Ireland had yellow bills.'

A visit to Wexford by Scott confirmed that the white-fronts there were also dark-coloured when he examined some birds that had been shot. This set off a scientific line of enquiry, but the Second World War intervened; by 1948 he and his colleague C. T. Dalgety had gathered enough evidence to propose a new race of white-front, quite distinct from the Russian geese, breeding west of the Greenland icecap and wintering in the British Isles, chiefly in Ireland.

This new race, the Greenland white-fronted goose, was readily accepted by the ornithological world and in the years that followed extensive studies, including ringing, helped expand the knowledge we have about them, notably their migration paths through Iceland into Scotland, Ireland, and that thin scattering into central Wales.

The reserve centre at the Wexford Slobs is shut at the moment so I visit the only hide that's currently open. My luck is in as I chance upon three Wexford-based birdwatchers – Graham Murphy, Nora Young and Declan Roche – who are having a whale of a time taking photographs of some mixed flocks of Brent geese and white-fronts. Graham is engendering envy with his latest purchase, a Nikon D850 full-frame camera which has Nora almost slavering, already calculating how to justify the expenditure should she ever buy one. They're a rum bunch, full of gags and good humour, and it's almost icing on the cake when the birds start to appear right in front of us, the trio snapping away like wildlife paparazzi. At one point we have a 'ringtail' hen harrier and two kestrels mobbing a buzzard, all right in front of the Pat Walsh hide, while a fly-past of whooper swans is like an advert for how white nature can get: dazzling, starch, virginal, pristine. There is a scattering, too, of Greenland white-fronts, but they are much outnumbered by the brents, which, in the distance, look like giant swarms of black insects as they rise and veer. On the lagoon in front of us some goldeneye ducks plop underwater, adding to the day's list and to the general mêlée of excitement as we tried to keep up with all that was going on. The three birders start to discuss where they would go next, having already started the day's watching and snapping at first light. They mention Carne Beach, but are torn between the desire to try somewhere new and staying here, where the birds seem to be magnetised to their cameras: they show each other pretty much every shot and Nora approves of the really good ones, saying, 'You've got the eye: if you've got the eye then everything else tends to be right.' They also discuss photoshopping images and I wonder if the classical bird photographers such as Eric Hosking would approve. I'm not sure, but I know he'd have loved the unbridled enthusiasm on display in the hide: a trio of very happy birdwatchers, verging on the exultant.

* * *

In Ireland the Greenland white-front was colloquially known as the 'bog goose', wintering on open peatlands with little human presence. But during the nineteenth century this habitat was extensively drained and cut for turf, or converted to forestry, but this all coincided, fortuitously, with the reclamation of Wexford Slobs from Wexford Harbour. The Greenlands first arrived here at the beginning of the twentieth century and by 1925 their numbers had increased, reaching 4,000–6,000 birds by the 1940s, leaving traditional haunts in the midland and western bogs. The Greenland white-fronts had virtually replaced the greylags on the North Slob at Wexford but by the 1950s there were signs of a parlous and worrying decline for the race, as numbers plummeted.

One interesting aspect of the Wexford area was the long history of local wildfowling which goes back to 1798 at least, when a ballad called 'Kelley the boy from Killane' made mention of 'my bold Shamelier with your long-barrelled gun from the sea.' The classic *The Fowler in Ireland* (1882) by Sir Ralph Payne-Gallwey noted an octet of fowlers in the area in the mid-nineteenth century: 'The fowlers of Wexford, of whom there are seven or eight, nearly all live on the Point of Rosslare, a bar of sandhills three miles long that protects the harbour from the sea. From this "coign of vantage" these men can spy the whole extent of ooze and water on which the birds are wont to alight. Their fowling is still very primitive, most of their big guns being ignited by flint.'

The first local fowler, in the eighteenth century, had lived in a smack right out on the ooze and his isolation earned him the nickname Robinson Crusoe. There was also Mollie Raven, a one-armed wildfowler who could hold her own with any man and lived an ultra-hard life fowling, fishing, and raking for cockles. Later, Andy Bent, the fowler who shot specimens for Peter Scott, was called 'Iron Man' because he punted in his bare feet and slept with the window wide open so he could hear the wigeon at sunrise, their high whistling calls acting as his alarm clock.

The target species included ducks such as wigeon, and the commonest geese they shot were brent geese. The fowler tried to navigate his punt, or 'float' as they were known locally, as close as he could to the waterfowl: 'The shooter lies face downwards, and paddles over either side if the water be deep; but if shallow, he pushes with two short setting poles. He directs his craft as straight on the fowl as he can steer her, and pulls the trigger by hand when in shot, dropping at the same time his paddles or poles, which, as usual, are secured by strings to the gunwale. The elevation of the gun cannot be altered, and a flying shot is well-nigh impossible. The Wexford men, nevertheless, bag large numbers of fowl, mostly Widgeon and Brent Geese, which latter, as usual, are misnamed "Bernicle."'

This local misnomer echoes the Latin name of the brent goose, *Branta bernicla*, and a historian just across the water, the seventeenth-century Pembrokeshire writer George Owen, once cheerfully explained its provenance, which was, as explanations go, strictly in the category marked bonkers: 'This fatherless bird is bred of no parent but engendered by secret nature out of some piece of timber remaining long in the salt water, out of which, upon long strings or ropes, shall be seen ten, twenty or thirty of these birds growing out of two shells, like mussel shells, having the perfect form of a fowl, some ripe, ready to fall off, having wings, legs and buds of feathers, hanging only by the bill.'

Yet Owen, to be fair to him, was only passing on the knowledge of the time: a belief that geese grew out of seashells, shook themselves into life, then flew away.

The guns the Wexford fowlers used were often very substantial, up to ten or eleven feet long, and carrying one to one-and-a-half pounds of shot. Imagine a drainpipe filled with explosives aiming lead shot across the marshes or fowling guns the size of mini-howitzers and you'll be close to it.

The area offered such good shooting that visitors came here in droves to try their hand, with some travelling a very long way to do so. One such shooter was the Saudi Arabian Prince, Faisal Ibn Saud, who came with his retinue to stay at Michael O'Connor's Shooting Lodge at North Slob. The Royal Prince came with his cousin, Prince Abadulla of Qusaibi, and they were escorted there by a representative from the British Colonial Office: John Philby, the father of the British undercover agent famously known as 'The Third Man'. They probably avoided playing 'I-Spy' for diplomatic reasons.

* * *

The naming of birds in the Wexford area is fascinating. The local Wexford dialect, known as 'Forth and Bargy', or 'Yola', had alternative names for many birds, and listing them is a delightful process. The red-throated diver was a far outer, while its relative the great northern diver was a say lamb or loon. The little grebe, sometimes known as a dabchick, was known in Wexford as a dipchick. There isn't a dialect name for the Greenland white-fronted goose, simply explained because the goose arrived here after the demise of Yola. It has an Irish name, of course, *Gé bhánéadanach*.

Some of the commoner water-birds had their own litany of names so that the grey heron was cauchees, cawchee, granny, granny goose, granny cureask, ganny gureask, *and* crane. Not only were brent geese known as bernicle, but the barnacle was also known by the same name. Wigeon too had a local name, the whinnard, while a mallard might be known as duuks, digger or dig, while a teal was locally called a tail. The number of names proliferated depending on how common they were. The same is true in Welsh, where a familiar bird, such as the pied wagtail, so closely associated with farming, has a string of names longer than its own tail. So, on a stretch of coast such as Wexford's, where the cormorants are common, the bird has been variously baptised as black diver, clack shag, black hag, frole, and the lovely-sounding cawmurl. The list goes on. A lapwing's names are a found poem in themselves: laupeen, lapeen, peewee, Philip-a-wee, Phillip-o-week and green plover. The jack snipe, which is smaller than a snipe, is therefore known in these parts as half snipe, though it's not quite that much smaller. The whimbrel, which arrives in May, is the Maybird, while the wood pigeon names are a little triad of great variety – quest, woodquest and cooloor, which carries a soft echo of its cooing. A lovely name. But the loveliest name of all, perhaps, is the collective term for small waders such as sanderling, dunlin and turnstone, all known as sea mice, which one can imagine scurrying along the shoreline.

* * *

Ringing and radio-tagging research has shown that the vast majority of Ireland's wintering white-fronts breed in Greenland, stopping off in Iceland. Hunting bans here, and ultimately in Iceland, boosted populations up to the turn of the last century. A severe decline since then is blamed partly on climate change impacts on the breeding grounds.

All these factors, plus the vital nearby access to sandbars for safe night roosts, have made the North Slob a 'honeypot' for this species. Yet they are, as we know, relatively new to the area. They were first noticed in the 1910s, though other geese, especially the greylag, had long been thriving on the new fields, as had smaller wildfowl. This made the Slob very popular with hunters. As the geese numbers in

Ireland declined, so concern about shooting grew and in the winter of 1982/1983 a moratorium was introduced – much earlier than the one in Wales of 2018 – and research intensified. This included marking schemes in Ireland, Iceland and Greenland, and helped find out a great deal about social structures in such a family-orientated bird, where virtually all of the goslings remain with one or other parent throughout their first winter. There are definite patterns of movement and faithfulness to the sites this goose uses: one individual was traced travelling to Greenland before falling in with a group of Canada geese and flying all the way to Pennsylvania, before returning to North Slob the following winter.

* * *

The conversion of the land on the North Slobs was the brainchild of, among others, Limerick's William Dargan, the brilliant engineer who established the Irish rail network (and helped set up the National Gallery). A major local figure was John Edmond Redmond, great uncle of the Nationalist Party leader. Legislation was introduced in the Houses of Parliament in London on 18 August 1846 to reclaim land on both the North and South Slobs.

They first created a polder, a landscape feature familiar in the Netherlands, but very rare here. This involved building a sea wall between the slob and the harbour area and a roughly semi-circular canal behind it, enclosing 2,400 acres. The work started in 1847 with an assault on the north side of the harbour, when labourers drawn from all parts of the county set to it with nothing more sophisticated than spades, sprongs, shovels, picks, and the sweat of their brows.

This canal intercepts flows of fresh water from the higher land surrounding the former marsh. The most challenging engineering feat was the construction of a pumping system to expel this water into the sea when canal levels rose.

The slob is still drained on this basis today, and the resulting land-scape has proved super productive for grazing and cereals. From an aesthetic point of view, however, other than the excitements of winter birds such as the geese, whooper swans and legions of waterfowl, it is a pretty dull prospect of flatlands, of arable crops unbroken by hedgerows.

Monocultural rye grass alternates with monocultural barley stubble and for the white-fronts it is all a diner's delight. The strolling geese avidly gobble up the rye grass, their stubby bills hoover up the shoots from spilt barley, and they are particularly partial to fodder beet. As seven-year old John Nolan from St Ibar's National School in Castlebridge once put it:

> My favorite food to eat,
> Is grass, corn and beet,
> Although Greenland is my home,
> To Ireland I like to roam.

That beloved beet is planted by the National Parks and Wildlife Service, and mechanically 'lifted' when mature, then left on the ground for the geese to savour. The birds like feeding out in the open, giving them the advantage of seeing danger at a distance. Then, over the course of the winter they graze and plump, plump and graze, putting on the necessary fat to make their next long-haul flight.

And with the lengthening days comes a growing excitement, as some inner clock triggers the need to migrate, to depart for the western edge of Greenland, to places such as the upland tundra of Eqalungmiut Nunât, 'Land of the Fisherfolk', on the edge of the Greenland Ice Sheet, and to the ice-smoothed, lichen-encrusted land around Kûp Akua, 'where the waters meet or mix'.

From the south of Ireland to the northern rim of the world they fly, their metronome wing beats a slow, feathery sky-drumming, as the days turn into dazzle and the air is cleaved by their determined chevrons.

PART THREE

THE OPEN SEA

'Out of the sea have come ideas, peoples, treasures and disasters – war bands, travelling saints, visiting giants, orange trees from wrecked galleons, wines from torpedoed freighters, Irishmen, pirates, even it is said the entire clan of Morgans, whose name means Born of the Sea, and who are sometimes said to to be descended from mermaids.'

Jan Morris, The Matter of Wales

17.

SAINTLY SEAWAYS

As tongue-twisters go, the name Modomnoc of Ossory is certainly in the premier league, but his is among the sweetest connections between Wales and Ireland. Modomnoc, also known as Dominic, was a descendant of the O'Neill clan in Ulster, one of the minor-league saints. A disciple of St David, and a talented beekeeper to boot, Modomnoc was known for talking to the insects while the bees he tended in special straw-filled hives formed frenetic clouds around his head. The bees produced super-abundant honey and he had to get help to carry the summer's harvest to the monastery.

After studying in Wales this apiarist saint left for Ireland in a small boat, but legend has it that as he travelled slowly west the bees duly swarmed after him as if Modomnoc's head was lathed in flower nectar. Alright, that last bit was a tad embellished but that's how these things work, changing from one teller to the next.

Modomnoc had only managed to get 3 miles out to sea before the little swarming bee-clouds joined him, forcing him to turn back. Worried that he would be depriving the monks at the Mynyw community of honey, he returned to land, there explaining all to St David. He in turn suggested that Modomnoc should resume his journey – if need be, bees and all, and with his blessing. As with many such tales, it wasn't until his third attempt that he settled his small charges in a temporary shelter on the boat and made the crossing.

Once he'd settled in his new home – a church he built at Bremor near the town of Balbriggan near Dublin – Modomnoc settled his nectar-seeking charges in a quiet corner of the monastery garden, where he planted the kind of flowers his workaholic charges loved best. It's little wonder Modmonoc became the patron saint of bees and beekeeping.

Modomnoc was just one of a small legion of holy men who plied the waters of the Irish Sea and beyond. It's now some 1,500 years since they took to the sea in simple craft to extend their missions, taking the western routes that led from the Mediterranean to Brittany, Cornwall, Wales and Ireland. Some of them even visited Rome and Jerusalem as part of their quest for spiritual enlightenment before setting up simple mission stations and religious houses, often in remote, or very remote, spots.

One of those was the place St David chose for an early church in a hidden Pembrokeshire valley leading to the sea, a place both isolated and elemental. This suited him fine. The vegetarian St David was notably ascetic, living on leeks and dealing with the lusts of the flesh by giving himself shock treatment by immersion in cold water. It seems to have worked, because he reputedly withstood attempts to tempt him, engineered by an Irish chieftain called Boia. Boia's wife sent her maids to dance naked in front of David and his monks, yet they refused their carnal blandishments, while a heavenly fire set Boia's house ablaze as if by way of divine response.

Other stories about his abilities abound. He was a miracle child, quite literally: The infant David wrought a miracle even at his baptism, giving a blind man sight, an act he repeated with his teacher Paulinus. Little wonder that St David's cult grew to be so popular, with more than a thousand churches dedicated to him. Of course, churches dedicated to particular saints might not have been established during the lifetime of the saint in question. Powerful cathedral churches placed their own patron saint over many of the churches in their control, so perhaps the number of churches dedicated to St David simply expresses the power of the see of St David's in the Middle Ages.

The Irish *Catalogue of Saints*, written circa 730, contains the first reference to St David's voyages and tells how the Irish were given mass by him and fellow travellers Gildas and Teilo from Brittany. The strong links beween Waterford and Wales meant that David's first contact with an Irish priest was early in his life. Shortly after his birth he was baptised in the small harbour of Porthclais by St Elvis, bishop of Emlech in Ireland. David, who would have many followers in Éire, used such small harbours to access the coasts of Waterford, Wexford and Wicklow, where he then possibly connected with Irish saints such as Aidan, Finnian of Clonard, Ailbe, Declan, and Senan, whom he visited at his settlement on the Shannon.

The early Welsh saints, seldom canonised by Rome, are often imagined as solitary holy men living the simplest possible life in a rocky cell. This form of stripped-down and pared-back Christianity owed its origins to the likes of the hermits of Cyrenaica and the Desert Fathers, whose presence in desert and sometimes sea-girt places is reflected in the many Welsh place names such as Diserth, or Dyserth, although it can also mean deserted place. St Martin, who became the Bishop of Tours, ushered in a new spirit in religion with the introduction of eastern mysticism coupled with the need to seek a 'desert' place for solitary contemplation and worship to the point of suffering in caves and caverns. Hardship was equated with holiness. Washing was seen as too much luxury and lice in hair and on body were regarded as 'pearls of God'.

A good example of a classic early Welsh chapel is St Govans, set in a cleft of Pembrokeshire rock, memorably described by Trevor Fishlock as seeming 'to have fallen from the cliff and lodged in the gully below like a shilling in a sofa.'* An earlier chronicler, Richard Fenton, noted the way in which the steep steps down to this remote holy site were 'worn smooth by the feet of the curious, the superstitious and the invalid who for ages have visited this pious isolation.'† You only have to

---

* Trevor Fishlock, *Pembrokeshire Journeys and Stories*, Llandysul, 2011.

† Richard Fenton, *Historical Tours Through Pembrokeshire*, https:// wellcomecollection.org/works/bz76fh54.

pause there awhile, listening to the wash of the waves and the whisper of the wind, to know something about the saintliness of things.

* * *

Sea routes from the south, reaching out towards the Mediterranean, brought the Gallic, Spanish and even the African world into contact with places such as southern Ireland and south-west Wales. The Celtic Church was a huge beneficiary of these sea-lanes, with an exchange of saints and scholars in both directions. A pivotal figure was St Illtud, who was a 'renowned teacher of the Britons, learned in teachings of the Church, in Latin culture and in the teachings of his own people,' and established Irish-style monasteries in his birthplace at Llantwit Major as well as in Bangor and Llandeilo. Similarly, Llanbadarn Fawr near Aberystwyth had close links with Ireland and was an important seat of learning: by the eleventh century it had a library bigger than Canterbury Cathedral or York Minster. Because of the production of illuminated mansucripts at such centres, monks became a small import market in themselves as they needed special products to help them produce their colourful manuscripts. Lapis lazuli came from Afghanistan and indigo from Europe to produce ink that was a deep, rich blue, while some of the pinks and purples came from a sunflower than shone in the eastern Mediterranean. Reds meanwhile came from cochineal, produced by crushing beetles from North Africa and southern Europe. A myriad of ingredients.

The main route from Ireland to Rome lay across south Wales, with trackways from Porthglais near St David's and thence to the south of the Preseli Mountains, to Carmarthen or Moridunum. From here an important branch of the route headed north-east following the wide valley of the river Tywi and skirting Brecon to connect with the lush watercourses of the rivers Wye and Usk. Travellers used the routes in both directions, of course. A twelfth-century manuscript, *De Situ Brecheniauc*, contains an account of Marchell, daughter of Tewdrig and mother of Brychan Brycheiniog, who followed this route from the area which is now Breconshire to Ireland, via Porthmawr, to marry an Irish prince. The journey was undertaken in a very harsh winter and many of the warriors who went with her perished en route because of night frosts which attacked the party with the savagery of a wild boar; Marchell, meanwhile, was wrapped up in her father's gift of a garment made of deep fur. This little story underlines the very strong connection between the early post-Roman kingdom of Brycheiniog and Brychan, a king who straddled history and legend, giving his name to the territory of Brycheiniog. Brychan – which means little badger – was the head of a very substantial family: he had twelve sons and twelve daughters, quite a sett.

In the so-called Age of Saints there were nine churches in south-west Wales dedicated to Brynach Wyddel – Brynach the Irishman – whose *Life* connects him with King Brychan. Churches dedicated to Brynach overlap with the presence of Ogham stones, notably in Brynach's most important church at Nevern in north Pembrokeshire. In Ireland there are several instances of Ogham stones being set up near the oratory or monastic cell of a Celtic saint, such as St Monchan's cell near Dingle in Co. Kerry.

Brynach was reputedly an Irishman of noble pedigree whose saintly adventures included slaying a monster on his way to Rome and travelling back to Wales, via Brittany, on the back of a piece of slate. He survived an assassination attempt by a woman whose advances he'd rejected and the would-be killers died from the effects of a plague of lice. He was then beset by evil spirits until a white sow and her offspring led him to the place where he should establish his church, after which he exerted a strange power over animals. Wild stags pulled his cart, a wolf shepherded his cow and when the animal was stolen the thief couldn't start a fire to roast it. Word spread about the saint like holy wildfire and soon he was pretty much beset by would-be disciples. So he took himself up a mountain, in this case Carn Ingli, the Mount of Angels above Nevern, where he conversed with angelic visitors, as was his wont.

For the early Christians, often upgraded to saints, the seas were superhighways: as the historian Gwyn Alf Williams put it, 'in the sixth century St David's was a veritable Crewe Junction of the

sea-routes which laced the Irish Sea and the Western Approaches.'*
Columba, for example, departed Howth near Dublin, bound for Iona
in a small leather boat, or curragh. This was a small boat made of
ox-hides sewn together, then stretched tightly over a wooden frame
– cowhide tugged taut on ribs of hazel – and sealed with wool grease.
Near Columba's landing place there's a bay called Port na Curraigh,
the port of the curragh. Teilo travelled from Wales to Rome in the
company of St David, and later took the sea-route to settle down in
Cornwall. The sea could also be an escape route: St Tysilio fled the
aptly named Church Island in the Menai Strait to either avoid Anglo-
Saxon invaders or the unwanted attention of his brother's widow.

Some saints travelled much, much further – such as Brendan of
Clonfort, a.k.a. Brendan the Navigator, who navigated across the
Atlantic in the company of fourteen other monks, making landfall in
Labrador, an extraordinary feat for a skin-clad boat crossing wild wide
ocean. They were looking for what they described as the 'Promised
Land', and using their knowledge that the world was round, 'like a
well-formed apple,' they headed west, following Hesperus, the
Evening Star, as their guiding celestial light.

Women peregrinators set sail as well, such as St Keyne, who left
Wales in a coracle and arrived in Cornwall where the village of St
Keyne commemorates her arrival. St Kywere, meanwhile, is thought
to have travelled on to Ireland, and carried on her missionary work in
Wicklow. Some of the earliest Irish monasteries were founded by
women. A famous nun was Brigit, named after Brígh, the Celtic
goddess of fire and light. When Gerald of Wales visited her monastery
in the twelfth century he saw a fire that her nuns carefully tended
'surrounded by a circular withy hedge, which men are not allowed to
enter.' Many churches in Wales are dedicated to her, such as
Llansanffraid (the church of St Bride's) while St Bride's Bay is a beautiful half-moon of sea named after her.

In the fifth century many saints or peregrini wandered the coun-
tyside, either alone or with a small band of followers, stopping to set

---

* Gwyn A. Williams, *When Was Wales?*, London, 1985.

up small beehive cells or maybe a wooden preaching cross. The place where such a holy man lived would be sanctified: a little church might grow up at the site, first in wattle and daub, then in timber and perhaps then in stone. These helped spread Celtic Christianity far and wide. Voyagers such as Seiriol, Cadfan and Deiniol were the basis for well-known cults, and these can help trace how saints were commemorated in various places. Thus Carantoc doubles-up as the patron of Dulane in County Meath under his Irish name Cairnach, but also appears on the coast of west Wales in Llangrannog and in Llandudoch.

One well-known coastal Welsh chapel is St Patrick's chapel on the shore at Whitesands Bay in Pembrokeshire. Here a rectangular mound stood in a field known as Parc-y-Capel close to the shore. When this was excavated in 1926 they found the outline of a rectangular chapel of a single-cell type with human remains under the west wall. Others might have been buried under the chapel floor, which was a feature of such Celtic chapels. This had been known as St Patrick's chapel going back to the reign of Queen Elizabeth, and Whitesands Bay – Porth Mawr – was an important point for pilgrims going to and from Ireland. They also travelled from this pilgrim port for other, more venal reasons, such as the copper and gold that was to be found in the Wicklow hills. But pilgrims far outnumbered prospectors. George Owen pointed out that 'there were formerly several chapels about St David's, which all belonged to the mother church, dedicated to several saints ... all the chapels are near the seaside and adjoining to the places where those that come by sea commonly landed. They were placed here to the devotion of the seamen and passengers when they first came ashore: other pilgrims us'd likewise to come to them.' The surrounding area, Dewisland or Pebidiog, connected with many places in Wales, Ireland, the Isle of Man and western England.

* * *

Patrick was captured by a raiding party as a young boy in Cumbria to be sold as a slave in Ireland. After six years he eventually escaped to Gaul on a boat carrying a baying cargo of hunting dogs. There he took the name Patrick and returned to Ireland to undertake missionary work in the north, setting up a church in a barn in Ulster and confronting the pagans on the Hill of Slane, an event which ended with King Laoghaire being baptised. Subsequent ecclesiastical publicists argued for his primacy over other saints, an argument which was clearly won, as anyone who has seen the Chicago river run green on St Patrick's Day will attest.

Stories abound about Ireland's patron saint: he managed to get rid of all the demons and snakes on the island; his crozier was actually the staff of Christ, given to him personally as a holy relic; he explained the concept of the Trinity to King Laoghaire using a three-leafed clover, more familiar perhaps as the shamrock. The place where Patrick grew up before he was seized by slavers was called Bannavem Taberniae, and the people of the Welsh village of Banwen, on the northern edge of the south Wales coalfield, have laid claim to this being Bannavem. The local historian and short story writer George Brinley Evans has managed to promote the idea so successfully that each year the likes of RTÉ interview him on or around St Patrick's Day.

Surprisingly perhaps, Patrick only has three Welsh churches dedicated to him, one being at Llanbadrig on the north coast of Anglesey. It's a remote spot with the name apparent also on a rocky islet half a mile offshore named Ynys Badrig (St Patrick's Isle). Also on the mainland, a cave with a freshwater well situated halfway up a cliff, was also named after him. There's a standing stone at the church itself which features carvings of crossed fish and palm trees resembling carvings found in Roman catacombs and churches in the Near East.

One of the most intriguing places connected with Patrick is Sarn Padrig, an undersea ridge south-westwards of the high peak of Cader Idris, designed by higher powers to make Ireland more accessible to saints. In truth it's what's left of a glacial moraine formed 20,000 years ago, when Cardigan Bay was full of cracking and shifting ice rather than sea-water. At very low water parts of the reef appear like a causeway, and local legend has it that a couple of centuries ago the remains of houses were sighted along this rocky spine. Miracles do happen.

18.

A TUMULT OF TEMPESTS

The Irish Sea can be a place of one raging gale after another, making shingle seethe, turning waves into battering rams, and causing the surf to boom like cannons. There have been great historical storms matched by more recent events such as 1957's Hurricane Carrie which on making landfall actually toppled the lighthouse at Bray, Co. Wicklow, into the sea, tempting local wags to suggest they now had the world's only lighthouse for submarines.

Shipping Forecast sea areas Lundy, Fastnet and Irish Sea, the ones which pertain in this book, often have a tempestuous time of it. As a storm gathers the weather map's isobars close and tighten until they look like the contours on the map of a steep-sided hill. The building sea rises like a wild green escarpment, mountainous waves pile up – towering 30 feet or more – to be topped by snowy peaks of spume. The barometer pressure drops, signalling a meteorological depression with all its attendant wet and windy weather. It all whips up, waves churning in wild slop and surge.

As the wind blows across the Irish Sea some big swells can form, leading to rough and heavy weather for those unfortunate enough to be at sea. Waves on an open sea can travel at almost three-quarters the speed of the wind itself so the swell can seemingly outpace the full brunt of a storm, acting as a precursor of heavy weather coming in – announcing it's time to well and truly batten down the hatches.

*   *   *

James Joyce, with his penchant for portmanteau words and neologisms – often banging two words together like a ship's blacksmith to create something new – would have had fun whipping up a verbal storm. The man who gave us 'the sea, the snotgreen sea, the scrotum-tightening sea' crossed the Irish sea pretty often, once to meet W. B. Yeats near Euston in London in a rare meeting of poetic minds. So Joyce might have served up some whipwinds and churnwinds, gale-blasts and blastgales – the latter blowing in the opposite direction of course. There'd be agitbroths of spumewhite and blastornado hell-winds setting off all the wild bells keening in the rigging. Oh had he but glorytime enough to madpen such stuff!

It's been suggested that 'One way of writing about the Irish Sea was to deny its roughness, as if to refute the suggestion that Ireland was not ready for incorporation into empire, a "strange country" resistant to improvement and exploitation. Such a defensive formulation began to emerge in the seventeenth-century, even as Cromwell's body started to churn up the sea.'* The earliest natural history of Ireland by the Dutch physician Gerard Boate appeared in 1672. It has a chapter calmly, or calmingly, entitled 'The Irish Sea not so tempestuous as it is bruited to be'. In this he was flying in the face of the opinion of the inveterate map-maker John Speed, who appraised the Irish Sea as one 'whose rage with such vehemency beateth against her bankes, that it is thought and said, some quantity of the Land hath been swallowed up by those Seas'. He wasn't alone in such a view. The Pembrokeshire historian George Owen backed up Speed's assessment when he maintained that the unyielding, land-eroding sea off Pembroke was 'dealeinge so unkindely with this poore Countrey as that it doth not in any where seeme to yeld

---

* In Claire Connolly, 'Too rough for verse? Sea crossings in Irish Culture', in Leerssen, J. (ed.) *Parnell and his Times*, Cambridge: Cambridge University Press, 2020. This chapter, originally delivered as the Parnell Lecture at Magdalene College, Cambridge is both touchstone and lodestone for *The Turning Tide*. This present volume would be all the poorer without it.

to the lande in anye parte, but in everye corner thereof eateth upp parte of the mayne.'

Boate, who hadn't actually visited Ireland before he wrote his natural history, nevertheless felt expert enough to investigate 'the Nature of the Irish Sea, and of the Tides which go in it,' averring that 'that part of the Irish sea which divideth Ireland from Great Britain, is very much defamed both by ancient and modern writers, in regard of its boysterousness and tempestuousness, as if it were more subject to storms and raging weather than any other, and consequently not to be passed without very great danger.' Boate goes on to challenge the wisdom of a proverb that suggests that something may be as 'as unquiet as the Irish Sea' by marshalling historical evidence that 'the Irish sea is quiet enough, except when by high winds it is stirred, so as not only in the summer, but even in the midst of winter people do pass it to and fro ... True it is that some ships do perish upon this, but the same happeneth also upon other seas, who are all subject to the disaster of tempests and shipwracks.' Such writing wasn't just natural history, it was also propaganda: it appeared at a time when attempts were being made to lure adventurers, planters and investors to settle in Ireland, and so promising calm passage and easy two-way access was an essential component of the colonial project. It's the same sort of flagrant abuse of advertising standards that had parched areas of Patagonia being described as lush with shoulder-high grass when attempting to attract Welsh settlers to move there in the middle of the nineteenth century.

*　*　*

The modern way of storm-spotting involves studying weather patterns, crunching data, using computer projections to tell us about what might happen today, tomorrow and ten days hence. In the old days you might have visited someone such as the blacksmith in Holyhead at his forge. Here in the mid-nineteenth century he would, with the aid of a barometer of local renown, concoct a daily weather forecast, beginning 'I prognosticate ...' His prediction was then pinned up on the gable wall of the nearby Lord Nelson pub 'and skippers of sailing vessels wind-bound read the predictions – generally of "stormy weather" – and then turned into the Black Lion.' In Holyhead another local weatherman called Wheldon was much revered, almost to the point of being an oracle: his weather-divining quadrant was hung reverently in St Cybi's church as if it were a holy relic. Then there was the very long-range forecaster Robert Roberts, whose forecasts were included in annual almanacs, based as they were on skilful use of his telescope, which he would use both to map the stars and pick up signals for the packet ships from a tower atop his house. It was a bit more scientific than a system described in *The Folklore of Wales*: 'In some parts of Wales the coast people say they see white hares before winter storms, and the howling of dogs foretokens a south-westerly gale.'

* * *

Stand on a wild day on a headland such as St Ann's Head near the mouth of Milford Haven and you may not see white hares but you'll swear you can hear the anemometers at the lighthouse whirr like kids' fidget-spinners above the seethe. Waves turn into churches, steeples, great wet crags of seawater. They build and they build and they build, before unleashing their furious force. Sieging seas such as those that manifest increasingly in the winter, when they seem to want to dismantle the land, undermining the very cliffs and rupturing the rugged headlands built of older, tougher rocks. The whirring silver cups of the anemometers of St Ann's Head register up to thirty gales a year and their speeds can register on the gauges as if on the speedometer of a Formula 1 racing car, blasting in at 100 mph.

The northern coast can be just as windy, as King George IV found out when contrary winds stopped him leaving Holyhead on the royal Yacht, *Royal George*, before he decided to continue his state visit on the steam mail-packet *Lightning*.

The Irish Sea fully earns its reputation as 'one of the worst hazards of the Atlantic crossing' secured by its 'baffling combination of havens and hazards.' The combination of strong tides and a shallow coastal seabed make navigation tricky. As one commentator assessed: 'The whole of this coast is dangerous, even to a proverb; and many sea captains have declared they felt more anxiety in going from Holyhead to Liverpool, than in their passage from the West Indies to England.'

Some stretches of water are said to be particularly dangerous, with jagged dentitions of rock jutting up from underwater reefs. One patch of sea between Dublin and Holyhead is said to be treacherous because the body of a widely despised man was said to be buried there. An oft repeated folk story, now deepened into legend, has it that Oliver Cromwell died in Ireland and was interred in its soil but the very earth rejected him, ejecting his coffin each and every night. It was finally cast into the sea, sinking down between Holyhead and Dublin, causing this stretch to be turbulent ever since, as if the very waters are troubled by his unquiet spirit.

September, at the tail end of the Atlantic hurricane season, can herald some ferocious storms, as I well know. The one in 1976 blew the roof off our newly erected bungalow on the south Wales coast, almost killing my father as the timbers and tiles came raining down. It was an Act of God that sent him outside for a smoke at just the right moment. I also remember it bringing in seabirds from deep ocean, storm petrels and grey phalaropes that made stormy days memorable for coastal birdwatchers. My dad wasn't so enthusiastic about the rare birds blown in, although he probably dragged hard at his Golden Virginia rollie with some sense of relief. Maybe went to chapel to give thanks.

One of the most dramatic Irish Sea shipwrecks – in a sea which specialised in high drama and high winds – was at Druidston Haven in Pembrokeshire. Here in 1791 a boat called the *Increase of Scarborough* ran aground, attracting the attention of locals, who swept in like gulls to see what they could salvage before she went down. Unbeknown to the plunderers, the ship was carrying a cargo of gunpowder, and in the act of scavenging, a piece of metal thrown onto the shore caused a spark which in turn ignited a mighty explosion, killing eight people.

There were other storms of equal severity. One threw up some pretty remarkable flotsam in nearby Newgale. This was a mad storm that Geraldus Cambrensis described in his *Journey around Wales*. It raged 'so fiercely that conger-eels and many sea-fish were driven on the high rocks and into the bushes by the wind, and there men came to gather them.' Cod on the rocks, perhaps, or herring hanging on blackthorn – which had its own poetic resonance, as there was a tradition of Pembrokeshire fishermen making simple hooks from the barbed thorns of this spiny tree. The storm also exposed sandy shores 'laid bare by the extraordinary violence of a storm' and 'the trunk of trees cut off, standing in the sea itself, the strokes of the hatchet appearing as if made yesterday.' Black, twisted and glistening, these tree trunks, set in beds of ancient peat deposits, revealed as the sand was scoured away, were stubborn remnants of a forest that grew here 5,000 to 6,000 years ago. The skull of an auroch – a huge kind of cattle that grazed hereabouts in prehistoric times – was discovered on this wind-battered stretch of coast in 2015.

* * *

Mike Alexander, who wardened Skomer Island for ten years, knows full well how winds can turn placid seas into raging torrents and can be strong enough to make breathing difficult. In his compendious book about the island, called simply *Skomer Island*, he recalls how, turning away from the wind: 'You are propelled forward, running and stumbling, almost out of control; it is exhilarating, frightening and quite overwhelming. It can be impossible to stand upright, and the storms can only be viewed by crouching low in the lee of the rock. Huge crashing waves carry "green water" over the cliff top, the saltwater running in rivulets over the saturated ground. Sea spray flying over the cliff tops is carried inland, to envelop and soak the island. Sometimes the foaming spindrift racing through the air is so thick and heavy it can give the impression of a snowstorm.'

In light of such ferocious winds, it's little wonder that some parts of Skomer Island are classified as 'Ballantine 1'. On the scale that measures the degree of exposure of a rocky shore to wave action, number 8 describes 'becalmed and sheltered shores' and number 1 the most exposed. Skomer Head is world-ranking in this sense, a top-ten chart topper when it comes to tumult.

Some historical storms in this sea-area have reached perfectly gargantuan proportions. The worst storm in British and Irish history was a cyclone from the north Atlantic that hammered in on the evening of 26 November 1703. It swept 'every obstacle before it from the surface of the earth.' Some thought the Day of Judgment had arrived early, not least when the tally of the dead – 8,000 people – was finally counted. It had been a calm day, but as darkness settled so did the wind pipe up, as the *Dublin Evening Post* recorded: 'About half past ten it rose into a high gale, which continued to increase in fury until shortly after midnight, when it blew a most fearful and destructive tempest.'

The usual warnings of bad weather had been absent. No rings around the moon, no red moons or red skies. No dogs eating grass, pigs showing distress or cats scraping chairs to intimate a storm on the way. But because this happened on 5 January, the Feast of Ceara, when the fairies held their revels in Erin, they got the blame for things going wrong or nature blowing up a storm. They set off quite a few storms. In *The Elder Faiths of Ireland*, Wood-Martin said of the fairies: 'That their last great assembly was in the year 1839, when violent disputes arose ... and the night following a large portion of the fairy host quitted the Green Isle, never to return. The hurricane they raised was long referred to by the peasantry as "The Night of the Big Wind".'

Irish fairies were said to be wingless and flew by whipping up a whirlwind, the *sidhe gaoithe* or *side chora*, and this one in 1839 was the wild, whirling mother of them all.

Fairy-originated or not, another storm in 1703 pounded the land like meteorological artillery. Houses rocked all over the country. In the Wicklow mountains, Ordnance Surveyor John O'Donovan felt his hostel rock under him 'like a ship.' On the streets of Dublin the aurora borealis burned brightly, 'mantling the hemisphere with sheets of red.' And of course there were many wrecks. Two dozen ships came to grief in the Irish Sea alone, including the sleek transatlantic liner the *Pennsylvania*, which was wrecked, then looted, off Liverpool.

Then there were the packets *St Andrews* and *Oxford* and the emigrant ship the *Lockwoods*, which lost fifty-two passengers, many of them from Ireland bound for New York under the aegis of the city of Dublin Steam Packet Company. In Ross, Co. Wexford the *Catherine*, out of Newcastle, 'struck on the south tongue of our very dangerous bar' and its crew abandoned ship along with its cargo of timber. Many fishermen lost their lives near the Skerries in County Dublin, where nine boats each carrying a crew of nine or ten men were tragically lost, leaving their tightly-knit communities marooned in grief. Some ships did get through, but as the *Liverpool Mail* reported, the 'mail, which left port at five o'clock on Sunday afternoon, did not reach Kingstown until four o'clock this morning, having occupied thirty-five hours in the passage, which was one of the most perilous on record.'

Assessing the aftermath, the *Dublin Evening Mail* described a 'sacked city with houses burning, others unroofed, as by storm of shot and shell, a few levelled with the ground.' In Wales it tore down much of the Menai Bridge, which was one of the engineering marvels of its day, and an essential link on the route between London and Dublin was broken.

One of the eyewitnesses to the cyclone of 1703 was the novelist Daniel Defoe, who had just been released from prison for his 'seditious' writings. Despairing and bankrupt, the storm – which left cows stranded in the branches of trees and set windmills ablaze by the mad friction of their whirling sails – must have matched his downcast, shattered mood. Nevertheless, as an eyewitness to such wholescale devastation, it offered him a powerful subject for his first book. *The Storm* melded his own words with eye-witness accounts from those who had experienced nature's wrath and thunder, such as Captain Soames, the Commodore of a Squadron of Men of War that had sought sanctuary in Milford Haven. From his ship *The Dolphin* he responded to Defoe's request for accounts of the wild winds:

Sir,

Reading the Advertisement in the Gazette, of your intending to Print the many sad Accidents in the late dreadful Storm, induced me to let you know what this place felt, tho a very good Harbour. Her Majesty's Ships, the Cumberland, Coventry, Loo, Hastings and Hector, all being under my Command, with the Rye a Cruizer on this Station, and under our Convoy about 130 Merchant Ships bound about Land; the 26th November at one in the Afternoon the Wind came at S. by E. a hard Gale, between which and N.W. by W. it came to a dreadful Storm, at three the next morning came the Violentest of the Weather, when the Cumberland broak her Sheet Anchor, the Ship driving near this, and the Rye, both narrowly escap'd carrying away; she drove very near the Rocks, having but one Anchor left, but in a little time they slung a Gun, with the broken Anchor fast to it, which they let go, and wonderfully preserv'd the Ship from the Shoar. Guns firing from one Ship or other all the Night for help, tho' 'twas impossible to assist each other, the Sea was so high, and the Darkness of the Night such, that we could not see where any one was, but by the Flashes of the Guns; when day light appear'd, it was a dismal sight to behold the Ships driving up and down one foul of another, without Masts, some sunk, and others upon the Rocks, the Wind blowing so hard, with Thunder, Lightning and Rain, that on the Deck a Man could not stand without holding.*

The aftermath was 'terrible to behold,' with ships hurled out of the harbour at Dale. One lay with a big rock driven through her hull, the vessel lifted from one side of the channel to the other as if she was nothing more than a balsawood model. One ship was forced 10 miles upriver while another, the *Pembroke*, was ignominiously hoicked onto a bridge. Captain Soames's final computations reckoned that 'nigh 30 Merchant Ships and Vessels without Masts are lost, and what Men are

---

* Daniel Defoe, *The Storm*, London, 2003.

lost is not known; 3 ships are missing, that we suppose Men and all lost.' It made for a grim inventory, even if there was the very small compensation in that none of Her Majesty's Ships had come to harm in the sustained blasts of wind.

Another almighty storm struck on 25 October 1859 when the steam clipper the *Royal Charter* was wrecked, with the loss of over 400 lives. This was the worst storm in living memory, with winds of over 70 mph, or Force 12 on the Beaufort scale. A total of 113 ships were wrecked, the trouble compounded by the fact that lifeboats could not be used due to the severity of the winds. Even on land the storm wreaked havoc. Llandudno's pier was turned to matchwood. And a ship such as the *Royal Charter* simply didn't stand a chance as it was driven onto the east coast of Anglesey. Charles Dickens, sent by *The Times* to cover the story, was sickened by what he saw as looters rifled the clothes of the dead. But what really made the headlines was the fact that the ship was carrying enormous amounts of gold, carried in boxes belonging to miners on their way to Liverpool from the Australian goldfields, as well as bullion stored in the hold, all worth millions maybe billions in today's money. Little wonder deep-sea divers have treated the wreck like some Holy Grail.

There were so many shipwrecks off the Anglesey coast that they actually had a home for shipwrecked sailors in Holyhead. The Stanley Sailors Home and Reading Room was built at the behest of W. O. Stanley and was opened by the Bishop of Bangor in 1871 with accommodation for shipwrecked sailors. It took in the survivors of the sinking SS *Apapa* for instance, which was torpedoed by a German U-Boat on 28 November 1917 when she was 2 miles off Point Lynas, on a voyage which had started in Lagos, Nigeria. The rescued men and women were greeted by Commandant Jane Henrietta Adeane, who had been an associate of Florence Nightingale, and had therefore ample experience of dealing with trauma. The scale of the work of the home is apparent in the figures for the period between 1914 and 1918: between those dates the Home cared for the crews of no fewer than fifty-five vessels, a total of 1,199 men who were looked after before they could be sent home.

A TUMULT OF TEMPESTS

*   *   *

But the wind isn't always terrible, or a gusting danger to shipping. It can be benign, plump the sails, add colour to the scene, or hurl crowds of kittiwakes and other gulls up towards the stratosphere like mad confetti. And useful, too, in gauging directions, as Pembrokeshire historian George Owen of Henllys advised back in 1603: 'A stranger might travel knowing in what direction of the wind his journey lyeth by the bending of the trees, as the mariner does his compass.'

Beautiful winds: the Irish have a lovely way of describing them. It's contained in the tenth-century *Saltair na Rann*, the *Psalter of Quatrains*, which ascribes a colour to winds from each direction. In P. W. Joyce's *A Social History of Ancient Ireland* he explains the belief that God had made 'four chief winds' blowing from the north, south, east and west, with eight subordinate winds between these points. The north wind was a harsh wind, therefore dark or black; the north easterlies were speckled or dark; the east wind, blowing directly, was a purple wind. South easterlies, on the other hand, were yellow, the south westerlies green or greyish green, the west wind was a dun colour, and the north westerlies, in turn, a dark brown or a grey wind. It's delightful to ponder the chromatics of this arrangement, a colourful arrangement of gale and bluster, a spectrum describing invisible blow and breeze. And the prevailing south westerlies, which sweep both Ireland and Wales, are said to be *glas*, which means both green and greyish blue in Irish and blue and green in Welsh. Such a wind comes from the direction of the Otherworld, where the shifting interchange of colours is entirely possible, being that boundaries blur in such places, and is not inconsistent therefore with the magic of such provenance. It all adds up to a vivid spectrum, a sort of beautiful, colour-inflected medieval synaesthesia:

From the East, the smiling purple,
From the South, the pure white, wondrous,
From the North, the black blustering moaning wind
From the West, the babbling dun breeze.

THE TURNING TIDE

It's lovely to picture the purple air-currents, steaming like imperial ribbons, or the prevailing blue winds, laving the land's edge, or indeed the dowdier, dun west wind adding its own reserved tint to the colourful, swirling mix. Before all settles into calm.

19.

THE WRECKING ZONE

The charts of the Irish Sea are littered with little symbols consisting of a horizontal line crossed by three equally spaced verticals – used by the Admiralty since 1920 to mark shipwrecks. St George's Channel in particular is fair peppered with them, having been described as the 'most dangerous of all British seas.' It is little wonder therefore that the list of ships lost on the sands and rocks of the facing coasts of Wales and Ireland is in the hundreds, a long and tragic litany. *Ankair. Turtledove. Croghan, Shadinsay. Topaz. Mellary. Witch.* Dangers abounded. On the Irish coast there were sands like the Kish Bank or a jagged range of rocky hazards – *sceir*, a sharp sea rock; *siorra*, a submerged, sharp rock rising almost to the surface of the sea; and the deadly *scor*, a rock completely concealed by the waves. War brought its deliberately hidden dangers, not least when German submarines turned the Irish Sea into an underwater shooting gallery.

Subject to such jeopardy, compounded by storms, fog and other navigational threats, the tragedies of wrecks heaped up like seawrack at the high water mark. One such involved the large American clipper ship *Pomona*, sailing from Liverpool to New York, which struck sandbanks at Blackwater on the east coast of Wexford in 1859, leading to the loss of 424 passengers, many of them Irish emigrants. This was the largest loss of life due a single shipwreck along the coasts of Ireland. There was an inquest into the multiple deaths which was duly reported in the *Wexford Independent*: 'Arranged side by side, they lay locked in the sleep of death, and the lifeless, which a few hours past were lighted up with life and animation, had become sickening objects, from which the heart recoiled … the eyes never seemed directed to that haven where shipwrecks are never known – where no dread is entertained of a tempestuous ocean, and where no unskilful mariner can cast them on the dreaded sandbank.'

This sort of travel was a peril in and of itself: ships heading for Canada would leave through the North Channel, to the north of Ireland, while others, bound for Boston or New York would round the south coast of Ireland via St George's Channel, skirting past the dangers of Tuskar Rock and the jagged rocks of Wexford Bay. Conditions on board such emigrant ships could be pretty horrific as they were often designed to carry cargo, not people. On-board provisions could be scant, or criminally lacking, and sanitary provision was terrible, leading to all the attendant problems of disease. The travellers might have already walked for miles from remote areas to reach the ship in the first place, and fatigue and insalubriousness soon led to sickness and often death. Even waiting to cast off from cities such as Liverpool might involve staying in filthy hovels.

Over 15,000 shipwrecks are estimated to have occurred on the coast of Ireland, many of those being ships from Wales, of course. The *Mary*, out of Caernarfon, wrecked at Ballybriggan in hammering seas in 1859. The *William Cardiff*, out of Cardiff, dashed on The Skerries. The Cardiff coaster *Anna Toop*, carrying sheet metal from Port Talbot to Derry, grounded on a bank near Arklow. The *Swansea*, sea-broken at Baldoyle. The list goes on and sadly on.

Wrecks were seen by some people on land as a beneficence, blessing coastal communities with unexpected treasure as items of cargo and perhaps ships' fittings bobbed to shore. There's a story about a prayer of the period that runs 'We pray Thee, O Lord, not that wrecks should happen, but that if there be any wrecks, Thou wilt guide them to these shores for the benefit of the poor inhabitants.' Another story, probably equally apocryphal, tells of a clergyman who is told about a nearby wreck as he's in the middle of a sermon. The same thing happens on another Sunday but on this occasion he does not say anything from the pulpit, waiting instead until he is at the church door, where he says, 'This time we all start fair!'

Dublin Bay in particular was infamous for its dangers to shipping. A description, penned in 1800, posited that 'The numerous wrecks that take place every winter, apparent from the masts, which are seen every here and there, peeping above the surface of the water, as it were, to warn others by their fate, are convicing proofs of the truth of this assertion.'

Indeed, the whole of the Irish Sea was fraught with dangers, as historian Roy Stokes reminds us in *Between the Tides*: 'The beat down the Irish Sea is one that has brought so many vessels, big and small, to the brink of disaster and beyond. Looking out to sea from either side of the channel, it seems to be a vast expanse of water. However, though only 45 miles lie between Ireland and Wales, large sailing vessels trying to get out of the Irish Sea and into the open water of St George's Channel dreaded having to tack back and forward, east and west, down the channel in bad weather and poor visibility.'

The city assembly in Dublin emphasised just such a point in a complaint of 1808 in which they stated that 'The Bay of Dublin is an open bay and a most dangerous roadstead for vessels during the continuance of strong north-easterly or south-easterly winds from which points violent storms frequently proceed during the most dangerous seasons of the year.' Captains had to steer clear of the Bennet Bank and the Burford Bank, both straddling the north of Dublin Bay, while closer inshore lay the shallow perils of the Rosbeg Bank, dead south of the Baily Lighthouse.

The entrance to the harbour itself, while still pretty narrow, is much safer now than in bygone days. A 1693 chart by Captain Greenville Collins shows the approach to Dublin harbour to be tortuous, with many sandbanks and shifting channels within it, not to mention the Bar of Dublin, a big sandbank which stretched right across the mouth of the channel. At low water there might be only five or six feet of water available. So ships often had to anchor off and wait for high tide and should the weather whip up they might be blown onto the sandbanks known as North and South Bull, jointly a graveyard of broken ships.

In light of such dangers it's little wonder that so many ships floundered or went down. The *Tayleur* – the largest sailing ship of her day, as big as the *Cutty Sark* – was wrecked in January 1854 when en route from Liverpool to Melbourne, taking emigrants to the booming gold fields. A storm arose which exposed the paucity of crew members: there should have been eighty men, but in fact there were only twenty-six and of those, eleven were young boys. To compound the problem, the semi-mechanical steering gear misfunctioned when they were within sight of land at Lambay Island, the Captain failed to take soundings, and the three compasses were wrong, because none had been recalibrated after taking on cargo. What must the captain have thought as the ship reared under him like a horse, the waves running wild as mustangs? The crew, scared for their skins, looked for a safe place, but everywhere was a hell hole – turning down metal cul de sacs, as the sea groaned and roared, nature ready to engulf their tiny lives. The ship's boats could not be launched because of the ferocious pounding of the waves, but luckily a passenger did manage to scramble ashore with a line which helped save some of the *Tayleur*'s passengers. Sadly, hundreds of them were lost, all women and children, and the seabed near the wreck is their terrible resting place, also littered with fragments of willow pattern pottery from the ship's cargo, which also included linen, tinplate and, ironically enough, tombstones.

* * *

Mail packets were wrecked all too often, such as the *William* from Holyhead, caught by a storm on entering Dublin Bay and smashed to pieces between Sutton and Raheny, with another mail boat lost off Howth six years later. Indeed there have been 400 known wrecks in Dublin Bay alone. The treacherous Kish Bank, for instance, claimed the Imperial East Indian *Comte de Belgioso* in 1783, possibly the richest ship to ever have sailed from Liverpool, going down with its cargo of silver bullion, 25 tons of root ginseng, copper coins, tar, porter and rum. There was also a consignment of rare and ornate clocks made by the London maker James Cox. On other reaches of the coast, ships were similarly stricken, marooned or stranded. There was the *Aid*, bound from Rome to Dublin and wrecked at Wicklow Head. It was carrying a small museum's worth of classical art including a statue of Venus, an Egyptian sarcophagus and Nubian granite tables. The *Moelfre Rose*, carrying coal bound for Donnelly's coal merchants, foundered in Dublin port itself. Further south, ships from Wales were lost near Wexford, such as the *Clementian* from Cardiff, which was running rum and sugar from Demerara to Greenock before it went down 3 miles west of Kilmore, while the *Thomas Booth*, a Milford Haven steam trawler, was completely wrecked on Wilkeen Rock near Carne Pier.

In 1807 there were two horrendous incidents in Dublin Bay, the loss of both the *Prince of Wales* and the *Rochdale*, which led indirectly to the establishing of Dún Laoghaire as a harbour of refuge. In total some 370 people lost their lives in the two wrecks during an easterly gale, when the hatches were duly battened down and the soldiers therefore trapped. There's a saying in Irish, *Bionn acuid féin ag an blifarrage*, which maintains that the sea must claim that which is owed to it, words which take on sombre, deeper meaning when considering such drownings. The sinking of the *Rochdale* occurred during the so-called Pensinsular War when regiments of men were brought over to Ireland before being shipped off to Spain. The *Rochdale* was washed in at Seapoint Martello Tower, while the *Prince of Wales* crashed ashore at Black Rock. The captain and half a dozen crew members managed to climb into a boat and row ashore, abandoning everyone else to their fate. They were subsequently put on trial for shirking their duties so criminally.

* * *

Salvage rights, or the rights to auction goods that had been rescued from a wreck, were the source of squabble and dissent, some of which was allayed by the foundation of the so-called Ouzel Galley Society, a group of prominent Dublin merchants who would arbitrate in difficult or disputed cases of ownership, deciding who owned what in the event of ships being lost or, more rarely, sometimes found. The wrecks of the sea, with their jetsam, flotsam, lagan and derelict, offered rich spoils for those who got to them first.

One of the inventions that allowed access to wrecks on the seabed was the diving bell, a huge example being that cast from iron, designed and commissioned by the improbably named engineer for Dublin Port & Docks, Bindon Blood Stoney. With men inside, the bell would sink to the seabed, able to rise or fall on a system of pulleys even when the oxygen supply diminished as the divers laboured. They could signal for a replenishing barrel to be lowered down from the tender vessel, but the act of moving the barrel to a place just below the bell in dark waters would have been one heck of a feat, not least as the men were working in air that was slowly becoming poisonous with exhaled, foul air. But salvage operations could be financially very worthwhile, as merchants, owners or underwriters might give half the cargo as a reward to the rescuer, or a quarter of something valuable such as silver.

* * *

The battle between the Allies and German U-Boats between January 1917 and the spring of 1918 was a key determinant in the outcome of the First World War, as shipping was attacked and supply lines severed.

The submarine campaign conducted by Germany aimed to starve Britain into submission before the Americans became involved. The Irish Sea, or Irish Channel, was far from being the 'quiet lake' the Admiralty described when dismissing requests for escort vessels for commercial shipping. There were 718 shipping casualties in what was to become known as 'U-boat Alley', which included the coast from

Antrim to Wexford, the North Channel, Irish Sea and St George's Channel, where wolf packs of submarines – including the larger ocean-going U-class, the coastal German Type UB and the Type UC minelayer – all worked in concert to sink or scupper enemy ships. One U-boat alone, the UC-65 under Otto Steinbrinck, sank forty-two ships in three months in spring 1917. Between 1914 and 1918 she sank 206 ships and damaged a further twelve. Fishing boats were attacked as well as merchant ships and troop carriers, while other targets included lightships such as South Arklow's *Guillemot*, attacked in March 1917. Meanwhile mine-laying U-boats laid their deadly eggs in previously safe channels at Blackwater, Arklow, and near the Kish Bank, targeting in particular ships carrying munitions from Dublin to the Kynoch plant at Arklow.

Because of the increasing submarine menace in the Irish Sea, Holyhead Naval Base was formed in 1915. A force of six destroyers and sixteen motor launches was stationed there under the name of the Irish Sea Hunting Flotilla, which would be augmented by eighteen motor launches belonging to the US Navy, six of which were permanently stationed at Holyhead. There followed a game of stealth and counter-stealth, much of it played out under the sea.

* * *

The greatest single loss of life in the Irish Sea came with the sinking of the *RMS Leinster*, a mailboat owned by the City of Dublin Steam Packet Company, which usually plied back and fore between Dún Laoghaire, then known as Kingstown, and Holyhead. Its anchor is now installed on the seafront at Dún Laoghaire as a memorial.

The *Leinster* defiantly kept the mail service running throughout the First World War. On 10 October 1918 she left Dún Laoghaire, her passengers entrusted into the care of Captain W. Birch. Painted in dazzle camouflage and armed with a single twelve-pounder gun, she was only a few hours out when she was struck by torpedoes fired by German submarine U-123. One hit the *Leinster* near the bow where twenty-one Dublin Post Office sorters were at work; only one survived. One hit the engine room, occasioning many casualties and spreading fear like oil on water. Sebastian Barry opens his 2014 novel *The Temporary Gentleman* with a bravura piece of writing imagining a similar troopship going down, describing how 'the deck broke into the waters, it smashed through the sacred waters like a child breaks an ice puddle in a Sligo winter, it made a noise like that of something solid, something icy breaking, glass really, but not glass, infinitely soft and receiving water, the deeps, the dreaded deeps … let the waters take us quickly.' The chill waters did take over 500 souls from the *Leinster* – many of them soldiers from the British Isles, Australia, Canada, New Zealand and the United States, who were duly buried in the Grangegorman military cemetery at Blackhorse Avenue in Dublin.

Rescue vessels had left the port of Kingstown with all despatch but it was too late for so many, while the survivors of the stricken *Leinster* were brought to hotels in Dublin. Meanwhile, a tragic harvest of bodies was washed ashore in both Ireland and Wales. The Irish poet and novelist Katharine Tynan was staying in Dublin's Shelbourne Hotel in the days following the loss of the *Leinster* and later chronicled the 'dreadful' atmosphere with 'the corridors full of the unclaimed luggage of those who had gone across for the weekend intending to return.' In Tynan's vivid description, 'the sea was giving up its dead daily and hourly during that week.' The story resonated with the longer history of lives and vessels lost in the Irish Sea and the wreck became part of what Gillian O'Brien has described as the 'ring of sorrow' encircling Ireland, 'binding together communities who have suffered maritime tragedies like beads on a rosary.'* Meanwhile, in the opinion of the Irish modernist writer Elizabeth Bowen, broadcast on the BBC during World War II, the loss of the Leinster exposed 'the cleft … between the two islands,' a 'natural tract of danger' at once political and environmental, its vulnerability intensified by conflict.

---

* Claire Connolly, Rita Singer and James L. Smith, 'Environmental Dimensions of the RMS *Leinster* Sinking', Environment & Society Portal, *Arcadia* (Autumn 2021), no. 32.

* * *

Barry Hillier of the Holyhead Maritime Museum has a family connection with this tragic *Leinster* story concerning Holyhead seamen. Richard Williams was the bosun of the City of Dublin Steam Packet Company and served on the *Connaught*, the sister ship of the *Leinster*, herself torpedoed in March when the ship was lost with fortunately only three lives lost. As he told me: 'The crew was then dispersed across other ships and so Richard lost his status as bosun and became a seaman on the *Leinster*. My wife's grandfather, Evan Rowlands, was serving on board the *Leinster* at the same time as Richard, as one of the three gunners. Evan had been in the Royal Reserve and been trained as a gunner on HMS *Caroline* and then worked on ships bringing bully beef from Argentina to Britain before transferring to the ships of the Dublin Steam Packet Company. Richard Williams lost his life when the *Leinster* went down but Evan Rowlands survived and made his way back to Holyhead immediately after the tragedy, possibly one of the first people back, and bearing with him the grim news. Relatives of those on the *Leinster* were very anxious, of course, even as Evan Rowlands tried to settle back into his life at 13 Wells Street.'

One day there was a knock at the door and standing there was the son of Richard Williams, who lived in Rock Street. He'd been sent by his mother to ask if there was any word about her husband. Evans's daughter Dorothy, known as Dora to the family, was the one who answered the door and invited Richard in. He was 13 at the time while she was 11. This was the first time they met but they became friends and the friendship blossomed and eventually they got married and settled down in Holyhead and had a daughter, Beryl. She had two grandfathers on the *Leinster*: one survived and one was lost.

* * *

Another tragic torpedo incident involved the *Lusitania*, hit by a torpedo off the Irish coast in May 1915. This was a turning point in the war, ratcheting diplomatic tensions between the USA and Germany pretty much to breaking point and leading ultimately to America joining the war two years later.

One of the passengers on board the *Lusitania* was Margaret Thomas, Lady Rhondda, who was travelling back from the United States in the company of her politician and industrialist father, D. A. Thomas. After the ship was struck she found herself clinging on to her father's lifebelt, convinced that she would be sucked under as the ship went down. There was debris everywhere and she found herself bound by a stray length of rope even as a sense of 'mounting terror' took hold of her. She escaped from the tangle of rope, managing to cling to a floating length of wood for almost three hours, indeed time enough to think of an improvement to lifebelts that might help someone in a similar situation, namely to tie on a bottle of chloroform so they could render themselves unconscious. Around her were many other desperate survivors along with a floating junkyard of flotsam including 'boats, hencoops, chairs, rafts, boards and goodness knows what else.' She was by this point beyond terror. As she later recalled: 'the sharp agony of fear is not there: the thing is too overwhelming and strong for that.' The sun hit her face at one point and then she passed out. Lady Rhondda was eventually picked up by a rowing boat, although she was believed to be dead. It was only when she was transferred to the small patrol steamer that worked the waters between Ballycotton and Kinsale, the *Bluebell*, that a midshipman saw that there was 'some life in this woman,' and duly attended to her.

The submarine menace would finally be defeated for, despite the fact that the German U-boats had excellent communication equipment, signals and messages could be intercepted. This gave the Allies the advantage and led to a growing sense of despair on the part of commanders such as Ernst Hashegan, who wrote: 'It is as though the very sea had gone over to the enemy; it seems as if electrified, so violently do attack and defence rage upon it. Every wave is a foe. The coastal lights are false: the sea marks treacherous. They listen-in for us, to hear the distant beat of our screws; and feel us with electric fingers along the sea-bed.'

If they could be heard the subs became ready targets. If war is sometimes about competition between opposing technologies then this time the Allies had the killer advantage.

*   *   *

There are some works of art that lodge like limpets in the mind: Marc Arkless's photographs in his 'Shipwreck' project did just that, staying with me long after I had seen them in the arts and craft pavilion at the National Eisteddfod. Some are studies of the sea's surface, unbroken nautical miles of waves under cloud-scudded skies, and might seem a little empty, offering little for the eye to settle on – that is, until you read the title, and more poignantly the longitude and latitude point of each one.

Marc's photographs are of things no longer there, ships which sundered, vessels wrecked; patches of sea that are resonant with loss and absence. I remember the one called 'Mewsford Point' most powerfully, its image of sunbeams raking the shimmering surface of the waves. Here the SS *Ionian* was hit by either a mine or a torpedo from German U-51 close to St Govan's Head. This was one of the largest ships to be lost on the South Pembrokeshire coastline and the wreck resulted in the loss of seven lives.

His black and white study of Thorne Island suggests another story, that of the *Loch Shiel* which went down there on 30 January 1894 when she was battered by an almighty gale. Bound for Australia, the *Loch Shiel* was laden with a cargo of gunpowder and whisky, and had sought shelter in Milford Haven from the battering winds. When she went down most of the passengers and crew managed to get to Thorne Island, while some of the others were rescued by the lifeboat out of Angle. The day following the storm saw cases of whisky being washed ashore, in scenes reminscent of Compton McKenzie's novel *Whisky Galore*, which depicts the effects of a similar alcoholic bonanza on a remote Scottish isle. In total some sixty cases washed onshore, and although no lives were lost in the actual rescue, two men died whilst swimming out to the wreck, while another died of alcohol poisoning.

* * *

The shores of the Irish Sea are peppered with memorials to those lost at sea, and the graveyards of many coastal chapels and churches contain drowned men. Wandering under louring, pewter skies in Maeshyfryd Cemetery in Holyhead, I see that the place is dominated as much by one memorial as it is by the two little chapels contained within its extensive walls. An unshowy granite cross set on a tablet of slate commemorates the loss of the HMS *Thetis*, a submarine lost in 1939, just a few weeks before the Second World War began. She was undertaking her first sea trial, launched from the Cammell Laird shipyards in Birkenhead into Liverpool Bay, and carrying more than the usual complement of some fifty crew members. On this occasion there were 103 on board, including naval observers and shipbuilders' employees. Something went amiss on her very first dive, and soon parts of her were flooded whilst the bow was firmly embedded in mud on the seabed. Only four men managed to escape; the other 99 died, trapped in this horrific steel tomb.

The *Thetis* memorial isn't the only substantial one in Maeshyfryd Cemetery. There's also one decorated with a large angel, a memorial to the crew of a ship named the *Primrose Hill*, which sank on 28 December 1900 on her way from the Mersey to Vancouver, breaking into pieces in just five minutes, with the tragic loss of over thirty lives.

A multitude of headstones telling a collective story of drownings can be found in Llansantffraed Church near Llanon in Ceredigion, just a field's breadth away from the sea, which gnaws energetically away at its edge. Here I find the grave of James Lewis James, aged thirty-seven, who died in a voyage from Rangoon to Rio de Janeiro in 1901, and Jenkin Evans, bosun on the cargo steamer the SS *Constantia*, who died in the sea near Whitby during the Great War. There is also Capitan Don Jose Manuel Segarra of the Spanish Mercantile Marine, whose body was washed ashore when the SSM *Benlluire* was wrecked hereabouts in 1915. There are local house names such as Ontario, and epitaphs in Russian, not to mention nautical *englynion* in Welsh, all ample reminders of the sea's connectedness. I pause at the grave of Evan Rees, who died on a journey from Philadelphia to Havana. He was twenty-eight years of age, his whole life in front of him, before the sea's wet arms pulled him under.

Similar graves can be found right around the Welsh coast. The churchyard at St Carannog's Church in Llangrannog, just a gull's hop from Llanon, contains the grave of two brothers, David and William Jones – the first died on his way back from Larash, Morocco and the latter drowned between Cardiff and Messina. Then there's William Lewis, who died in Payta, Peru and James Jenkins, drowned between Carrickfergus and Swansea. The names create an aching litany of loss – Able Seaman Evan Iorwerth Rosser Morgan, torpedoed near Trinidad; Christopher David Lewis, master with the merchant navy, bombed by German aircraft off Flamborough Head; sailor Simon Davies, killed on a voyage from Freetown to New Orleans – all testament to the way the sea connected such communities with the world, but also of its perils, and sometimes lack of mercy. As Mali Parry Jones, one of the twenty-five volunteer members of the Porthdinllaen lifeboat, cautioned me, 'One of the most dangerous things is when someone says they know the sea. You can never be comfortable on it. The sea has its own mind and you can be caught out in seconds.'

*   *   *

Life countermanding death, wrecks are now often havens for wildlife. The first divers to reach the wreck of the *Queen Victoria* near Howth on the northern rim of Dublin Bay saw a 'very large old encrusted lobster, who had set up home in the boiler's condenser.' The maritime historian and diver Cormac Lowth, meanwhile, encountered the biggest cod he'd seen between the engines of the sunken *Bolivar*, along with that typical loner of such new reefs, a 'conger eel with a head the size of a knee,' and shoals of wrasse and pollack. When the fiming team making *Wonders of the Celtic Deep* for BBC Cymru Wales explored the twisted wreck of the *SS Gwynfaen* in Caernarfon Bay, they found underwater life in veritable profusion: darting shoals of bib, common lobsters with their dark blue and yellow carapaces, pollack – a member of the cod family – and bloody henry starfish. There were bright flashes of Caribbean blue and orange as the gender-fluid cuckoo wrasse sped by: a remarkable, hermaphrodite species which can change sex according to circumstance. There was also the appropriately-named coral, Dead Man's Fingers, clinging onto the rusting girders of this iron-hulled, cargo-bearing steamship alongside giant sea urchins that graze on barnacles. Such wrecks are as busy and bright as coral reefs, full of flashing fins and marine fecundity.

20.

FACES AS GREEN AS THE SEA

Poor nuns. When the writer Margiad Evans took the boat from Fishguard to Waterford, passing the flashing pulse of the Strumble Head lighthouse, she felt more than a little queasy. Yet she could draw a little solace from the plight of some of her fellow travellers, who were probably a deeper shade of jade: 'I'm glad when we go up on the Bridge & she begins to fling her head up & down and the lights of Goodwick go out in the sea while Strumble makes quick and furious gestures on our portside ... The nuns were sick. Mike said they never said a word to each other all night but were sick into their bowls sitting bolt upright.'*

The nuns, in turn, would not have been consoled to know that the church recognised their plight. In St Davids Cathedral there's a wooden carving depicting four men in a small boat in turbulent seas. Carved from solid oak, the scene depicts one man being violently sick over the side while the expressions of his mates seem to suggest their being all at sea in knowing how to help with his discomfort: one is patting him on his back to help while another's hands outreach heavenwards, as if pleading with God for help and safe passage. Some divine Dramamine.

The story associated with this carving is that of the sixth-century St Govan who, with two companions, was sent by his Master, St Aelfyw,

* Margiad Evans, *The Nightingale Silenced and Other Late Unpublished Writing*, Dinas Powys, 2020.

from St Davids Cathedral to Rome, to obtain a copy of the true Mass. During the journey St Govan nearly died of seasickness. A late medieval Welsh poem from the fourteenth century, '*Cywydd I'r Llong*' (Ode to The Ship) by Iolo Goch, lists the many discomforts suffered by those who travelled on boats, from the sheer stench to the weakness of the simple steering system and the incessant rocking motion: or as he says, '*rocian a wnai bai o beth*'. The poem was composed about the same time that John Cabot travelled to Newfoundland and belongs to a medieval tradition of works which describe heroic sea voyages, although judging by the tone of it Iolo was not exactly enamoured of the waves.

To alleviate her seasickness Margiad Evans took to mother's ruin, but the gin wasn't strong enough, or maybe she hadn't taken enough. Luckily 'the Capitano lent me the Chart House and I slept in the top of the ship among the whines of the wind & the tall plungings of the waves. The heartburn was worse than ever. I thought I'd never shut an eye but saw the broad moonlight through a corner of the window & the desk light steady. Lord how she leapt and sunk & how I saddened the gin in me.'

Gin wasn't necessarily the best tipple. John Gamble, a physician, traveller and writer from Strabane, Co. Tyrone and author of such works as *Sketches of history, politics and manners taken in Dublin and the north of Ireland* (1811) suggested, 'Wine or spirits is bad; though, of the two, the latter diluted with water is preferable. The drink I would recommend is a highly-taken bottled porter, soda or seltzer water.' Former army surgeon Gamble further recommended copious draughts of fresh air to cope with this 'nauseous disease', encouraging 'every person who goes to sea for the first time to keep upon deck as much as possible; it is the most effectual method of avoiding sickness.' Should fresh air not be sufficiently restorative, Gamble's gambit is for a person to 'betake himself to his berth … with his head low and firmly pressed to the pillow, endeavoring to lose all motion of his own, and to accommodate himself to the ship's.' If all else fails, Gamble suggests 'a small opiate plaster, applied to the pit of the stomach.' In this he was anticipating the advent of medications such as the aptly named Quells, perhaps, where hyoscine hydrobromide temporarily reduces the effect of movement on the balance organs of the inner ear and the nerves responsible for nausea. Seasickness is literally in your head.

One of the captains who regularly crosses St George's Channel has seen many of his colleagues on the Stena Line ferry from Dublin to Holyhead succumb to seasickness, even to the point of being very ill. Some who work the summer have to give up when winter brings its storms and swells. Captain Mark Roberts has been tempted to tell them it's all in the mind, as he explained to BBC Wales news in a piece to mark the twenty-first anniversary of the route in 2011. He freely admitted, however, that it was easy for him to say as 'I come from a long line of seafarers in my family and I'm fortunate enough to have never experienced seasickness.'

That said, every sea voyager is subject to the vagaries of the weather, subject to the roil and lift, the stomach-unsettling pulse of the waves. The novelist Joyce Carey recalled the simple dangers of a ferry crossing from Liverpool to Derry, when he was eight years of age. He (his first name was Arthur but he bravely chose Joyce as a pen name) was 'wedged firmly between two aunts while they smoked their cigarettes and guarded themselves from flying into the Atlantic at every roll of the ship by nothing better than their shoe-heels hitched against the two-inch gunwale. For we sat behind the boats where there were no rails.'* As if smoking wasn't dangerous enough.

Motion sickness could mar even the most romantic trip. A well-heeled vicar's daughter, Elizabeth Bower, was on an eight-week honeymoon trip around England, Wales and Ireland in 1837 with her husband the Rev. Henry Tregonwell Bower and a companion called Mary. On the return leg from Ireland she set off to cross the sea to Holyhead. It was a calm day, the ship cleaving the waves, its wake a white triangle, conditions calm enough for Mrs Bower to indulge in a spot of art: 'So begins my aquatic career in style, first

---

* Christopher Harvie, 'Garron Top to Caer Gybi: Images of the Inland Sea', *The Irish Review*, No. 19, Summer 1996.

taking two slight sketches of the rapidly receding shore & then standing with Henry at the bow of the vessel & watching the magnificent waves breaking around us till two wettings cooled my ardour & sent me astern. But all this enjoyment was not destined to be of very long duration for … I was taken suddenly worse & was obliged to take myself with all speed to the sofa in the cabin … the sea became very rough & for some time I dare not raise my head from my pillow but after a while I recovered enough to laugh at my companions in misfortune, especially at the appearance of Mary at the bottom of the stairs attended by the steward who was holding a basin under her nose with as much composure as if it had been a plate of bread and butter.'*

In her sea-borne travelogue *Two in a Boat* the former National Poet of Wales, Gwyneth Lewis, describes a voyage from Milford Haven, following the wakes of mariners such as 'prehistoric metal traders, the Vikings bartering Welsh slaves, Normans exchanging agricultural goods for tanned leather, honey and tar, and later ships bearing cargoes of wine and raisins, lemons and oranges.'

But as she and her husband leave Milford Haven for Ireland and the fog lifts on a perfectly windless July day Gwyneth is beset by seasickness: 'I sat rigidly on deck, trying to hold my head steady. Going below to boil a kettle or use the heads was out of the question, as it immediately made me ill. All I could usefully do was keep a good lookout on deck and try my best not to be sick. The moment we left the sight of land I cried, "Look, Leighton! No walls, no floor!" as I looked queasily at the gently heaving, sprung dance-floor of the sea.'

Lewis disliked being laid low in this way and feels despondent about being a wallflower at the sea's lurching discotheque. Consolingly, her husband says that her being there with him is comfort enough. They plough on, through millpond waters, and by the time they reach the trawler-packed harbour at Kilmore Quay, and walk on dry land, they are both grinning like Cheshire cats, having completed the first

---

* Liz Pitman, *Pigsties and Paradise: Lady Diarists and the Tour of Wales, 1795–1860*, Llanrwst, 2009.

international leg of a journey intended to take the two of them across the unanchored otherworld of the Atlantic Ocean.

In her brilliant Parnell lecture, 'Too Rough for Verse: Sea Crossings in Irish Culture', Claire Connolly garners many instances of green-faced writerly queasiness. Novelist Maria Edgeworth, for instance, penned a letter in 1791 from an inn in Holyhead, wearily reporting that 'a thirty-three hours' passage' had left her family sick and sorry: 'all the sick pale figures around me with faint voices send their love to you and my uncle'. Her fellow novelist Mary Granville (Mrs Delaney) wrote about the sea with a mixture of weariness and phlegmatism, reckoning a little bit of suffering is worth it to get to journey's end: 'Don't apprehend anything from the sea. It is a disagreeable element to deal with, but it never hurts me any longer than whilst I am on board, and though I must confess, and I fear you will find whenever you make me happy by coming here, that a ship is a most unpleasant thing, yet the happiness it is to convey me to is a full amends for a few hours distress, and the passage is seldom more than forty hours, and often not much more than half that time.'

Then there is Elizabeth Bowen's novel *The Last September* (1929), set in a big house in Cork during the Irish War of Independence in which Lois draws on the remembered miseries of the sea crossing to feed an 'inner blankness': 'She was lonely, and saw there was no future. She shut her eyes and tried – as sometimes when she was seasick, locked in misery between Holyhead and Kingstown – to be enclosed in a nonentity, in some ideal no-place, locked and clear as a bubble.'

Connolly also directs us to *The Lonely Girl*, being the closing part of the hugely successful and controversial *Country Girls Trilogy* by Edna O'Brien. It gives us the lives of two women, Cait and Baba, in 1950s rural Ireland and then in England, which is a different land: a place of immorality and temptation. A pregnant friend asks Cait to send abortion pills from England, a reminder of the many women in twentieth- and early twenty-first-century Ireland who travelled to the back streets of Liverpool with their pregnant shapes 'pushed out of sight on the Liverpool boat.' The trilogy's reception in Ireland was nothing short of stormy: banned by the Irish censor because of its sexual content and even burned by one parish priest, presumably incendiary with rage. Being banned, however, made the book more desirable for many readers and those who stood in moral censure had to watch the slim books climb rapidly up the bestseller list.

At one point the two young women leave Ireland on board the *Hibernia*, the waves below them churning filthy and unclean: 'Baba waved a clean hanky, and we leaned on the rails and felt the ship move and saw the dirty water underneath being churned up. "Like a hundred lavatories flushing," Baba said to the foamy water as the seagulls rose up from their various perches along the rails and flew, slowly, with us.'

As they leave their native land far behind, Baba prepares for life in London by doling out seasickness tablets 'in case we puke all over the damn ship': 'If I'm sick, 'twill spoil everything, Baba said as she burped, and then put a hand towel over her new dress, for safety's sake.'

* * *

The emptiness of the sea, the darkness and giddiness of its moods, the lurch and lilt of a ship subject to the whim of the waves, it was all enough to unsettle a stomach. Even John Masefield who ran away to sea at an early age and hymned the sea in his well-known 'Sea-Fever' suffered from sickness throughout his life. It didn't put him off returning to the sea, again and again.

* * *

The experiences of characters such as Baba and Cait, or indeed John Masefield, would chime with many as they crossed, nervousness settling acidly in the pit of the stomach. The future started at a foreign port and many were carrying their own baggage of anxiety, if not of despair. Given such tests and travails on the sea-crossings, ones that made poets such as Louis MacNeice curse 'the bloody boat home', it was easy to see why another poet, the Welsh nationalist Harri Webb

– who once opined that 'One damp green country/Is much like another'* – avoided the boat altogether. He wrote this comparison of Wales and Ireland, mind you after having flown over the sea, describing his 'Return Visit' from the cramped comfort of the airport bus, having seen, from the air, how 'two hundred miles more/into the Atlantic a different light/Tinges the clouds.' It was a surefire way of avoiding getting as seasick as nuns.

---

* Harri Webb, *Collected Poems*, Llandysul, 1995.

21.

WOMEN OF THE SEA

Fishing and sea-going were traditionally seen as the purview of men, while history under-records women's achievements or even their presence. There were, of course, some remarkable women of the sea who pioneered, breaking, if not a glass ceiling, then certainly some unwritten rules of the waves.

Sailors from Wales learned their trade both in the hard school of the waves and more formally in navigation schools. It was little wonder that so many of them became sea-captains, while Welsh crews added their accents or the Welsh language itself to the Babel of bustling waterfronts all over – in Rio, Shanghai, Marseilles, Yokohama and Sydney. When the Welsh barque *Gwydyr Castle* hove into harbour in Valparaiso in 1906 the crew found fifty ships at anchor, a dozen of which were under the command of a Welshman and four of which had a captain who came from the port of Nefyn in north Wales. This was not an uncommon occurence.

The sea ran in men's blood. In Cardigan Joseph yr Asyn (Joseph the Donkey, a Biblical name if ever there was) owned three ships and lost each one in a storm. Tragically he also lost each of his four sons, who drowned in wrecks off Java, the Scillies, Rio de Janeiro and the coast of Ireland. It was little wonder that women gathered each day at the shipping office at places such as Llangrannog to read Lloyd's List to see if a ship had safely reached its destination, be it in Vladivostok, Athens or Fremantle.

* * *

Many men would have learned their nautical skills at a local school run by one of the most remarkable Welshwomen who ever lived: Sarah Jane Rees, more commonly known as Cranogwen.

Sarah was born on 9 January 1839 to a sea captain of uncommon ilk. Education, scanty enough for boys at the time, was in very short supply for girls; yet with her parents' backing Cranogwen demanded to be taught to read and write, rather than acquire such skills as dressmaking. Accomplishment in household chores was the norm, as if such drudgery were the stuff of female ambition. When the time came for her to leave school she was forced to take a job in nearby Cardigan, where she was apprenticed to a dressmaker – but deep down Cranogwen was having none of it. She argued that she wanted to go to sea with her father and he readily acquiesced.

Her dad captained a schooner which sailed and traded all the way around the Welsh coast and occasionally ventured further afield to places such as France. Sarah took to the sea with alacrity, mopping up knowledge and skills with ease, always eager to learn more about all the various aspects of navigation and ship handling. While it was rare to see a girl on board a ship, it wasn't entirely unknown; but Sarah Jane's aptitude and enthusiasm did set her as a breed apart. She appreciated the danger of the sea but concomitantly loved the freedom, the wind plumping the sails, the apparent boundlessness of a sea yet lapping at the far horizon. On one occasion she overruled her father when they were caught in a storm near Strumble Head. He wanted to take the vessel to shore but she thought otherwise and as an early biography, *Cofio Crangowen* by D. G. Jones tells it, 'A storm rose between the two of them; at last she stamped her foot with force on the deck, she challenged the experience and authority of her father, and forced him to bend to her judgment.' Not only was it a feisty show of defiance, it also probably saved both their lives.

After three years of voyaging with her dad the strong-willed Sarah returned to school to satisfy her craving for more knowledge. In Ysgol Twmi, in the nearby village of New Quay, the art of navigation was one of the most prominent subjects. From there she went on to enrol in a school in Cardigan before rounding off her nautical education in Liverpool and London, where a combination of book-learning coupled with all the experience she had gained on her father's schooner helped her gain a master's certificate, and thus the right to both sail and command ships anywhere in the world. In this she was fairly unique, as it was beyond uncommon for a young woman to gain such a sought-after piece of paper, with all its attendant rights and privileges. Along the way she learned not only about the use of charts, but also their unreliability.

The world was now very much her oyster and she could have chosen to settle anywhere, but Cranogwen – by now a tall, dark, striking woman – chose to return home, where she found herself at the helm of the British School. There, in addition to teaching boys and girls, she also admitted adults who could plump for studying the art of navigation, the thick heavy charts to hand. She taught celestial navigation and the use of sextants, showing her charges how to recognise the stars and which ones to expect to see. Some would leave their dependency on the North Star behind and learn how far south they were when they could see the Southern Star. In school, small, eager hands handled big brass seaman's dividers, cautious about their sharp ends. Sarah turned local boys into mathematicians with a sense of wide oceans. To do this she had to overcome the engrained prejudice that argued that a woman couldn't or shouldn't have such a position. Over the years many men learned the art of sail from her, with many of them becoming officers or master mariners themselves before going on to captain their own ships. Cranogwen's life journey, or voyage, took her in another direction – indeed in many directions – as she became a pioneering activist for women's rights, a spirited advocate of temperance, a celebrated poet – whose bardic name became her well-known moniker – the editor of a magazine for women, a persuasive preacher, and the founder of a home for destitute girls in the Rhondda valley. It was as if she rolled many lives into one frenetic one, as if her life wasn't a single vessel but a whole fleet of ships.

Cranogwen wasn't entirely alone as a woman teaching the skills of the sea to men. In north Wales, on the banks of the Menai Strait in Caernarfon, Ellen Edwards taught over 1,000 sailors over a period of six decades.* Like Cranogwen, Ellen's father was a sea captain and a successful one at that, who decided in 1814 to give up the seafaring life in order to establish a navigation school in Amlwch on the northern rim of the isle of Anglesey. He had travelled the seven seas and seen the world, but retired when Britain's war against France made things too dangerous for merchant vessels. Cargo might be plundered and crews taken as prisoners of war, so Ellen's mother put pressure on her husband to give up the sea at a time of such real and present danger. It was natural that the inquisitive Ellen should pick up some of the knowledge from her now-landbound father. At the time Amlwch was one of the busiest ports in Wales, due in great part to the proximity of Parys mountain with its plentiful mineral deposits, especially copper. By the 1920s copper production was declining, but the business of shipbuilding around Amlwch Port was taking up the slack. Ellen's father set up a navigation school and there was a ready source of students who wanted to learn about navigation and mathematics, including his own children, who could therefore teach themselves.

About 1830 Ellen Edwards moved to Caernarfon, where she established a navigation school. It was a town with its own maritime ferment where no fewer than 3,000 ships used the port each year. Edwards's teaching skills were very much in demand in town, where the population could swell by extra thousands when crews were in port, with all the attendant problems of prostitution, pollution, drunkeness and minor crime in the ascendance. The Edwards school had an enviable success rate: thirty students on average passed their examinations set by Maritime Boards of Scotland, England and Ireland each year. At the time Wales didn't have its own such board,

---

* The young historian Elin Tomos's blog about Ellen Edwards complemented a hugely informative conversation we had about this pioneering teacher on the edge of Caernarfon's much-changed Victoria Dock. https://hanesmenywod. cymru/ellen-evans-e-tomos/.

therefore many of Ellen's candidates travelled to sit their exams in Dublin, where the Welshwoman's success was noted in the local press even as she changed the competence of generations of north Walian sailors. As one reporter noted in 1863, 'No less than fifty Welsh mariners have passed their examination as master and mates in Dublin since the first day of January 1863, and that to the satisfaction of the examiners, who are as competent as any in the United Kingdom. Perhaps sixty years ago there were not fifty masters in Wales that knew the art of navigation.' Among her school's many successful alumni were Captain Robert Thomas, who was in charge of the *Meirioneth* when she broke the world record for the fastest trip to San Francisco and back; Captain Thomas Williams, the maritime superintendent of the Black Line who at various times had charge of the *Lightening*, the *City of Sydney* and the *City of Melbourne*; and Captain John Pritchard, who was captain of the record-breaking ocean liner, the *Mauretania*. As student numbers increased so did the staff: Ellen's sister Lydia moved in with her and became an additional teacher.

Ellen's connection with the sea further deepened in a personal way in 1833 when she married Captain Owen Edwards, with whom she had a daughter, Ellen Francis Edwards. Ellen senior, like Cranogwen, turned her students into mathematicians, so the young men acquired an understanding of sines, cosines and tangents, as geometry helped them to take measurements, to help them find out where they were in the world, quite literally. Students might handle, then appreciate the value of weighty sextants, learning it was impossible to use one without a proper horizon, also becoming literate, but more importantly highly numerate, able to make the necessary calculations, plotting a course as well as a position.

Those such as Ellen Edwards and Cranogwen who taught navigation probably benefited from the chronometer, an instrument that had recently been invented by the English carpenter and clockmaker John Harrison. This revolutionised sea travel, as longitude – and therefore direction – would be marked by time difference from a fixed point – Greenwich was established as Prime Meridian in 1884 – rather than by a reliance on celestial navigation.

Harrison submitted his first chronometer to the Board of Longitude in 1736, and built two more large, heavy chronometers over the course of the next nineteen years. Captain James Cook took one with him to the Antarctic and the South Sea Islands in 1772 and lauded its performance even under severe temperature and climate fluctuations. They were expensive to produce at first, but the cost of manufacturing chronometers eventually decreased, and so, by 1825, each ship of the Royal Navy had at least one on board. By mid-century, chronometers were considered indispensable devices on most sea voyages.

But life at the school wasn't all smooth sailing. Reports commissioned in 1837 to look at the state of education in Wales – known as the Blue Books because of their binding and commonly referred to as the 'Treachery of the Blue Books' because of their content – did their damnedest to besmirch Ellen Edwards's good name, dismissing her as being perfectly unsuitable to run such an establishment. The same men also criticised schools in Holyhead for not teaching enough navigation. They were critical to a fault. In the case of Caernarfon, the principal architects of the attack were two local men, the conniving vicar of nearby Llanbeblig, the Reverend Thomas Thomas, and James Foster, the headmaster of the National School, who opined that 'All the navigation that has been learned here as a science has been taught by an old woman of Carnarvon,' even though Ellen was only thirty-seven at the time. Why did they attack her so? Foster was a dedicated Anglican and a Tory to boot, who abhorred chapel-going Nonconformity. This theory seems to be borne out by the fact that their report mentioned not only Ellen's age but also that she was a Baptist, as if suddenly that was a crime. Despite this the local paper, the *Carnarvon and Denbigh Herald*, regularly posted news of the school's success, as the little factory of navigators continued to produce qualified students.

Sadly, tragedy befell the small family in 1860 when Edwards's ship, the *St Patrick*, sank near the beach at Colwyn. Following her husband's death Ellen received a very small pension of £6 and ten shillings from the Sailors' Society, a paltry sum. As a consequence a campaign was organised when Ellen turned 70, in which the Harbour Trust, encouraged by Sir Llywellyn Turner, a former mayor of Caernarfon town, put pressure on the Government to ensure a decent pension for a woman who had given so much. Though she never received such a pension, she was given £75 from the 'Royal Bounty' fund in recognition of her valuable work bridging navigation and education. It wasn't enough but it was something.

Her funeral in 1889 was attended by a great many mariners and her gravestone's epitaph speaks eloquently of her teaching gifts:

Distaw weryd Mrs Edwards dirion
A gywir gerir, gwraig o ragorion.
Athrawes oedd i luoedd o lewion,
Y rhai uwch heli wnânt eu gorchwylion.
Urddas gaed trwy addysg hon. Ni phaid llu
Môr ei mawrygu tra murmur eigion.

The silent earth of gentle Mrs Edwards
Is truly loved, a woman of excellence,
She taught a multitude of brave souls
Who attended to their duties o'er the brine.
Their dignity was gained through her teaching – Seafarers all
Will not cease to praise her, for as long as the oceans murmur.

The life of Kate Tyrrell, Ireland's first woman to be a sea captain, is not dissimilar to that of both Cranogwen and Ellen Edwards, or indeed Betsy Miller, from Saltcoats in Scotland, in that she too was the daughter of a sea-captain who took an early interest in marine affairs. Tyrrell was born in 1863 in Arklow, County Wicklow, the second of four daughters. Her father, Edward Tyrrell, was a sea captain who owned a shipping company that transported cargo between Ireland and Wales.

Arklow itself was historically intimately associated with the sea, and in particular with fishing. References to fishing grounds off the coast at Arklow can be found in Patrician legends and scattered in medieval documents. Over the centuries the activity of fishing and the area became synonymous, so that by the 1800s the 'Arklow Fishery' denoted both the practice and the place. The entry for Arklow in Samuel Lewis's *Topographical Dictionary of Ireland* (1837) opens: 'This place ... appears to have been occupied as a fishing station since time immemorial.'

As a child, Tyrrell loved hanging around her father's shipyard; by the time she was twelve, she was filling out shipping journals for him and giving him an attentive hand with the book-keeping. Tyrrell gradually became indispensable to her father, and as she grew older, Tyrrell's father promised her that she would one day own a ship herself. Then sorrow moved in to live with them. By the end of 1882, Tyrrell had lost her mother and a younger sister to tuberculosis. Defiantly, she took over running the household while also managing the book-keeping for her father's business.

In 1885, Tyrrell's father bought a Welsh schooner, the 62-ton *Denbighshire Lass*, which he registered in Kate's name. She sailed it home from Wales by herself, and the two used it to transport cargo such as coal, bricks, iron ore and textiles. In July 1886, Tyrrell's father died from a heart attack, and Tyrrell took over the family business. She sold off several ships and became the sole owner of the *Denbighshire Lass*. Despite her ownership, however, as a woman she was not permitted to have her name on the ship's official documentation, as the law of the day did not recognise female shipowners or sea captains. As a temporary solution, a trusted male employee put his name on the documents, while Tyrrell ran all business operations, inspected repairs, and captained the crew.

In 1888, Tyrrell lost another younger sister to tuberculosis. Her last remaining sibling – the eldest Tyrrell sister – took over managing the household affairs, while Kate supported them both through the shipping business. Tyrrell spent most of her time captaining the *Denbighshire Lass* personally, becoming adept at navigation and all aspects of sailing. She was known for being a stern enforcer of order on board her ship, intolerant of any drunken crew members on duty.

Throughout the 1890s, inspired by the growing women's suffrage movement, Tyrrell fought to have her name officially recognised on the ship's ownership documents. She succeeded at last in 1899, when she was finally acknowledged by shipping authorities as the owner.

The *Denbighshire Lass* continued to sail throughout World War I, navigating landmines in the Irish Sea without incident, despite having no insurance. It was the first ship to fly the new Irish tricolour flag at a foreign port, which made it an ensign fully in keeping with Tyrrell's defiant stances in life, flying proudly aloft.

22.

NETS AND LINES

For many years herrings were the silver coinage of the Welsh and Irish coasts. On the west coast of Wales a herring fishery was recorded as far back as 1206: the chronicles contained within *Brut y Tywysogion* suggests that there was a great quantity of fish landed at Aberystwyth, 'so much that the like had never been seen before.' A place such as Tenby in Pembrokeshire was given the Welsh name Dinbych y Pysgod ('little fortress of the fish') and here, as in so many other towns, herrings were sold by the meise, or five hundred fish, with an extra one kept to one side for every two-score counted – a sort of slippery wet abacus, or simple loss adjustment. They helped create communities, wealth, and even language: the Cornish language has a lovely word, *golowillions*, for the shining scales of herring left on clothes after cleaning fish, while the Breton language has the very similar *golou uilhenn*, sparkles of light for the same sparkling phenomenon. In Waterford the argent-bellied fish themselves were simply and lovingly known as 'little darlings'.

In Ireland and Wales, as elsewhere, herring was an indispensable component of the diet, not least because they could be eaten fresh or preserved. They were also an important element of fasting days, so much so that, after Lent, happy Dublin butchers would lead 'herring funerals' in places to celebrate the fact that their customers would once again be eating meat. This involved 'beating' a herring through the town on Easter Sunday before it was thrown into the sea, at which time a quarter of lamb, beautifully bedecked in ribbons, would be displayed in the window.

Fishing completely transformed some coastal communities. With good herring runs a tiny place such as Aberdyfi on the Gwynedd coast could transform into something like the Alaskan salmon season, complete with flotillas of netters and fishers. As one of the earliest Port Books, *A Survey of Creeks and Havens*, attested in 1565: '… being a haven and having … but only three houses whereunto there is no resort; save only in the time of the herringe fishing at which tyme of fishing there is a wonderful great resorte of ffyshers assembled from all places within this Realm with Shippes, Boottes and Vessells.' There was even a captain from among the herringers who was chosen to be the admiral of this varied fleet.

A pivotal lawsuit dating back to 1685 gives a further glimpse of the importance of herring. There had been a protracted argument over whether Aberystwyth beach fell under the purview of the parish of Aberystwyth rather than the parish of Llanbadarn. What was at stake? Well, the vicar of Llanbadarn claimed every tenth fish caught as part of the tithes, or church taxes. Three of the oldest inhabitants went to court to support the fishermen, arguing that they had always caught the herring under the high-water mark, which was therefore not in any parish whatsoever. They also mentioned a ritual whereby the incumbent of St Mary's would stroll down to the beach to bless their endeavours, offering prayers before the men set out. If his blessings translated into a catch they would thank him on their return by giving the vicar some herrings by way of thanks.

The last known place in Wales where fish were actually blessed was Tenby. A small chapel stationed on the rocky projection of the shore was appropriated solely for the performance of this singular service.

In Gwynedd, north Wales, the herring ran and ran. By reputation the best ones came from Nefyn, where the season extended from September through January, when boats would return loaded to the gunwales with plump specimens which had 'bellies like inn-keepers and backs like farmers.' At the peak of the industry, in the 1920s, they sold for twopence a fish and of course the whole town thrived as a consequence, as the maritime history enthusiast Meinir Pierce Jones told me: 'There were three salt-houses in Nefyn. I was talking recently to a woman in her late eighties who remembers going to one as a little girl to ask them to cut her a block of salt so that her father could preserve the fish.'

Salt was a key necessity for preserving fish, of course, and a loophole in the law allowed unlimited exports of rock salt from a port such as Liverpool to Ireland, where it could be sold at a much lower price than in Britain, where the duties on salt were punitive. This led to extensive salt-smuggling along the western edge of Wales. Salt and fish were both very valuable, therefore, and intimately linked. Thomas Pennant, writing in 1771, describes a catch of herrings in great abundance, worth about £4,000, being taken from Porth Ysgadan (Port of Herrings) to Ynys Enlli, Bardsey island. These might be salted on shore, or be taken to be cured in Dublin

To give some idea of the scale of fishing one can cite the example of the *Richard and Jane*, which took a cargo of fifty casks of white herring, eighteen casks of red herring, and two and a half barrels stuffed with cod from nearby Porthdinllaen to Chester.

And fish, more fish. Nefyn herring were traded in France and annual exports were measured in thousands of barrels. There was a ditty about them, which rejoiced in their plump character:

Penwaig Nefyn, penwaig Nefyn,
Bolia fel tafarnwyr
Cefna fel ffarmwrs.

Nefyn herrings, Nefyn herrings
Bellies like inn keepers
Backs like farmers.

Fresh herring with bright red eyes were particularly treasured, and eaten locally. Bloatered ones, pickled in brine or dry salt soon after they had been captured, might be spread on a bed of ferns on a sunny day before being packed in willow hampers to be moved, then sold.

Red herrings (though not the sort beloved by Maigret and Miss Marple) were smoked, the fish having been split, cleaned and pickled slightly before being smoked in a smoke house, using oak chips should they be available.

*   *   *

Fishing had long been a key component of the local economy in Pembrokeshire; historian George Owen of Henllys stated that it 'is one of the chiefest worldly commodities, wherewithal God has blessed this country.' Cleddau oysters, salmon, trout, cockles and eels were all part of the area's rich wet harvest. Fish traps were also commonly employed along the coast in medieval times and earlier.

The town of Fishguard has a Scandinavian name derived from *fiski-gardr*, an 'enclosure for catching or keeping fish.' The fish trap itself is to the north-west of Fishguard Harbour, lying just below the entrance road to the ferry terminal. It is first shown on the early maritime charts of Lewis Morris dating from 1748, and the hooked portion of the trap is locally still renowned as a good place to catch bass, which gather there in large numbers to feed on the scuttling population of crabs. Fry gently in oil, add lemon.

The town of Milford, now known as Milford Haven, became the biggest herring port in England and Wales in 1924 when no fewer than 124,000 barrels of herring were landed. The port had first started life with the arrival of Nantucket whalers but attempts at expansion – and to corner some of the lucrative passenger market across the Atlantic – came to naught. The port therefore concentrated on fishing and the opening of the docks in 1888 allowed steam trawlers and fishing boats equally to ply their trade. Thomas Wood assessed the developments very favourably: 'That much derided and despised fish trade has come in very opportunely for us and yields a very consider-able revenue … It is a trade we did not either cater for, or look forward to … but it helps to pay, and in fact does pay for the expenses of the docks.' By 1904 there was a fleet of 200 fishing boats working out of Milford and the switch from importing ice from Norway to ice made in the port's own factory in 1890 was a further boost, as was the opening of a substantial fish market in 1908 with links to the railway. H. V. Morton, impressed by the speed of fish processing here, averred that 'no port can turn a herring into a kipper faster than Milford Haven.'

During the First World War the fishing fleet here was engaged with mine-sweeping and submarine-hunting and the docks themselves were taken over by the Admiralty, the port itself being used as a base for mine-sweeping operations. Work resumed quickly after the war. Some 124,000 barrels – 6,000 tons – of herring were landed in 1924–25, and by the 1930s there were 12,300 men afloat on Milford vessels, in a port that could easily compete with English centres such as Fleetwood, Hull and Grimsby. Auctions at the fish market attracted up to 140 merchants, who would send their purchases by train direct to Billingsgate in London. In 1946 the port broke its own record with an annual haul of 60,000 tons of fish, an enormous biomass hauled out of the sea. But decline set in and by 2005 what had once been the largest herring landing station in England and Wales only handled a single ton. The same story was repeated in ports such as Holyhead, where the number of fishermen dwindled and thus so did the catch. It had been so different in the past.

Many villages such as New Quay, Llangrannog and Aberporth along the Welsh coast had long found prosperity in fishing, especially after laws were passed in 1705 and 1718 which guaranteed fishermen a shilling per barrel for red herring and two shillings and eightpence for salted white herring. A further act in 1750 rewarded any vessel with a deck weighing 30–80 tons which joined the herring fleet while the advent of steam engines accelerated the growth of the industry and its legion of associated small ports, since vessels powered in this way were not at the mercy of the winds and could pull otter nets through the water. In his *Topographical Dictionary of Wales* Samuel Lewis noted a lucrative herring fishery in Aberaeron in 1830, 'in which about thirty boats with seven men to each are engaged,' while in nearby St Dogmaels and at the mouth of the river Teifi a fleet of herring boats 'are commonly from eight to twenty burthen with masts and sails, but mostly open, without decks and manned by six to eight men. The herrings generally make their first appearance … between the middle and end of September, which is considered the best part of the season, as they will bear carriage to distant markets and harvest being commonly over, the fishermen can be spared from agricultural labours.'

*   *   *

While herring was the boom species in the Irish Sea there were plenty of other fish, and the plenitude of stocks had long been noted. During the time of the Irish Famine an assessment made by a man called Richard Valpy seemed to suggest that fish might be the answer to this, the direst of situations: 'Few of the resources of Ireland are perhaps more capable of affording extensive and speedy relief than the sea-fisheries, and in such an industry no delay occurs in the return for capital and skill applied, and the yield is almost miraculous.' There is some evidence that coastal communities fared better in the Famine because of fishing, especially as some people caught basking shark, a fish as big as an elephant, off the west coast – and in sufficient numbers, truth be told, for it to be a tradition. The waters of Ireland, Valpy suggested 'present a general length of 2,346 statute miles, and with but little variation, abound in all the various kinds of fish in common use. Cod, ling, haddock, hake, mackerel, herrings, whiting, conger, turbot, brill, bream, soles, plaice, dories and salmon are the sorts most commonly met with; but several others are by no means uncommon, as gurnet, pollock, skate, glassen, sprats, etc.'*

He went on to argue that fish from the Nymph Bank on the south coast of Ireland were superior in quality and could be sent to markets such as Gravesend in four or five days and from there moved speedily to satisfy the London market. And that market was indeed penetrated, and at speed.

---

* Richard Valpy, 'The Resources of the Irish Sea Fisheries', *Journal of the Statistical Society of London*, 1848.

NETS AND LINES

* * *

The deeper waters of the Irish Sea were worked by trawlers out of Fleetwood in Lancashire, Milford Haven, or Irish ports such as Wexford and Waterford. The new types of trawlers gave a new lease of life to Dublin fishermen too, ranging the length and breadth of the Irish Sea, from the coast of County Down to Dungarvan Bay in the south, and across to the Isle of Man in their search for such tasty species as sole and turbot.

A government report in 1835 found that there were about thirty cutters fitted out in Dublin and Kingstown to fish in what it described as the English system, with a further forty boats fishing with the use of lines. By 1829 there were 64,000 men involved in the Irish sea fisheries. A description of a trip undertaken on a trawler from Ringsend, published in the 1880s, hauled in a vivid, wriggling description of what might be encountered in a catch: 'The produce of the trawling net, when turned out on the deck, is certainly a curious and interesting sight: comprising skate, ray, brett – being another name for brill, turbot, conger eel, John Dory, gurnard, both red and grey, cod, haddock, soles, plaice, herrings, mackerel, flounders, squids, being small cuttlefish and piles of queer things about which naturalists get enthusiastic, such as sea-mice, star-fish, sea-urchins, feather stars, brittle stars, seaweeds of beautiful colours and forms … Sometimes a small porpoise is taken. The conger eels are large – up to seven or eight feet long. Turbot are bled by an incision on the underside of the tail and they bleed very freely. This keeps them firm. They are left under the boat on deck, and must be shaded from the moonlight which would injure them – at least that's what the men say. The fish are not packed in hampers until the vessel is going into port to land them, as they would spoil sooner by so doing.'

Sadly, too much competition in part did for fishing, with the price per pound dropping to a single penny in the Dublin markets in 1820, when a combination of the newly-formed Dublin Fishery Company and the busyness of visiting English trawlers turned ample supply into a glut, prompting a collapse in prices.

THE TURNING TIDE

* * *

But how things changed. In 1999 I met a man called Dafydd Phillips, a sparkle-eyed Llŷn fisherman in his sixties, who has worked the inshore waters around Morfa Nefyn since he was old enough to walk. Sitting by his beach hut, his eyes sparkling like Alpha Centauri, he recalled one night when he set three nets. When he returned to them in the morning in the little boat he calls *Y Tanc* he had caught no fewer than 12,000 herring. All his friends ate fish that day. And the next. And the day after. Some possibly grew tiny silver scales on the back of their hands from eating so many. Or maybe that's just a fisherman's tale.

There were other days of glut and plenty, such as the one when Dafydd and his son Matthew, a chef in Criccieth, took part in the annual mackerel race, where contestants see how many fish they can catch in two hours. Using rods baited with nothing more sophisticated than strings of white feathers they caught almost 2,000 of the zebra-striped fish. But over the half-century he's been fishing these waters, Dafydd has seen a steady decline in fish stocks, which he puts down to overfishing. 'It's like the Dead Sea here sometimes. That's what we call it. The Dead Sea,' his eyes dimming slightly as he adamantly made his point about the fishery's slow, steady but certain diminishment.

23.

THE FISHGUARD WHALE

I can trace my long fascination with whales to reading John Steinbeck's diary of his trip on board a biological research vessel. *The Log from the Sea of Cortez* is full of wonder at the interconnectedness of things. As he writes, 'The true biologist deals with life, with teeming boisterous life, and learns something from it, learns that the first rule of life is living.'

Grey whales start their gargantuan migrations northwards from the Sea of Cortez, or Gulf of California, so when I had a chance to look for them on a trip to the Farallon Islands, off the coast of northern part of the state, I jumped at the chance. Our luck was in, because we saw a fair few, both mothers and calves, breaching and pushing determinedly on as part of a journey that is the very longest mammal migration. It takes the creatures from the warm waters of Baja, California to the deep chill of the Bering Sea, a total of 12,500 miles.

It was a grand day in so many regards. Dumpy little birds, rhinoceros auklets, performed skittering forward rolls on the sea's surface as they tumbled desperately to take off. Big schools of Pacific white-sided dolphins scythed out towards the great fathom-drop of the Continental shelf. The whales, too, seemed to keep us company, their spouting a celebration of air in water, water in air. That night I was watching TV when I started to weep quietly. Before long I was shuddering at the memory of the day. It was something about the sight of the determined animals, the sheer purpose in their movement, that had triggered a deep emotional response. Call it Steinbeckian.

I remember some years ago the then Pembrokeshire warden for the RSPB, Ian Bullock, enthusing knowledgeably about whale species at a marine policy launch. One fact lodged in my mind like a barnacle, namely that the heart of the blue whale is the same size a Morris Mini car. And then another. The beat of its heart can be heard up to 2 miles away, helped by the fact that sound carries over four times as far in water as it does in air.

The blue whale, known in Welsh and Irish respectively as *Y Morfil Las* and *Míol mór gorm*, is the largest of all the whale species. Indeed, it is the largest known animal ever to have inhabited the world, growing up to 110 ft and weighing up to 200 tons, or the weight of thirty-three elephants. It is also long-lived – anything up to a century – and its mottled blue colour is unique among whale species, making it stand out in so many ways.

Sadly, most of the whales recorded on the Welsh and Irish coasts are strandings – whales coming inshore either dead or dying, sometimes with no explanation or rationale. One of the most famous of these was a blue whale that became stranded on the Swanton sand bank below the Fort in Rosslare.

This individual – a young adult, 25.2 metres or 82 feet long – was migrating up the east coast of Ireland, but had the misfortune of being caught by the low tide and was duly stranded at a sandbar in Wexford. It was discovered there on 25 March 1891, struggling pitifully in the shallows for two whole days before it was ultimately put out of its misery by a local fisherman, Ned Wickham, who dispatched it with a home-made harpoon lanced in under its flipper. It was then put up for public auction at Rosslare: its meat and blubber were swiftly sold, and finally its skeleton, too, which was bought for £250 by the Natural History Museum in London. They finally got around to putting it on display in 1933, when they opened their special whale gallery. The animal itself was nicknamed Hope, and you can still see it hanging in the big hall, swimming above the bright shoals of selfie-taking tourists.

Recent analysis of the chemical make-up of its baleen, the flexible plates that hang inside its mouth in lieu of teeth, have revealed three phases of the animal's life. Dr Clive Trueman from the University of Southampton used radioactive isotopes to chart its journeys, which included, seven years before its death, swimming in the subtropical waters of the Atlantic, in places such as Cape Verde – famous for its history of whaling – or off Mauritania. The whale would have followed the usual pattern of migration, which takes the big animals from summer feeding grounds around Iceland and Norway, then up into the Arctic Circle before a movement south to avoid the encroaching ice. Furthermore, Dr Trueman found patterns of carbon isotopes consistent with her being pregnant. Hope probably gave birth to a calf in waters south of the Azores. It's a singular instance of science fleshing out a creature's life story long, long after its death.

* * *

Sightings and acoustic detections in recent years have shown that these blue titans occur during the summer and autumn in Ireland, appearing along the edge of the continental shelf, in waters of around 700m depth. At sea, a blue whale might announce its presence by the spout of air-blast, which can be as much as 10 metres or 33 feet high, before its long back appears, then the small dorsal fin as it plunges underwater again, rarely exposing its tail. It swims very quickly indeed and was often much too fast for whalers in olden days, outpacing them at a lick. Even if it should be struck by a harpoon it would powerfully swim away, pulling the line behind it in its wake like so much dental floss.

The bomb-gun changed all that, as it was used to plant a lethal charge in the animal's body and, by dint of this, the species was hunted to the very brink of extinction. It was mainly chased for the oil contained in the blubber that surrounded the body. Baleen whales such as the blue whale were thought to contain superior fine oil and lots of it: one whale might yield as much as 10 to 20 tons. A gargantuan whale killed at Walvis Bay, south-west Africa, in 1928 produced a record 50 tons, which was then variously used for the manufacture of soap, margarine, machine oil, waterproofing or glycerine, being the basis for the explosive nitroglycerine. It was little wonder that sea-hunting skills – married to avarice and lethal technology – almost did for the species. It takes a long time for them to reproduce, having only one calf at a time; recovery is thus very slow after such depletions by whaling. It is estimated that the current North Atlantic population of this magnificent animal still stands at around only 400 individuals.

It is great to know they are coming back, albeit slowly. Blue whales were sighted – and indeed filmed – in 2012 by the Irish Air Corps flying over the Porcupine Bight, a sea area set way off the coast of south-west Ireland. Additionally, acoustic monitoring studies in the North Atlantic – conducted by US researchers from Cornell University – have indicated that upwards of fifty blue whales pass through Irish offshore waters in late autumn and early winter on what is their south-bound migration. How different things are nowadays for the blue whale in the Irish sea, in 'this passageway which once proved fatal for the easy access it allowed to British and Irish hunters, a kind of ceta-cean shooting alley,' as Philip Hoare memorably put it in *Leviathan*.

The recovery was allowed by the various moratoria on whale hunt-ing around the world, with some inglorious exceptions. Thankfully, the seawaters off the coast of Ireland were designated as Europe's first whale and dolphin sanctuary in 1991, and a total of 25 cetacean species have been recorded there. Recent years have seen a surge in sightings of big whales such as fin whales, which blow spectacular columns of water, fire-hosing spouts to heights of 7 to 8 metres, as they make powerful exhalations at the sea-surface. These beautiful creatures are increasingly seen off the coasts of Cork and Waterford as they propel through the depths in search of krill, sprat and herring. A humpback whale even appeared in the path of the Irish Ferries vessel *Ulysses* near Howth Head in July 2010. More recently, in the summer of 2021 humpbacked whales were spotted off the coast of Wales – one near the island of Grassholm and the other sighted offshore at Tresaith, while long-finned pilot whales have also been sighted.

THE FISHGUARD WHALE

*　*　*

Nature has a gift for producing the unexpected. Take the example of the leatherback turtle washed ashore on Harlech beach, Gwynedd, in September 1988. It was approximately 100 years old when it died, drowned after being trapped by fishing lines. It was the largest and heaviest turtle ever recorded, measuring almost 9 feet in length and weighing 2,016 pounds. Or that piratical seabird, the long-tailed skua, which novelist Cynan Jones happened to chance upon in May 2021. 'A most astonishing thing,' as he Tweeted, 'a bird I thought near-mythic,' which appeared near land his grandfather farmed in Llanrhystud on the Ceredigion coast.

*　*　*

Porpoise are sleek, fast mammals which delight the eye on many an Irish Sea crossing. It's been estimated that over 36,000 porpoise live in the Celtic Sea between southern Ireland and Wales. Harbour porpoises can be seen easily in many inshore waters, especially in calm sea conditions. One of my favourite spots is Strumble Head near Fishguard where, on a good day, the animals seem to goosepimple the grey surface of the sea as their little bodies briskly appear then dip away. Both sides of St George's Channel support good populations and ferry trips are often blessed with sightings, often early on during a crossing as the animals seem to like harbourages. They are particularly abundant between Howth Head and Dalkey, off Co. Dublin, where boat-based surveys conducted by Irish Whale and Dolphin Group produce some of the highest counts anywhere in Ireland.

Porpoise live life in the fast lane and travellers on the ferries connecting Ireland and Wales might think they're being overtaken by these speedy mammals. The harbour porpoise is 1.5 metres long and can scythe through the water at speeds of 25 kilometres per hour. They become sexually mature at the age of three and from then on can have a calf a year: one of the oddities of the species is that the female can both lactate and be pregnant at one and the same time. They are relatively short-lived, with a life span of some nine or ten years.

They spend 5 per cent of their time on the surface of the water, but when they are underwater they become very active acoustically as sound helps them navigate, forage, socialise, and communicate more generally. They use ultrasonic clicks on a narrow, high band frequency, and do so in a way comparable to the way bats use echolocation: that the clicks are reflected off objects, so giving the mammals a picture, albeit a rapidly changing one, of their marine surroundings.

The harbour porpoise is sometimes described as Ireland's smallest whale – as opposed to the smallest baleen whale, the minke whale – and takes its place on that list of twenty-five different species that have been sighted in its waters. Oddities occur and keep on occuring. There was the bowhead whale seen in Carlingford Lough, a species normally seen in areas of pack ice, so this one was very much displaced. Then there was the pigmy sperm whale, stranded in Dublin, alive but in very poor condition.

Luckily it's quite easy to see live ones. There are eight species of whale and dolphin which can be seen, say, in Dublin Bay, often from land; Howth Head is a good place to spot porpoise, and Dalkey Head to the south is a good place for dolphins. Some years bottlenose dolphins take up residency hereabouts, as did three individuals in 2012, gambolling in the water to the delight of anyone fortunate enough to see them.

* * *

Let's cross back over to Welsh waters for a complementary ceteacean spectacle. Bottlenose dolphins in Cardigan Bay are often seen in summer, when the females move closer inshore, following the mackerel shoals. They can be an uplifting, joyous spectacle as they hunt in swift and agile packs, skittering over the waves in high-speed chases, sometimes throwing fish in the air with carefree abandon as if they have some to spare. The ones off the Ceredigion coast are sufficiently distinct a population to have their own 'dialect' of clicks and signature whistles, the latter helping to identify an individual much as humans have names. Seeing them in New Quay is always a champagne moment, as these frisky, balletic animals dance in aquamarine delight.

* * *

Sometimes, whales manage to really grab the headlines. On 30 October 1954 *The Times* carried an unusual story under the headline 'Film whale walks out':

> Ships off the coast of Wales and south-west England were warned yesterday to look out for a dummy whale, which was described as a 'possible hazard to navigation.'
>
> The whale, a 75ft model weighing 12 tons, being used for the filming of *Moby Dick*, broke away while being towed off Fishguard on Thursday. Coastguards and an R.A.F. flying-boat searched for it yesterday without success. The film company's unit at Strumble Head was towing the whale in a rough sea, filming a scene. When the tow-ropes parted the assistant director, Mr K. O. McClory, jumped on the back of the whale. He fixed another tow-rope, but the whale broke away again and was lost sight of in the rough seas, drifting away in the fog.
>
> The fake whale, built by Dunlop in Stoke-on-Trent, was later sighted by an ocean liner and the director John Huston believed it eventually bumped into a dike on the shores of Holland.

The Great White Whale they had built for filming was constructed so that it could be towed by a tug. They made several such models, each made of steel and wood and covered in latex. Each required eighty drums of compressed air and a hydraulic system in order to remain afloat, costing between $25,000 and $30,000. Huston lost not one but two of them, adding to his already punishing financial woes. 'They were being pulled with nylon cables two inches thick, but the force of the waves in this bad weather was so great that when slack in a cable was taken up, the damn thing broke like a guitar string.'

It wasn't just the whale that was lost. Leading man Gregory Peck – playing the terrifying Captain Ahab – was on board the model when it snapped loose.

Within moments, the 'whale' was swept out to sea, with Peck towed helplessly in its wake. He later recalled watching the shoreline recede from view and thinking what fun the newspapers would have the next day detailing his demise on the back of a giant whale.

Luckily coastguards rushed to rescue Peck who, having recently starred in *Roman Holiday* alongside Audrey Hepburn, was one of the world's most famous, and thus most expensive, leading men.

The mishap-prone *Moby Dick* was filmed around Fishguard, Youghal in Ireland – where there is still a Moby Dick Bar – and the Canaries. The trouble began even the moment they started filming. They arrived in Fishguard to get the White Whale scenes in what the director described as the 'worst winter weather in the history of the British Isles.' Mini-disaster begat mini-disaster. Two special power-rescue launches capsized outside the harbour. A high gale sent the *Pequod* – adapted from a three-master which had been a sea-going aquarium and tourist attraction on the Scarborough coast – running desperately for Fishguard harbour. The wind was blowing directly in the harbour mouth and their engines couldn't make any headway. Once they cleared the port's entrance the cable to the tugboat bringing them in suddenly snapped.

Huston even had to play God. When they were filming the whale sequences they had men out in longboats, which 'was risky in bad weather, and when the seas became dangerously high, we'd bring the longboats back to the ship. But it was in precisely this kind of weather that the cables could snap and the whale would begin to drift away. So we were confronted with a choice: save the men or save the whale.' Properly, he chose men: Huston wasn't Ahab, obsessed by a whale. He still wanted to make a film about it, though.

According to John Huston, it was: 'The most difficult picture I ever made. I lost so many battles during it I even began to suspect that my assistant director was plotting against me. Then I realized it was only God. God had a perfectly good reason. Ahab saw the White Whale as a mask worn by the Deity and the Deity as a malignant force. It was God's pleasure to torment and torture man ... The picture, like the book, is a blasphemy, so I suppose we can just lay it to God's defending Himself when he sent those awful winds and waves against us.'*

And God kept on defending himself. When the American producers came over to find out why they were so far behind schedule the Hollywood moguls came out by power launch to visit the *Pequod*. Huston enjoyed seeing their faces as they cleaved though gigantic swells, their 'faces green and agonised.'

*   *   *

While whaling is often historically associated with places such as Nantucket, on the eastern seaboard of the United States, there were ports in Britain such as Hull and Whitby very much connected with the deadly trade. In 1733 the first act granting bounties to the whale fisheries was passed, offering twenty shillings a year per ton for vessels fitted out for hunting. This gradually increased to forty shillings per ton, which encouraged a greater take-up by nineteen ships. In 1754 Milford in Pembrokeshire joined the whaling 'fleet', although to begin with only two ships from the port were involved.

The southern whale fishery, which mainly chased after the sperm whale, had been created by the Americans, following the capture of a single animal in 1712 by a Nantucket whaler. The nascent industry grew at a lick. Among the aforementioned Quaker settlers in Milford were fifteen families arriving in 1792 and led by Samuel Starbuck and Timothy Folger. The families had originally requested the British government should set up whaling stations in the UK as early as 1785. The War of Independence, which came to an end in 1783, had interrupted the American whaling business – Quakers refused to fight for either side in the conflict – and many of the whalers sought refuge elsewhere. The British government offered incentives to the American whalers to invest in Milford Haven and promised them 'the right and

---

* John Huston, *An Open Book*, New York, 1980.

privileges of natural-born subjects.' Why? The authorities were keen to avoid an over-reliance on American supplies of oil and other products of the whaling industry. As part of their relocation package the settlers negotiated the construction of docks and quays, a Quaker meeting house as well as a dedicated burial ground in Priory Road. Houses were erected in the New England manner. Today's street names in this port which once sported a dozen whalers duly commemorate this history: there is Dartmouth Street, Starbuck Road, Nantucket Avenue, Fluke Street.

Eight years after the arrival of those first families their number grew with the arrival of Ben Rotch, described as 'a gentleman of great commercial knowledge, connections and property' who was also a Quaker and a well-established whaler, and he brought his ships. His daughter Eliza described how on arrival: 'My father began immediately to build stores and a dwelling house and ships began to arrive from America, full freighted with sperm oil. The business attracted the artisans necessary for carrying it on and houses sprang up on every side and Milford became a scene of activity unknown before. The author of so much prosperity was deservedly popular and his prompt pay secured him plenty of workmen. The oil imported from the United States was landed, the casks coopered and then reshipped in small coasting vessels to London. This with the outfitting of his ships for the South Seas made a thriving business for a variety of trades and introduced some new shops into the town.'*

Ships ventured to these southern seas to hunt for whales but also imported whale goods from the other side of the Atlantic, and thus could avoid the punitive taxes on goods being brought into Britain. There was money to be made and Milford was making it. By 1814, however, the brief boom was bust. Rotch got into financial difficulties and relocated to London. Whaling had changed and Milford no longer fitted the picture.

The Quaker Meeting House still stands in Milford. Inside there is a commemorative tapestry into which is woven a couplet by perhaps

---

* https://gwallter.com/books/wales-and-whales.html.

the finest Welsh language poet of the twentieth century, Waldo Williams, taken from his poem '*Y Tangnefeddwyr*' ('The Peace-lovers'). Quakers are renowned for their pacifism so *The Encyclopaedia of Wales* entry for Milford notes how 'It is paradoxical that so pacific a people followed so bloody an occupation.' Certainly it seems un-Biblical, for as the first book of Genesis explains: 'And God created great whales, and every living creature that moveth, which the waters brought forth abundantly, after their kind. And God blessed them, saying, Be fruitful and multiply, and fill the waters in the seas.' It doesn't say go out and kill them. So it is a wee bit perplexing how the Quakers were, as Herman Melville put it in *Moby Dick*, 'the most sanguinary of all sailors and whale-hunters. They are fighting Quakers; they are Quakers with a vengeance.'

Some of those buried in the Milford graveyard – Abigail Barney Starbuck and husband Samuel, Daniel Starbuck and his wife Alice, and Samuel and Lucretia Folger Starbuck – share a surname with the famous coffee chain but also with the chief mate of the whale-hunting *Pequod*. He was a Nantucket native who 'though born on an icy coast, seemed well equipped to ensure hot latitudes, his flesh being hard as a twice-baked biscuit.' Their names here aren't spelled out, the humble headstones simply marked with initials, for these are appropriately quiet, almost anonymous markers to people who crossed the Atlantic to play out their brief moment in an equally brief chapter in the bloody history of whaling.

Ireland too has its own brief chapter in the history of whaling. Strandings around the island were always important and such natural booty was keenly fought over in medieval times. To give an idea of their value, in 1295 a man called William Macronan was fined two cows and 10 shillings for appropriating a stranded whale for his own use, and there was a court case in Co. Kerry disputing the Crown's right to such discoveries. One Robert de Clohulle argued, like his father before him, that 'great whales are reported wreck of the sea.' A few centuries later, the charter of the City of Waterford gave the mayor fishing rights over salmon and the like but notably excepted whales and sturgeons.

Short-lived attempts were made to establish whale fisheries in Donegal Bay in the 1730s and 1760s after which there was no active whaling until the early twentieth century. In 1908 the Arranmore Whaling Company established a shore factory on South Iniskea Island, killing seventy-six whales of five species under licence that year. The Blacksod company followed suit, setting up at Ardelly Point in Co. Mayo. By 1909 the Iniskea operation was running very profitably, taking 100 whales annually, which in turn produced 29,000 barrels of oil, 53 tons of guano, 124 tons of cattle food and over 14 tons of whale bone. The company employed thirty men on the whalers and sixty-five men at the factory but five years later, as demand for whale products dwindled, the station was abandoned, even though the one at Ardelly Point remained active after the First World War, closing down in the 1920s.

* * *

Wales had a contingent of whalers even more recently. Two whaling expeditions set off from the port of Holyhead, with local crew members recruited in such nearby coastal villages as Amlwch between 1936 and 1941, going far south, to the Antarctic. An initial recruitment drive in 1936 by Unilever, at one time the world's largest purchaser of oils and fats, was so successful that soon other whaling companies looked to Holyhead to supply men. So important was whale oil that the British government declared it a 'national defence commodity.' Although most men were employed on the factory ships, processing the whales, a few of the more experienced north Walian sailors worked on the catchers. The names of whale ships became as well known in Holyhead as those of mail boats: the *Southern Princess*, *Southern Empress*, *Terje Vike*, *Sven Foy* and the *Hectoria*. Whales' eardrums, often decorated with painted faces, were to be found, and still are in many homes on the island. Barry Hillier, guiding me through the cornucopia of objects in the Holyhead Maritime Museum, also showed me their collection of whales' teeth, along with a dagger that was used to strip the whale blubber in what was nothing less than a 'Fordist production line,' as Robert MacFarlane once memorably described whaling.

Barry remembers three sets of whale teeth in his grandmother's house in Amlwch, 'and you'd find others parts of the whale, pieces taken out of the throat for instance present in many homes in Holyhead.' They were mementos of how tough, weather-beaten men worked on the ships in the winters of 1939 and 1940, driven in part by the necessities and deprivations of the Depression, which meant companies could more easily recruit workers for testing journeys. The enticements were enough to get a Holyhead man to swap hemispheres, north for south. One, John Pritchard, signed a contract with the Southern Whaling and Sealing Company Ltd, which guaranteed him nine pounds and ten shillings a month, with a small bonus for every barrel of whale oil they brought back. After a six-month journey Mr Pritchard returned with £100 in his pocket, a princely amount in those days. He really had to earn it, mind, in frigid Antarctic waters, working twelve-hour days cutting up carcasses or cleaning fuel tanks, which needed to be emptied in order to store the whale oil on the return leg.

* * *

It is difficult for many people to reconcile magnificent animals with the barbarity of their slaughter, especially when one thinks of the rich complexity of their lives. The author Manchan Mangan lists a Irish proverb, or *seánfhocal*, which runs '*Saol trí mhíol mhór saol iomaire amháin, saol trí iomaire saol an domhain*' ('Three times the life of a whale is the lifespan of a ridge, and three times the life of a ridge is the lifespan of the world').* As a whale was believed to live for a thousand years, a ridge of cultivated land would, by this simple computation, last three thousand – and history and archaeology bear this out, with

---

* Manchan Magan, *Thirty-Two Words for Field*, Dublin, 2020. I might not have encountered this book were it not for researching this present volume: I cannot recommend it enough, a delight in all regards.

three-thousand-year-old field patterns still visible in places in Ireland, or on an island such as Skomer in Wales. If you carry on the multiplication then, three times the span of a ridge's 'life' makes nine thousand years, taking us back to the time when Neolithic man first began to exchange planting for hunting and started settling, claiming the earth as surely as the sea rejected any such act of ownership.

So the whale is, on top of everything else, an intriguing measurement of time. One thinks again of the grey whales off California and their simple magnificence, born in the sea and borne by the sea, their submarine bodies like enormous floating tanks to carry capacious oxygen supplies, buoyed up by the waters of the great wide ocean. Heading onwards, hopefully forever onwards, making of time itself a long journey, from warm seas to cold and then back again. Then repeat.

24.

ALWAYS LEAVING

The Irish and migration have always been fellow travellers. When the eighth-century poet Sedulius arrived at a European monastery, the abbot welcoming him to the place enquired if he had left his home country 'due to the unsettled state of the country or the Irish habit of going away.' Similarly the German historian and philosopher Walafrid Strabo wrote that wandering was 'the condition of the Irish.' And they moved in staggering numbers: between 1801 and 1921 some 8 million people went away, to America or to Britain. Their new homes were in places such as London's Kilburn and Cricklewood, and perhaps after a good night on the Guinness (other fine stouts are available) Irish roisterers might be heard singing a song which included the refrain:

The sea, the sea ...
Long may it roll between England and me

The words might hold meaning for many, many Irish who fled the catastrophe of the Famine between 1845 and 1849 and in the twentieth century left to look for work in the hospital wards and building sites of England, helping rebuild post-war Britain.

* * *

The Irish had long travelled in hope, some seeking their fortune. The Limerick novelist and playwright Gerald Griffin must have had an ambivalent idea about emigration. He had been left behind with a brother and two sisters when the rest of the family left for Pennsylvania. His story, 'The Half-Sir', one of the three long *Tales of the Munster Festivals*, published in 1827, paints a pantomimic picture of frenetic travellers leaving Dublin. The busy throng seems infected by the Midas touch, many of them hoping they would find, as did Dick Whittington, that the streets of London were solidly paved with gold blocks: 'The pier was crowded with passengers who were waiting to see their effects safely stowed before they took their own places in the vessel, with clamorous jingle-men and ragged, half-starved porters; members of the exiled parliament made up for the winter campaign; and adventurers of every description, who devoutly believed that gold and fame grew like blackberries upon hedges everywhere but in poor Ireland – and who, if they did not actually suppose that the houses in London were tiled with pancakes, and the streets paved with wedges of gold.'

Many of them might have left from Kingstown, now Dún Laoaghaire, where the poet Caroline Bracken can see the ferries – many, fittingly, with literary names – come and go from her window. Her poem 'Story' tells how:

From my window I watch ferries sailing in and out of Dublin
   Port
WB Yeats, Ulysses, Swift
they carry our stories songs and poems to Liverpool and
   Holyhead.
Many years since I made that change-at-Crewe journey
to Kilburn or Cricklewood
and their bedsits full of bricklayers, bus drivers and cinema
   ushers
sick for a city they would no longer recognise
the Luas, Dart, Samuel Beckett Bridge

Dún Laoghaire was both port of departure and, for many, a vale of tears. Those leaving from disparate parts of Ireland might be standing on home soil for the last time, contemplating what they were leaving and the vexing challenges that lay ahead. In his autobiography, *Self Portrait*, the Irish playwright, novelist and publican John B. Keane described that Janus experience of looking forwards and backwards at one and the same time: 'When I boarded the train at Listowel that morning it seemed as if everyone was leaving. It was the same at every station along the way. Dún Laoghaire, for the first time was a heart-breaking experience – the goodbyes to husbands going back after Christmas, chubby-faced boys and girls leaving home for the first time, bewilderment written all over them, hard-faced old stagers who never let on but who felt it worst because they all knew only too well what lay before them.'

Other accounts, such as the one in John Healy's *Death of an Irish Town*, describe the same sort of 'emigrant train' as if awash with tears: 'The train would pull into Charlestown to a crowded platform ... The Guard's door slamming shut was the breaking point: like the first clatter of stones and sand on a coffin, it signalled the finality of the old life. They clutched and clung and wept in a frenzy ...'*

Some people would plan long and thoroughly while others might leave on a whim, taking advantage of the £5 fares for the crossing to seek a better future. Still others would acquire a trade, be it carpentry or mechanics or whatever to prepare them for the boat. Richard Power, author of such novels as *The Hungry Grass*, tells the story of one such spur-of-the-moment life decision, when a young man from the Aran islands goes to wave goodbye to his friend but hops on board instead: 'He brought a pal to the quay one evening on the cart. They went for a drink to pass the time while they were waiting for the steamer. In the end Cóilín went away with him. He left the horse and the cart on the quayside. He left the door open. He abandoned the dog even, barking after him on the quay.'

---

* Quoted in Clair Wills, *The Best Are Leaving: Emigration and Post-War Irish Culture*, New York, 2015.

A railway station was a sort of emotional epicentre for feeling, as recalled by playwright Tom Murphy, who grew up in County Galway: 'I think the most important feature of my growing up was the emigration from the family. Somebody always seemed to be arriving or going away. A lot of emotion centred around the little railway station in my home town of Tuam.'

The statistics backed up the notion that everyone was leaving, with no fewer than 400,000 upping sticks in the 1950s, swelling the ranks of those born-in-Ireland-but-now-living-in-Britain to over 1 million, becoming the largest migrant population in the land. The exodus included priests, brothers, and nuns, crossing to serve the spiritual needs of those travelling for more worldly reasons and to bring round the pagan country across the sea. There were doctors, lawyers, and other educated women and men. But the great bulk of those emigrating were rural poor, leaving behind the hardscrabble farms for the post-war towns and cities of England. As they left they took a glass or three, pouring down the Dutch courage to buoy them up for a new life. John B. Keane, bound for the Irish enclave of Cricklewood, noted a depth of sadness to the travellers which matched that of the sea that lapped outside: 'The younger men were drunk – not violently so but tragically so, as I was, to forget the dreadful loneliness of having to leave home. Underneath it all was the heart-breaking, frightful anguish of separation …'

Those on deck watched their country, the familiar landmarks of their home turf, slide past in the sad panorama of departure. Caroline Bracken's poem, as it continues, watches them go, raising a metaphorical hand to the departing travellers:

They would know the sweep of Dublin Bay though
the cross on Bray Head, Killiney and Howth Hills
Dún Laoghaire's piers outstretched like a mother's arms
the red and white Pigeon House chimneys
Sandymount Strand and the Shellys walk
the Liffey stink

'They' were lured by the prospect of jobs and by the stories returning migrants recounted, as they stood another round in their fancy clothes. Cheaper transport back to Ireland had helped accelerate the movement of Irish migrants back home, though the majority still went the other way. Gary Brown's poem similarly charts a trip made by millions:

Pulling away game fully now towards open seas, seaward,
Belting and breaking freewheeling further and further
Holding up a long distance mirror of mature memories
Raheny, Sutton, Baldoyle and Binn Eadair speeding now
Almost skipping past The Kish the beckoning beacon
Of hope in hostile defiance of tempests and time,
Welcoming as it waves you god speed from the holy ground
Towards Holyhead.
Journeys of memos and missals, monies and moribund
    messages
Of lives beginning and declining, deaths, births and marriages
Announced backwards and forwards across this stretch of
Sometimes stormful sea

Crossing stormful seas could be a terrible experience, as those forced to leave Ireland on a ghastly armada of coffin ships knew, driven out of their homes and country as a consequence of the famine that swept across the land like a scythe. Driven by greed, shipowners crammed as many emigrants as they could into wildly inadequate vessels, where life on board was unsanitary in the extreme. They overpacked the creaking ships to the extent that the Plimsoll line came into being, showing the maximum height the water could rise on a ship's hull, thereby limiting the weight of cargo, or indeed passengers, they could carry.

* * *

When *The Times* of London compiled a report about the situation in Ireland in 1846 their reporter found a million desperate people dying from starvation. During the next five years another million would emigrate, driven by sheer need to find food and a new life in Britain but mainly in America, leaving a country which would see its population reduce by 20 per cent and not see a recovery until the 1920s. These were additional to the 'spalpeens', or seasonal migrants who crossed to Scotland and England to look for work as, say, summer harvesters. This big movement was commemorated in a poem, 'The Exodus' by Lady Wilde, which declared:

> A million a decade! Calmly and cold
> The units are read by our statesman sage
> Little they think of a Nation old,
> Fading away from History's page:
> Outcast leaves by a desolate sea
> Fallen leaves of Humanity!

The often arduous transatlantic journey is also detailed in Joseph O'Connor's riveting and bestselling novel *Star of the Sea*. It details the myriad hardships on board the creaking, leaking, incompetent concoctions of oak and pitch and nails and faith, 'bobbing on a wilderness of viciously black water which could explode at the slightest provocation.' For those travelling in steerage – the 'beggared spalpeens from Carlow and Waterford' – and the 'evicted farmers from Connaught and West Cork' who shared spaces with legions of scurrying fat rats and thus the predations of diseases such as cholera. The cosseted life of those in First Class was very different, with champagne and socialising, underlining the deep unfairness of the time.

Some chapters in *Star of the Sea* open with a roll call of passengers who have died during the twenty-six-day journey and are summarily buried at sea. Sixty-one-year-old Hannah Doherty of Belturbet. Paudrig Foley, farmhand of Roscommon. Bridget Shouldice, aged serving woman, now insane, from Birr Workhouse. Evicted tenant Daniel Adams of Clare. As much sad litany as grim captain's log, the lists show how people from all over Ireland, of all ages and all walks of life, traversed the ocean not in search of a better life but simply for the right and means to live: many never saw the unwelcoming, often frozen harbourage at New York. On their huge journey they faced illness such as typhus and unsanitary conditions that encourages mass infections and many, many succumbed.

Leaving was often sorrow-drenched. Samuel Harvey left Belfast bound for New York in 1849, taking loan of a telescope so he could survey the land he was abandoning. 'Oh, thou spot of earth, endeared by a thousand ties and fond recollections, your receding form but little knows with what sad feelings your unhappy exile bids you his last farewell.'

Seeing a country empty of its people as they turned emigrants saddened many observers. The *Waterford Chronicle* lamented the loss of so many young men. In 1846 it suggested that 'It was lamentable to witness crowds of fine, hardy young men and women rushing along our quays on Thursday night and getting their little substance on board the steamers, which sailed for England next morning, thence to take shipping to America. How long will this state of things continue? When will the severance of family, affection, the banishment of children of our soil, cease to exist?'

Not all of the emigrants were leaving of their own free will or need. Convict ships transported many, including a great number of women and children. Indeed, between 1845 and 1853 a total of fourteen female convict ships left Ireland, bound primarily for Van Diemen's Land or Tasmania. A single ship such as the *Waverley* – which departed in 1847 – carried 134 women convicts on board, as well as thirty-three children. These were horrible passages in so many regards. The last such convict ship, the *Midlothian*, left in 1852.

*   *   *

Most emigrants from Ireland passed through Liverpool, which had grown to be the most significant migrant hub in Europe, in part because of its earlier expansion as part of the slave trade. Those leaving

Dublin bound for Liverpool would join huge gatherings at the quayside, as the *Dublin Freeman* reported: 'During Friday, the appearance of the quay was like the approaches to one of the monster meetings of 1843 ... Drays, carts, cars and jaunting cars ... piled with boxes, beds, chests, household stuffs, together with pyramids of children – proceeded from early dawn to late at night to the steam packet stations.'

Those leaving Dublin were often crammed like anchovies in the hold, such as the unfortunates who travelled on the *Dundalk* in January 1853, which was 120 passengers over its official capacity of 350. A worse incident occurred in 1848 when emigrants travelling on the *Londonderry* between Sligo and Liverpool met a storm and when the crew battened down the hatches they cut off their air supply with many dying as a consequence.

When the emigrants got to Liverpool they would have to run the gauntlet of confidence tricksters – variously known as 'runners', 'man-catchers', 'crimps' and 'land sharks' – as Thomas Reilly, who travelled from Dublin to New York in 1848, averred: 'You would hardly believe, were I to tell you, all the tricks, cheats, plots and chicanery of every kind which I had to overcome. If a man had seven senses, it would take five hundred senses, largely developed, to counteract the sharpers of Liverpool and New York.'

A letter to the Dublin paper *Nation* confirmed the situation as an Irishman now resident in Liverpool warned of 'a system of plunder and bare-faced robbery.'

> I will think of her valleys with fond admiration
> Though never again her green hills will I see.
> I am bound for to cross o'er the wild swelling ocean
> In search of fame, fortune and sweet Liberty.

The dream of America, as popularised in songs such as this, persuaded many people to cross the ocean. The French geographer Paul Vidal de la Blanche suggested they carried 'their shells' with them, meaning the customs, language, and their songs. This was certainly the case for the

Welsh who left Ceredigion bound for Ohio. One of the early emigrants, George Roberts, described how the travellers would on fine afternoons gather on deck to pray and sing. A vessel carrying another cargo of emigrants left Aberaeron in 1839, bearing 175 passengers including four young men who led the spectators gathered at the quayside in a poignantly pertinent hymn of departure:

Bydd melys lanio draw
'Rôl bod o don i don
Ac mi rhof ffarwel maes o law
I'r ddaear hon

Sweet will be the landing over there
After sailing wave on wave
And I'll say farewell forever
To our native land.

The Welsh didn't emigrate in anything like the numbers of the Irish or the Scots but rather saw hundreds of thousands of people flowing *into* the country to fuel the industrial revolution like coal, and to aid in the production of iron and steel. Some did, though, leave many small ports on the Welsh coast bound for places such as New York, Quebec and Boston, often sharing space in the hold with a cargo of slate. Some ships carried 800 passengers, equivalent to two jumbo jets but without anything like the conveniences. Passengers were crammed in like sardines in a barrel, in conditions one captain likened to the Dark Ages. Things were so bad that an Act of Parliament had to be passed insisting that owners had to provide rations of food, which of course suggested that they had previously been sufficiently inhumane to not provide so much as a scrap.

Then there was the horrible presence of disease, which spread so easily in the confined dark – typhus, cholera, dysentery, all taking a deadly toll. Jonathan Edwards from Rhymney wrote in his diary as he crossed the Atlantic, outlining the sheer, miserable hell of it all: 'Death is using his sword very easily now and a more frightening storm than any we have seen sprung up. Two died last night and six today ... Five died last night and two at midday. It is extremely heart-breaking with our fellow emigrants groaning so with cramp and dying so suddenly ... Seven died today but we are not sure whether they are all dead or not, but we are sure they are thrown overboard without ceremony ... Our hearts are bled to see our friends dying. There was a woman crying bitterly having seen her baby thrown into the sea.'*

Life for the living was unpleasant beyond: as Robert Williams, who sailed out of Liverpool in 1844, reported: 'it is almost impossible to imagine the appearance of the people aboard, their clothes in rags and in their caps as if they had been a living room for bugs and fleas.'

* * *

Meanwhile, the Irish continued to leave in incredible numbers, a sixth of the population leaving the country during the Second World War, seeking work in fields or factories or joining the armed forces: a one-way traffic very much condoned, if not actively supported, by the government, who did not want poverty and discontent causing trouble at home. It was better to assist the passage of its people and encourage them to go elsewhere.

There was transatlantic traffic coming the other way, of course, and of a very different kind – not least in the heady days of the giant liners, when rival companies would compete to see which could claim the Blue Riband for crossing the ocean in the fastest time. One of the most famous and fastest hove into Fishguard, being Cunard Line's *Mauretania*, built jointly by the company and the government to steal back the prize from the sleek ships of the Germans who had long held the trophy.

The *Mauretania* had made her maiden voyage from Liverpool in 1907 and had soon claimed the Blue Riband for both the westward and eastward journeys, a prize she would hold for twenty years. In the

---

* Alan Conway (ed.), *The Welsh in America: Letters From the Immigrants*, Minnesota, 1961.

early twentieth century the public craved faster and faster crossings to their destination, including by land, and so Fishguard was chosen for its proximity to London, speeding its development as a port of call for Atlantic liners. Such passengers included Prince Albert and Prince Radziwell, not to mention the thousands who crossed the sea for the Coronation of King George V.

The *Mauretania*'s arrival at Fishguard on 30 August 1909 was cause for celebration, and crowds gathered on a hill at Goodwick, many in their Sunday best. There was the excitement of some 900 American mailbags coming ashore in tenders and men in boaters waiting for the train for Paddington. New records were set as the journey time from New York to London shortened to 5 days, 3 hours, 32 minutes. America seemed to have arrived in Pembrokeshire and soon there were 15,000 passengers arriving every month. The *Aquetania* called on her return voyage to New York and five special trains were required to take 600 passengers on to London. But the First World War changed all that and the Great Western Railway courted the bosses at Cunard, lobbying for Fishguard as the preferred port, but they instead plumped for Southampton; the uncertain political situation in Ireland had played into their thinking, and passenger numbers coming via Pembrokeshire duly trickled away. The ill-fated *Lusitania* was the last great liner to visit Fishguard on 14 September 1914, and her story adds to the catalogue of loss and sorrow connected with these seas, these self-same waters that acted as conduits for people, connecting them with their new lives as they carried hope with them along with their luggage.

25.

OUT WITH THE CHICKENS

The ferry hoves out of Rosslare, leaving land's edge. In a sense every bit of coast is a Finisterre (from the Latin finis terrae, meaning 'end of the earth'), although some places underline this more heavily, with cliffscapes of geological high drama, where fulmars wheel. The soft, low-slung cliffs of south Wexford are crumblier, as if the land is more tentative, which will have consequences as sea levels rise. Today the waves are a complex metallurgy; beaten tin, ruckled pewter and bright threads of mercury rimmed with sunlight.

At the opening of her marvellous trilogy of books – *Under-the Sea-Wind*, *The Sea Around Us* and *The Edge of the Sea* – Rachel Carson describes the sea's elusive and indefinable boundary. It's a strange and beautiful place and an area of unrest. She gives us the patterns: how waves have broken heavily against the land's edge, the tide pressing forward over the continents before receding and then returning. It is a quotidian pattern, Carson tell us, that is repeated and repeated over millennia: 'For no two successive days is the shore line precisely the same. Not only do the tides advance and retreat in their eternal rhythms, but the level of the sea itself is never at rest. It rises or falls as the glaciers melt or grow, as the floor of the deep ocean basins shifts under its increasing load of sediments, or as the Earth's crust along the continental margins warps up or down in adjustment to strain and tension. Today a little more land may belong to the sea, tomorrow a little less.'

Land's boundary slowly drifts away in our wake. From the observation deck of the ferry the magical white gleam of the autumn sun shines golden and smooth on the sea's surface. I am keeping my eyes peeled for a diminutive member of the same family as shearwaters, a bird hardly ever seen. By anyone. I keep my eyes peeled but am today disappointed.

That elusive bird is our smallest seabird, the storm petrel, a flying fleck of a thing that weighs hardly an ounce. It looks a bit like a house martin because of the contrast between its sooty-black upper parts and white rump. Storm petrels are also known as 'Mother Carey's chickens', believed by sailors to be the souls of drowned seamen. Mother Carey herself was the very antithesis of a caring mother, representing, rather, the very incarnation of an unforgiving, cruel and wrecking sea. She might even have been married – if not in complete harmony – to Davy Jones, the owner of that dark underwater locker where the drowned souls are contained as if in some existential treasure chest. Sailors knew the birds because they would turn up in bad weather, like small augurs of storm and ruin. It was believed that the souls of the dead would transmigrate into the birds, thenceforth left doomed to forever wander the endless oceans. More prosaically, it may be the case that they are called storm petrels because they are frequently swept inland after gales, simply blown in by storms.

In another deep-ocean version of an urban myth, Mother Carey is a corruption of Mater Cara, the Mother Beloved, or the Virgin Mary. Should some of these little birds be spotted by those on board ship they would be seen as presaging a storm, but also seen as a divine sign to the faithful that Our Lady would always answer their prayers and keep them safe from danger.

The Latin name of the bird, *Hydrobates pelagicus*, tells another story. The Hydrobates component combines water and walking, a reference possibly to St Peter, who could walk on water and did so at Christ's invitation on the stormy sea of Galilee. *Pelagikos*, in turn, means 'of the sea' from which we get the word 'pelagic'. As they feed over the ocean waves the tiny webbed feet of the storm petrels dangle weakly, pattering the surface, or perhaps 'Petering' the surface, as they nibble zooplankton in the churn of the sea.

Crew members on board the *Rienze*, heading from Belfast to New York in 1849, taught passengers about the various birds that followed the ship, and about how storm petrels embodied the souls of dead sailors. Not everyone bought into the story. 'It is all nonsense about Mother Carey's predicting storms,' remarked one emigrant. The sailors, however, were more circumspect, afraid should any passenger injure the birds and so engender bad luck. Superstition was as much a part of life at sea as the wind in the rigging.

Coincidentally, some exhausted birds did alight on the *Rienze*, including some storm petrels, which were immediately caught and stuffed. The fate of other wildlife on such ships was different: the surgeon superintendent on board the *Thomas Arbuthnot*, which was taking 194 Irish 'orphan girls' to Australia in 1849, had a shark they caught on the journey cooked in butter and promptly served up for supper.

*   *   *

I have spent memorable evenings on Skokholm Island, catching storm petrels in the safe pockets of mist nets (fine mesh, almost invisible) whilst listening to the tiny purr of the nesting birds in their underground burrows. I've used recordings of the birds to attract birds to be caught, and it's a technique that has revealed nesting sites in stone walls, rock cavities and small burrows in soft ground on islands which they had not previously been known to inhabit. Under cover of night the small birds flew around us, invisibly soot-black against a background of moonless sky – soft bullets, dark hurtles, feathery breaths. Tiny whooshes in all directions: incoming whispers.

Storm petrels are great wanderers and they have habit of visiting other colonies or prospecting new ones, so there is often traffic between Skokholm and Bardsey, from Skokholm to Irishtearaght, and from the Channel Islands and Brittany to west Wales. They are rather sparsely distributed in the southern Irish Sea but are more numerous south of St George's Channel and out into the Bristol Channel and especially in the Celtic Sea frontal region south-west of The Smalls, where they often associate with common dolphins.

The old quarry on Skokholm is a prime location to find them. The bird in the hand weighs just 30 grams, tiny morsels of life which seem quite unsuited to far-flung wanderings in open ocean. Being so small they are very vulnerable on land, and on islands such as Skomer and Skokholm are subject to the swooping predations of sharp-eyed little owls. The petrels migrate south after the end of the breeding season, following the coasts of Britain and Ireland and out into the Bay of Biscay. By the end of the year the birds have moved along to the western edge of the Iberian peninsula and in winter the birds – often young ones fledged that year – have persevered on to the coasts of Mauritania and the warm tropical seas off West Africa. The adult birds progress even further, crossing the Equator and its doldrums as far as the Tropic of Capricorn and the Namibian coast. There warm currents from the Indian Ocean meet cold waters brought by the Benguela Current surging all the way from the Antarctic, making this stretch of water between Namibia and Natal a fecund area for commercial fishing. Here the redoubtable little storm petrel can also happily find its small, busy pickings amidst the sea's plenty.

Ireland, meanwhile, has the largest breeding colonies in the world of this bird, with important sites such as Bull Rock off County Cork, Inishtearaght, Skellig Michael and Inishvickillaun in Kerry, and Rathlin island in Donegal. The storm petrel is also abundant in numbers as it feeds off the south coast of Ireland in the months of July, August and September.

The Irish name for storm petrels is *gearr úisc*, gearr being short for gearrcach, or fledgling, and *úisc* meaning grease, animal oil or fat. This tiny bird, the same size as a house sparrow, has to carry a lot of energy supply with it as it flies and patters across wide oceans, and does so in the form of oil and fat deposits, which plump up its body. If a bird is killed the body can no longer store the oil and it is released into its digestive tract. So a petrel's corpse, duly threaded through with a tarred wick, became a macabre candle, the light coming out almost as a last breath from its clogged windpipe. It's interesting that one of the folk traditions of Wales is the *cannwyll corff*, the corpse candle, being a spectral candle that appears in the window of a house in which someone has recently died. Like a greased fledgling, lit in remembrance.

The distinguished Irish poet Richard Murphy once found a storm petrel's nest in the skull of a hermit on Ardoileán, or High Island, which is set in the sea 3.5km off the north-west corner of Connemara. The 80-acre island is graced with early Christian beehive cells from the seventh century as well as the oratory of the derelict hermitage, and Murphy had a dream of restoring them. Deliberately marooned on the island which he had bought from the owner of the Pier Bar in Cleggan on a mad whim, Murphy slept on the hard ground, 'writing continuously, sometimes in the dark.' From these studiedly solitary experiences flew out bright words, such as those in 'Stormpetrel', a song sung to the eponymous bird, which he baptises the gypsy of the sea, or the 'guest of the storm'. This remote rock had long attracted isolates and heavy-duty ascetics such as St Fechin and St Gormgall, not to mention possessing an ancient well whose waters were said to have turned to the colour of blood after the Battle of Clontarf in 1014. Little wonder, then, that Murphy reached for his religious lexicon when writing about the churring sound of the small birds in his autobiography *The Kick*: 'The whisper of little wings increases as they brush close to my head, like a swift breeze,' he wrote, just as: 'Storm petrels are beginning to stutter and purr underground ... burrowing under mounds of ecclesiastical debris. Their tiny, gurgling voices transmit hope of renewal if not of resurrection, as the hatched birds in the burial ground of their origin cry out for food.'

When Murphy finds himself writing by torchlight in St Gormall's oratory, 'the stone is humming and mewing, throbbing and piping, while under the starlight there's a continual vibration of innumerable wings ... occasionally a voice from underground utters a piercing cry, followed by a rush of wings ... souls in purgatory working on a severe passage to paradise ...'

A man could not be lonely, he averred, when he had the company of thousands of birds and a life he never knew existed. In keeping with the religious tenor of expression the poet is soon edging towards epiphany, joyously alive in his apparent solitude as the small birds orchestrate the night: 'I feel inexpressibly happy … nothing will stop the music of the masonry until the birds come to the end of their dance and vanish before daybreak.' For Murphy the underground, nocturnal murmurings were the very 'pulse of the rock/You throb till daybreak on your cryptic nest/A song older than fossils/Ephemeral as thrift/It ends with a gasp.' In a neatly complementary poem called 'High Island' he sketched their return to the nest on this 'shoulder of rock … set high in the sea' and the petrels' 'quiver in flight' which is like brushing long wavy hair.

* * *

The storm petrel properly belongs to the sea and land is not its true habitat. It is just a night-time domain during brief summer, and yet it must visit land to breed. This fact might well have been in the mind of a lovesick sailor who once carved his name on a petrel's bill, before tossing the small body into the waves. He watched the little corpse bob and drift, hoping it would carry news of his well-being to his far-off love. It was statistically improbable but this was an act deeply inflected with hope and romance.

* * *

The Pembrokeshire naturalist R. M. Lockley once saw some storm petrels on a visit to Cape Clear island in the south-west of Ireland. He and his wife were given a lift on the 30-foot *Inishclear*, a trip complete with barefoot girls dancing to Irish songs as the boat tacked between Long Island and Castle Island to gain the open bay. Then they see the bat-winged forms of petrels dancing about them, above ocean swell luminiscent with swarming plankton: '*Father* Carey's Birds they were, insisted the young man they called Padruig; though he couldn't be bothered to explain why. He, the girls, all of them seemed in a dream of joy at the end of their day ashore at Schull. They sang and chattered, and chattered and sang, subsiding sleepily into the refrain "Rolling home, rolling home to dear old Cape Clear!" in time with the swaying of the boat. It was so dark we could no longer see the storm petrels except as dim shapes, and imagine we heard their faint cries …'*

Mother Carey's chickens. Now, here, *Father Carey*'s Birds. The pattern of their fishing life has also given the bird its Irish name of *Peadairín-na-stoirme*, Little Peter of the storm. So many names for the little avian tyke.

*　*　*

The last time I saw one of the Little Peters was on a gale-tossed September crossing from Fishguard to Rosslare, the weather whipped up by meteorological events far away – Cuba or Antigua maybe, the sort of mad highway-sign-upending hurricanes that send field reporters on The Weather Channel into apoplexy. My luck was in, even if the boat was now a lurching rollercoaster, with many of my fellow passengers green at the gills as they stumbled about in aquarium light.

I went out on deck, finding it hard to find a safe spot where I could use my binoculars. There was a defiant group of two, now three storm petrels, flapping gainly into the surging wind, and it seemed almost impossible to see how a bird the size of a budgie and with a wing size to match could not only survive but thrive in the toss and tumult of wide ocean. The little birds seemed completely at ease despite the whipping gusts of wind and car-washes of spray. They hugged the tops of the waves, their webbed feet pattering along the surface before the little wings would sway and veer, the head dipping to feed on things invisible to me. One bird went under the surface, merging from the roil of the water with its wings already open to lift upwards. I lost sight of all but this one bird in sheeting rain now threatening to turn

---

* R.M. Lockley, *Flight of the Storm Petrel*, Vermont, 1983.

horizontal and I had to constantly wipe the lenses of the binoculars in order to keep the petrel in sight.

On it went, its black wings aflutter like one of those city moths that change colour to a muted camouflage because of air pollution, reducing in its dimensions until it was little more than a speck. Now it was at the very edge of binocular range, jinking, fluttering, diminishing, until the bird was a tiny smudge on the grey page of the sea, until it reduced to nothing more than the size of a final full stop.

PERMISSIONS

Some parts of Chapter 5, 'Enlli', first appeared in *Caught by the River*.

Thanks to Caroline Bracken in Dún Laoghaoire for permission to use her poem 'Story' and to Gary Brown for allowing me to quote extensively from his poems and songs.

Extracts from the poems 'Enlli' and 'Gannets', which appear in Christine Evans's *Selected Poems* (Seren, 2014) are used with the kind permission of the publishers.

Extracts from *The Kick: A Memoir of a Poet*, by Richard Murphy reproduced with the kind permission of Cork University Press, Boole Library, University College Cork, Cork T12 ND89, Ireland.

Lines from Tony Conran's verse play *Branwen* (Gwasg Carreg Gwalch, 2003) used with kind permission.

Lines from Roland Mathias's poem 'Terns' are taken from his *Collected Poems* (University of Wales Press, 2002). Copyright the estate of Roland Mathias.

Extracts from Harri Webb's poems 'Enlli' and 'Return visit' are taken from the *Collected Poems* (Gomer, 1995, edited by Meic Stephens) and appear with the kind permission of Ruth Stephens. Copyright Ruth Stephens.

BIBLIOGRAPHY

Allen, Nicholas, *Ireland, Literature and the Coast*, Oxford, 2020.

Anonymous, *I am the Border, so I am*, London, 2019.

Adams, Sam (ed), *The Collected Poems of Roland Mathias*, Cardiff, 2002.

Alexander, Mike, *Skomer Island*, Talybont, 2021.

Bala, Iwan, (ed). *Hon*, Llandysul, 2007.

Barrington, Richard, *The Migrations of Birds at Irish Lighthouses and Lightships*, London/Dublin, 1900.

Bolger, Dermot, ed., *Wexford Through Its Writers*, Dublin, 1992.

Bourke, Edward, *Shipwrecks of the Irish Coast, Vol 1, 1105–1993*, Dublin 1994.

Bourke, Edward, *Shipwrecks of the Irish Coast, Vol 2, 1932–1997*, Dublin, 1998.

Bourke, Edward, *Shipwrecks of the Irish Coast, Vol 3, 1582–2000*, Dublin, 2000.

Bowen, Elizabeth, *The Last September*, London, 1998.

Bowen, *Saints, Seaways and Settlements in the Celtic Lands*, Cardiff, 1988.

Brett, David, *A Book Around the Irish Sea: History Without Nations*, Dublin, 2009.

Brooke, Michael, *The Manx Shearwater*, London, 1990.

Burrow, Steve, *Tomb Builders*, Cardiff, 2006.

Cabot, David and Ian Nisbet, *Terns*, London, 2013.

Carr, Peter, *The Night of the Big Wind*, Belfast, 1992.

Carradice, Phil, *A Town Built to Build Ships: A History of Pembroke Dock*, Pembroke Dock, 2006.

Carradice, Phil, *The Last Invasion: The story of the French landing in Wales*, Pontypool, 1992.

Carradice, Phil and Roger MacCallum, *Pembroke Dock Through Time*, Stroud, 2009.

Chadwick, Nora, *The Celts*, London, 1970.

Childe, V.G., *The Prehistory of European Society*, Penguin, 1958.

Clarke, H, Dolley, S. and Johnson, R., *Dublin & the Viking World*, Dublin, 2018.

Cocker, Mark and Richard Mabey, *Birds Britannica*, London, 2005.

Colfer, Billy, *Wexford: A Town and its Landscapes*, Cork, 2008.

Cowsill, Miles, *Fishguard-Rosslare, 1906–2006*, Ramsey, 2006.

Crampin, Martin, *Depicting St David*, Talybont, 2020.

Davies, Damian Walford and Eastham, Anne, *Saints and Stones*, Llandysul, 2002.

Davies, John, *A History of Wales*, London, 1994.

Davies, Norman, *The Isles*, London, 2000.

Davies, William, *The Story of the Irish Mail: A London train to Ireland via Holyhead*, Llanrwst, 2016.

Dee, Tim, *The Running Sky*, London, 2010.

Defoe, Daniel, *The Storm*, London, 2003.

Tony Denton and Nicholas Leach, *Lighthouses of Wales*, Lichfield, 2011.

Devoy, Robert, et al, *Coastal Atlas Ireland*, Cork, 2021.

Dochartaigh, Kerri ní, *Thin Places*, Edinburgh, 2021.

Doherty, Andrew, *Waterford Harbour: Tides and Tales*, Cheltenham, 2020.

Ebenezer, Lyn, *Y Pair Dadeni: Hanes Gwersyll Fron-goch*, Llanrwst, 2005.

Ekin, Des, *Irish Pirates*, Dublin, 2021.

Evans, Margiad, *The Nightingale Silenced and Other Late Unpublished Writing*, Dinas Powys, 2020.

Fishlock, Trevor, *Pembrokeshire Journeys and Stories*, Llandysul, 2011.

Fishlock, Trevor, *Fishlock's Sea Stories*, Bridgend, 2004.

Fishlock, Trevor, *Fishlock's Wild Tracks*, Bridgend, 2001.

Foster, Roy, *The Oxford Illustrated History of Ireland*, Oxford, 1989.

Fox, A.D., Norriss, D.W., Stroud, D.A. and Wilson, H.J. *Greenland White-Fronted Geese in Ireland and Britain*, Dublin, 1994

Freeman, *St Patrick of Ireland*, New York, 2004.

Gerald of Wales, *The History and Topography of Ireland*, London, 1992.

Gooley, Tristan, *How to Read Water*, London, 2016.

Gower, Jon, *Wales at Water's Edge: A Coastal Journey*, Llandysul, 2012.

Green, Jonathan, *Birds in Wales, 1992–2000*, Blaenporth, 2002.

Gruffydd, Elfed, *Ar Hyd Ben 'Rallt*, Llanrwst, 1999.

Hague, Douglas, *Lighthouses of Wales*, Aberystwyth, 1994.

Hegarty, Neil, *Dublin from the Ground*, London, 2007.

Hegarty, Neil, *The Story of Ireland*, London, 2011.

Hoare, Philip, *Leviathan*, London, 2008.

Hughes, D.Lloyd and Dorothy Williams, *Holyhead: Story of a Port*, Holyhead, 1967.

Huston, John, *An Open Book*, New York, 1980.

Hutchinson, Clive, *Birds of Ireland*, Waterhouses, 1989.

Huxley, Julian, *Memories*, London, 1970.

Ifan, Dafydd Guto, *Llên Gwerin y Môr*, Llanrwst, 2012.

James, David, *Of Monks and Seawolves*, Pembroke Dock.

Jackson, Derek, *Lighthouses of England and Wales*, Newton Abbot, 1975.

Jenkins, J. Geraint, *The Inshore Fishermen of Wales*, Cardiff, 1991.

Jenkins, J. Geraint, *Welsh Ships and Sailing Men*, Llanrwst, 2006.

John, Angela, *Turning the Tide: The Life of Lady Rhondda*, Cardigan, 2014.

Jones, Alun R., *Lewis Morris*, Cardiff, 2004.

Kee, Robert, *Ireland: A History*, London, 1981.

Killeen, Richard, *Historical Atlas of Dublin*, Dublin, 2011.

Kurlansky, Mark, *Cod: The Biography of the Fish That Changed the World*, London, 1998.

Lewis, Gwyneth, *Two in a Boat*, London, 2005.

Liptrot, Amy, *The Outrun*, Edinburgh, 2006.

Lockley, R.M., *Flight of the Storm Petrel*, Vermont, 1983.

Lockley, R.M., *I Know an Island*, London, 1947.

Lockley, R.M., *Letters from Skokholm*, Wimborne Minster, 2010.

Lockley, R.M. *Shearwaters*, London, 1947.

Lockley, R.M., *Whales, Dolphins and Porpoises*, Newton Abbot, 1979.

Long, Bill, *Bright Light, White Water: The Story of Irish Lighthouses and their People*, Dublin, 1993.

Lovegrove, R., Williams, Graham and Williams, Iolo, *Birds in Wales*, London, 1994.

Loyn, Henry, *The Vikings in Wales*, London, 1976.

Mac Amhlaigh, Dónall, *Exiles*, Cardigan, 2020.

Mackinder, H.J, *Britain and the British Seas*, London, 1902.

Magan, Manchan, *Thirty-Two Words for Field*, Dublin, 2020.

Matheson, Colin, *Wales and the Sea Fisheries*, Cardiff, 1929.

Lockley, R.M., *Flight of the Storm Petrel*, Vermont, 1983.

Merrigan, Justin and Collard, Ian, *Holyhead to Ireland: Stena and its Welsh Heritage*, Stroud, 2010.

Miller, Kerry and Wagner, Paul, *Out of Ireland: The Story of Irish Emigration to America*, London, 1994.

Moffat, Alastair, *The Sea Kingdoms: The History of Celtic Britain & Ireland*, London, 2001.

Murphy, Richard, *The Kick: A Memoir of the Poet*, Cork, 2017.

Mwyn, Rhys, *Real Gwynedd*, Bridgend, 2021.

Nairn, Richard, David Jeffrey and Rob Goodbody, *Dublin Bay: Nature and History*, Cork, 2017.

O'Brien, Edna, *The Country Girls*, London, 2017.

O'Carroll, Aileen and Don Bennett, *The Dublin Docker: the Working Lives of Dublin's Deep-Sea Port*, Newbridge, 2017.

O'Leary, Paul, *Irish Migrants in Modern Wales*, Liverpool, 2004.

O'Toole, Fintan, *Heroic Failure: Brexit and the Politics of Pain*, London, 2018.

Osmond, John, *Real Preseli*, Bridgend, 2019.

Panes, Graham, *Voyages of the Celtic Saints*, Llanrwst, 2007.

Parker, Mike, *Coast to Coast*, Llanrwst, 2003.

Pitman, Liz, *Pigsties and Paradise: Lady Diarists and the Tour of Wales, 1795–1860*, Llanrwst, 2009.

Price, Neil, *The Children of Ash & Elm*, London, 2020.

Pritchard, Rhion, Julian Hughes, Ian Spence, Bob Haycock and Anne Brenchley (eds), *The Birds of Wales*, Liverpool, 2021.

Redknap, Mark, *The Vikings in Wales*, Cardiff, 2000.

Redknap, Mark, Sian Rees and Alan Aberg, *Cymru a'r Môr, 10,000 o Flynyddoedd o Hanes y Môr*, Talybont, 2019.

Richards, John, *Maritime Wales*, Stroud, 2007.

Roberts, Askew, *The Gossiping Guide to Wales*, London, 1882.

Roberts, R.E, *Holyhead and the Great War*, Holyhead, 1920.

Roche, Richard and Merne, Oscar, *Saltees: Islands of Birds and Legends*, Dublin, 1977.

Rowe, David and Christopher Wilson, *High Skies – Low Lands: An Anthology of the Wexford Slobs and Harbour*, Enniscorthy, 1996.

Rowlands, John, *Holyhead: People, Prosperity and Poverty*, Holyhead, 1989.

Rutt, Stephen, *Wintering*, London, 2019.

Skidmore, Ian, *Gwynedd*, London, 1986.

Stokes, Roy, *Between the Tides: Shipwrecks of the Irish Coast*, Stroud, 2010.

Strackland, Jean, *Strands: A Year of Discoveries on the Beach*, London, 2012.

Templar, Dale, Anne Gallagher and Sally Weale Weale, *Wonders of the Celtic Deep*, Cardiff, 2021.

Thomas, J.E., *Britain's Last Invasion: Fishguard 1797*, Stroud, 2007.

Thomas, R.S., *Autobiographies*, London, 1997.

Thompson, William, *The Natural History of Ireland*, Vol 2, London, 1850.

Vaughan-Thomas, Wynford, *Wales*, New York, 1981.

Wernquest, Rachel, ed., *Dublin Port Diaries: Dockland Stories, Nicknames & Dictionary*, Dublin, 2019.

Williams, Gwyn A., *When Was Wales?*, London, 1985.

Wills, Clare, *The Best Are Leaving: Emigration and Post-War Irish Culture*, New York, 2015.

Articles, etc.

Annual Roseate Tern newsletter, 2019, RSPB et al, compiled by Chantal Macleod-Nolan.

Greenland White Fronted Goose Study: Report of the 1979 Expedition to Eqalungmiut Nunât, West Greenland. Greenland White-fronted Goose Study, Aberystwyth, 1981.

Connolly, C. (2020) 'Too rough for verse? Sea crossings in Irish Culture', in Leerssen, J. (ed.) *Parnell and his Times*, Cambridge: Cambridge University Press, 2020.

Connolly, Claire, Rita Singer, and James L. Smith. 'Environmental Dimensions of the RMS *Leinster* Sinking.' Environment & Society Portal, *Arcadia* (Autumn 2021), no. 32.

Evershed, Jonathan, 'The Irish Sea: Both Barrier and Gateway', *Planet*, 242.

Harvie, Christopher, 'Garron Top to Caer Gybi: Images of the Inland Sea', *The Irish Review*, No.19, Summer 1996.

Roberts, Owen T., 'The Cots of Rosslare Harbour & Wexford', *The Mariner's Mirror*, Volume 71, issue 1.

Roper, Brian, *Divining the genius loci of Môr Hafren: A literary map of the Severn Sea*, unpublished PhD, Swansea University, 2018.

Springer, Mary Rice, 'Diaries of the Asgard', https://www.anphoblacht.com/contents/24233.

Tomos, Elin, 'Ellen Edwards', https://hanesmenywod.cymru/ellen-evans-e-tomos.

Went, Arthur, 'Whaling from Ireland', *The Journal of the Royal Society of Antiquaries of Ireland*, Vol 98, No. 1, 1968.

Williams, Lucy, 'The Development of Holyhead', *Transactions Anglesey Antiquarian Society*, 1950.

'The History of Chronometers', Smithsonian Museum of American History. https://amhistory.si.edu/navigation/type.cfm?typeid=10.

ACKNOWLEDGEMENTS

Thanks hugely to Jonathan de Peyer at HarperNorth for having faith in the book and steering it safely to port, for editing it judiciously and generally making it better. It's been a pleasure working with you. Diolch yn fawr iawn.

Alice Murphy-Pyle plotted a steady course when it came to marketing and publicity.

And thanks to Holly Ovenden for producing the beautiful jacket art, which made the book a handsome object indeed, and also to John Taylor for his deft map-making skills.

Thanks also to my wife Sarah, for listening to me wittering on about sea-things late at night and for reading the manuscript with a close eye. Gyda diolch a chariad cyn ddyfned a'r môr.

Sincere thanks also to …

Members of the Ports, Past & Present team for their support, insights and good humour, namely Sarah Baylis, Claire Connolly, Aoife Dowling, Liz Edwards, Jonathan Evershed, Maria Fitzgerald, Victoria Genn, Rita Singer and James L. Smith. Special thanks thanks to Mary-Ann Constantine and Martin Crampin for reading chapters in their specialist fields and making useful suggestions.

Darryl Hughes and members of the Dublin Bay Old Gaffers Association for allowing me to sit in on their lectures during lockdown.

Graham Murphy, Nora Young and Declan Roche for their hilarious company in a bird hide in Wexford and to Graham especially for the splendid photo taken on the day.

David James, Pembroke Dock.

Tony Murray, Wildlife Ranger for South Wexford, the Irish National Parks & Wildlife Service for his time after a hard day's work.

Gareth Huws, Anglesey Antiquarian Society.

Barry Hillier, Holyhead Maritime Museum.

Catrin M.S. Davies, who produced the BBC Radio Cymru series 'Ar Lan y Môr', for sending me the unedited interviews and to the contributors I've quoted, namely Meinir Pierce Jones, Mark Lewis Jones and Mali Parri-Jones from the Porthdinllaen lifeboat crew.

Suz Mendus for lending me some lovely phrases from her own work.

Cynan Jones for answering my queries and for that future negroni.

Gary Brown for sharing his father's stories, for a great night at a performance of his play *The Buttonmen* and gifting me poems to use.

A marvellous morning was had in the company of Niall Keogh who took me to see brent geese rise at first light over Dublin.

There was great *craic* when I met Declan Byrne and John 'Miley' Walsh of the Dublin Dock Workers Preservation Society and I am grateful to Alan Martin for his help in sourcing images from their huge and important collection of photographs.

Harper
North

BOOK CREDITS

HarperNorth would like to thank the following staff
and contributors for their involvement in making
this book a reality:

Laura Amos
Hannah Avery
Fionnuala Barrett
Samuel Birkett
Katie Buckley
Sarah Burke
Fiona Cooper
Alan Cracknell
Jonathan de Peyer
Charlotte Dolan
Tom Dunstan
Kate Elton
Simon Gerratt
Monica Green
Natassa Hadjinicolaou
Tara Hiatt
Graham Holmes
Ben Hurd
Patricia Hymans

Megan Jones
Jean-Marie Kelly
Taslima Khatun
Samantha Luton
Oliver Malcolm
Rachel McCarron
Alice Murphy-Pyle
Adam Murray
Holly Ovenden
Genevieve Pegg
Agnes Rigou
James Ryan
Florence Shepherd
Zoe Shine
Eleanor Slater
Emma Sullivan
John Taylor
Katrina Troy
Kelly Webster

For more unmissable reads,
sign up to the HarperNorth newsletter at
www.harpernorth.co.uk

or find us on Twitter at
@HarperNorthUK

Harper North